The Accursed Share

Volumes II and III

Translated by Robert Hurley

The Accursed Share

An Essay on General Economy

Georges Bataille

Volume II

The History of Eroticism

Volume III

Sovereignty

ZONE BOOKS · NEW YORK

1991

© 1991 Urzone, Inc.
ZONE BOOKS
611 Broadway, Suite 838
New York, NY 10012

Originally published in France as *L'Histoire de l'érotisme*
and *La Souveraineté* in Georges Bataille's *Oeuvres
Complètes* (vol. 8), © 1976 by *Editions Gallimard*.

Printed in the United States of America.

Distributed by The MIT Press,
Cambridge, Massachusetts, and London, England

Library of Congress Cataloging in Publication Data

Bataille, Georges, 1897–1962.
      The accursed share.
      Translation of: La part maudite.
      Includes bibliographical references.
      ISBN 0-942299-20-5 — ISBN 0-942299-21-3 (pbk.)
      Contents: v. 1. Consumption – v. 2. & 3. The
history of eroticism and Sovereignty (1 v.).
      1. Economics. 2. Economic history.
3. Economics – Moral and ethical aspects. I. Title.
HB173.B35513   1988   330   87-34072

*The act of copulation and the members
employed are so repulsive, that if it
were not for the beauty of faces and the
adornments of the actors and unbridled passion, nature would lose the
human species.*

—LEONARDO DA VINCI

*Between the normal man who confines
the sadistic man to an impasse and the
sadistic man who makes this impasse a
way out, it is the latter who knows
more about the truth and logic of his
situation and whose knowledge of it is
deeper, to the point of being able to
help the normal man to understand
himself, by helping him to change the
conditions of all understanding.*

—MAURICE BLANCHOT

Contents

VOLUME II: THE HISTORY OF EROTICISM

              Preface   13

PART ONE   INTRODUCTION
              Eroticism and the Reflection of the Universe
              in the Mind   21

PART TWO   THE PROHIBITION OF INCEST
       I   *The Problem of Incest*   27
      II   *Lévi-Strauss's Answer*   39
     III   *The Transition from Animal to Man*   51

PART THREE   THE NATURAL OBJECTS OF PROHIBITIONS
       I   *Sexuality and Dejecta*   61
      II   *Cleanliness Prohibitions and the*
           Self-creation of Man   67
     III   *Death*   79

PART FOUR   TRANSGRESSION
       I   *The Festival, or the Transgression of Prohibitions*   89
      II   *The Phaedra Complex*   95

III *Desire Horrified at Losing and at Losing Oneself* 103

IV *The Object of Desire and the Totality of the Real* 111

PART FIVE THE HISTORY OF EROTICISM
I *Marriage* 123
II *Unlimited Fusion, the Orgy* 129
III *The Object of Desire* 137
IV *Nudity* 149

PART SIX THE COMPOSITE FORMS OF EROTICISM
I *Individual Love* 157
II *Divine Love* 167
III *Limitless Eroticism* 173

PART SEVEN EPILOGUE

VOLUME III: SOVEREIGNTY

PART ONE WHAT I UNDERSTAND BY SOVEREIGNTY
I *Knowledge of Sovereignty* 197
II *The Schema of Sovereignty* 213
III *The Historical Development of the Knowledge of Sovereignty* 225
IV *The Identity of the "Sovereign" and the "Subject," and Consequently of the Understanding of Sovereignty and Self-understanding* 237

PART TWO SOVEREIGNTY, FEUDAL SOCIETY AND COMMUNISM
I *What Is the Meaning of Communism?* 261

II *The Collapse of Feudal Societies and the*
    Great Revolutions   277
III *The World of Denied Sovereignty*   291
IV *Sovereignty within the Limits of Soviet Society*   309

PART THREE   THE NEGATIVE SOVEREIGNTY OF COMMUNISM
             AND THE UNEQUAL HUMANITY OF MEN
        I   *Equivalence and Distinction*   329
        II   339

PART FOUR   THE LITERARY WORLD AND COMMUNISM
        I   *Nietzsche and Communism*   365
        II   *Nietzsche and Jesus*   373
        III *Nietzsche and the Transgression of Prohibitions*   395
        IV   *The Present Age and Sovereign Art*   411
        V   427

             Notes   431

VOLUME TWO

The History of Eroticism

Preface

> ...soon we'll be united for good. I'll lie down and
> take you in my arms. I'll roll with you in the midst of
> great secrets. We'll lose ourselves, and find ourselves
> again. Nothing will come between us any more. How
> unfortunate that you won't be present for this happiness!
> — Maurice Blanchot

I

The lowliest and least cultured human beings have an experience of the possible — the whole of it even — which approaches that of the great mystics in its depth and intensity. It only takes a certain energy, which is not infrequently available, at least in the first years of adulthood. But this intensity and depth are equaled only by the stupidity, the vulgarity — and even, it must be said, the cowardice — of the judgments they express concerning the possible which they attained. These judgments contribute to the ultimate failure of an operation whose meaning escapes them. Nothing is more widespread: by chance a human being finds himself in an incomparably splendid place; he is not at all insensitive to it, but he can't say anything about it. At the same time there occurs in his mind the sequence of vague ideas that keeps conversations going at full tilt. If it is a matter of erotic life, the majority are content with the most vulgar notions. Its foul appearance is a trap into which it is rare for them not to fall. It becomes a reason for placid contempt. Or they deny this awful appearance and go from contempt to platitude: *there is nothing filthy in nature,* they affirm. We manage in any case to substitute empty thinking for those moments when it seemed to us, however, that the very heavens were opening.

I wanted in this book to lay out a way of thinking that would measure up to those moments – a thinking that was removed from the concepts of science (which would bind their object to a *way of being* that is incompatible with it), yet rigorous in the extreme, as the coherence of a *system* of thought exhausting the totality of the possible.

Human reflection cannot be casually separated from an object that concerns it in the highest degree; we need a thinking that does not fall apart in the face of horror, a self-consciousness that does not steal away when it is time to explore possibility to the limit.

II

My intention, moreover, goes beyond a desire to compensate for the humiliation resulting from the fact that men turn away from their intimate truth, that they flee from it. This second volume continues an effort whose object is a general critique of the ideas that *subordinate* men's activity to ends other than the useless consumption of their resources. It is a matter of discrediting those ways of looking at the world that are the basis of servile forms.

It has seemed to me that in the end the servility of thought, its submissiveness to useful ends, in a word its abdication, is infinitely dreadful. Indeed present day political and technical thought, which is reaching a kind of hypertrophy, has gotten us ludicrous results in the very sphere of useful ends. Nothing must be concealed: what is involved, finally, is a failure of humanity. True, this failure does not concern humanity as a whole. Only SERVILE MAN, who averts his eyes from that which is not useful, which *serves* no purpose, is implicated.

But SERVILE MAN holds the power nowadays in all quarters. And if it is true that he has not yet reduced all of humanity to his principles, at least it is certain that no voice has denounced the servility and shown what made its failure inevitable.... That may be difficult to do.... All the same, two things are equally clear: no one has yet been able to contest the right of SERVILE MAN to be in power – and yet his failure is monstrous!

The impotence of those who are revolted by an otherwise tragic situation is less surprising than it seems. If the failure of SERVILE MAN is complete, if the consequences are terrifying, it is just as certain that the principles that utilitarian thought opposed have long been without vigor. To the extent that they survive their time, they are left with the empty prestige that is tied to the final defeat of those that vanquished them. But here there can only be the tedious rehashings of regret.

I feel quite alone in seeking, in the experience of the past, not the principles that were put forward but the unperceived laws that drove the world, laws the ignorance of which leaves us headed down the paths of our misfortune. The past, which did not accept servitude, lost itself on *devious* byways, constantly going astray and cheating. We lose ourselves in an opposite direction, in the fear we have of such senseless actions and such shameful trickery. But this humanity, seared by bad memories, has no other paths than those of a past that did not know how (and was not able) to follow them with enough consequence. Everything once *served* the interests of a *few*; we have finally decided that everything should serve the interest of *all*. We see that with use the most pernicious system is the second one, *in that it is less imperfect*. This is not a reason for returning to the first. But – if we do not make *consumption* the *sovereign* principle of activity, we cannot help but succumb to those monstrous disorders without which we do not know how *to consume* the energy we have at our disposal.

III

The paradox of my attitude requires that I show the absurdity of a system in which each thing *serves*, in which nothing is *sovereign*. I cannot do so without showing that a world in which nothing is sovereign is the most unfavorable one; but that is to say in sum that we need sovereign values, hence that it is *useful* to have useless values....

This made it extremely difficult to uphold the principle of the first volume of this work, where I analyzed the relationship of production to consumption (to nonproductive consumption).[1] I was showing, of course, that production mattered less than consumption, but I could not then prevent consumption from being seen as something useful (useful even, finally, to production!...).

This second volume is very different, describing as it does the effects in the human mind of a kind of consumption of energy generally considered base. No one therefore will be able to shift from the asserted sovereign character of eroticism to the usefulness it might have. Sexuality at least is good for something; but eroticism.... We are clearly concerned, this time, with a sovereign form, *which cannot serve any purpose.*

Perhaps it will seem improper to have made activity that is disapproved, that is usually connected with shame, the key to sovereign behaviors.

I will have to excuse myself by saying that no one can act *usefully* without knowing that individuals committed to usefulness, which is his own object, all answer in the first instance to the demands of eroticism. Consequently, from whatever point of view we consider it, whether we see it as an unvarying form of man's willful autonomy, or rather we insist on inquiring about the energy pressures that condition our decisions and activities at every stage, nothing interests us more than forcing out the *secrets* of eroticism.[2]

Moreover, this dual character of my studies is present in this book: I have tried, in an epilogue, to outline the consequences of the coherent system of human expenditures of energy, where eroticism's share is substantial. I do not think, as a matter of fact, that we can touch upon the underlying meaning of political problems, where horror is always in the background, unless we consider the connection between work and eroticism, eroticism and war. I will show that these opposed forms of human activity draw from the same fund of energy resources.... Hence the necessity of giving economic, military and demographic questions a correct solution, if we are not to give up the hope of maintaining the present civilization....

IV

I am aware of the small chance I have of being understood. Not that Volume I of *The Accursed Share* was not given a genuine reception, and precisely in the circles I wanted to reach. But my ideas are too new.

From the reactions of the most qualified persons, I saw at first that these ideas were appetizing, that they aroused interest, but I also very quickly saw that they took a long time to digest. Not that I saw in the objections that were made to me[3] anything other than misunderstandings to clear up. But the distance is considerable between the customary representations and those I offer instead.

Unfortunately, I fear that the present work may be entirely unsuitable for reassuring those whom my first book interested. My determination to question man's totality — the whole of *con-*

crete reality — will be unsettling once I begin to deal with the *accursed* domain par excellence.

I do not now wish to dispel a malaise that I have deliberately provoked; I believe this malaise is necessary. Let one consider the abyss that is open before humanity! Could minds ready to draw back from horror possibly measure up to the problems put in front of them by the present time, *the accursed time par excellence?*

I would like, however, to prevent a misunderstanding that might result from my attitude. My book might be seen as an apology for eroticism, whereas I only wanted to describe a set of reactions that are *incomparably* rich. But these reactions I have described are essentially contradictory. Follow me closely here, if you will: *Human* existence commanded an abhorrence of all sexuality; this abhorrence itself commanded the attractive value of eroticism. If my perspective is apologetic, the object of this apology is not eroticism but rather, generally, *humanity.* That humanity does not cease to maintain a sum of stubborn and in-compatible, *impossibly* rigorous reactions is something worthy of admiration; indeed, *nothing merits the same degree of admiration....* But on the contrary, the laxity and lack of tension, the slackness of a dissolute self-indulgence detract from *humanity's* vigor; for *humanity* would cease to exist the day it became something other than what it is, entirely made up of violent contrasts.

PART ONE

Introduction

Eroticism and the Reflection of the

Universe in the Mind

1. The Primary Incompatibility of the World of Eroticism and the World of Thought

We never grasp the human individual – what he signifies – except in a delusive way: humanity always contradicts itself; it goes suddenly from goodness to base cruelty, from extreme modesty to extreme immodesty, from the most attractive appearance to the most odious. We often speak of the world, of humanity, as if it had some unity. In reality, humanity forms *worlds*, seemingly related but actually alien to one another. Indeed, sometimes an immeasurable distance separates them: thus, the criminal world is, in a sense, farther from a convent of Carmelites than one star is from another. But not only do these various worlds exclude and ignore one another, this incompatibility also concentrates in a single individual: when he is with his family this man is a good-natured angel, but when evening comes he wallows in debauchery. The most striking thing is that in each of the worlds to which I allude, ignorance, or at least disregard, of the others is the rule. Even the father playing with his daughter *forgets*, as it were, the disreputable places where he enters as an inveterate pig. He would be surprised in these circumstances to recall the filthy individual he has remained, breaking all the delicate rules he observes in the company of his daughter.

In a comparable way, men who at home are only peaceful obliging peasants who bounce their children up and down on their knees, in wars are capable of burning, pillaging, killing and torturing: the two worlds, in which they behave so differently, remain unconnected to one another.

What gives partitions of this sort an intangible solidity is that that reflective, coherent thinking which alone has formed a rather durable image of man – the image that in theory presides over the construction of my book – itself forms, by itself, a determinate world. The admissible judgments concerning man, always having a coherent, reflective form, are those of the world of thought, which by definition has little or no contact with the disapproved worlds (and which even keeps aloof from certain acknowledgeable but disturbing worlds[1]). I'm not saying that thought, constituted as such, is unacquainted with that which it calls "inhuman," or foul or shady, but it cannot really integrate it; it knows it from above, through condescension, from the outside: all *that* is strictly a subordinate object for it, which it considers arbitrarily, without recognizing its own involvement, in the way that medicine regards the diseases.

It will never incorporate this accursed domain into *conceivable* humanity, which alone is constitutive of thought.

Yet one might believe that psychoanalysis considers the entire sexual domain without reservation.... That is true, but only superficially so. Even psychoanalysis is obliged to define it scientifically as that element from the outside which is unassimilable, in theory, to clear consciousness. Doubtless, for psychoanalysis the concrete totality without sex is inconceivable, but the thought that is proper to science is nonetheless regarded as *actually* inviolable, as if sexuality, which played a part in its formation, thereafter no longer modified it, or if so, only in a superficial way: for psychoanalysis, sexuality and thought stay on opposite planes; like the others, psychoanalysis is a science that considers abstract facts, isolated from one another, occasionally influencing one another. In this way it retains the moral privilege of abstract thought, always worthy of great respect. It accommodates the sexual element, but this is insofar as its developments reduce it to abstraction, from which the concrete fact remains manifestly distinct.

But it is possible, beyond this correct procedure, to envisage another in which the arrogance of science or of thought could not be maintained, where eroticism and thought would no longer form separate worlds.[2]

2. The World of Eroticism and the World of Thought Are Complementary to One Another; and Without Their Congruence the Totality Is Not Fully Realized

I will hold to a starting principle as my book progresses. I will consider the sexual fact only in the framework of a concrete and integral *totality*, where the erotic and intellectual worlds are complementary to one another and are situated on the same plane.

Of course the place of sexual life is humanly delimited by a prohibition: sexual life is never unreservedly free; it must always be confined within the bounds that custom sets. It would be useless, certainly, to oppose the prohibition by denouncing it: it is not *human* to say that only freedom accords with *nature*. In fact, man sets himself essentially apart from nature; he is even vehemently opposed to it, and the absence of prohibition would have only one meaning: that *animality* which men are conscious of having left behind, and to which we cannot aspire to return. But it is another matter to deny that abhorrence of nature, built into our essence, which sets our proprieties against animal simplicity, another matter to comply with the *judgments* that ordinarily

23

accompany the prohibitions. In particular, *thought* is compelled by the morality implied in the prohibitions; further, it let itself be formed in the world devoid of sensuality, which the prohibitions marked off. Thought is asexual: one will see this limitation – antithetical to sovereignty, to every sovereign attitude – make of the intellectual world the flat and subordinate world that we know, this world of useful and isolated things, in which laborious activity is the rule, in which it is implied that each one of us should keep his place in a mechanical order. If I consider, rather, the *totality* which exceeds on all sides the reduced world of thought, I know that it is made up of distances and oppositions. But I can never, without turning away from it, let go of one of its parts for another. For the popular voice, "it takes all kinds to make a world," prostitutes and saints, scoundrels and men whose generosity is boundless, but that voice is not that of established thought, which reduces man to the neutral part and denies this integral ensemble, combining the giving of oneself and the tears with the massacres and the revelry.

I don't intend in this way to declare a vague judgment concerning men, but rather to define a way of thinking whose movement corresponds to the concrete character of the totality that is offered for reflection.[3] I would like to set forth this method by using it rather than by analyzing it separately. But I needed to begin by saying that my purpose, to talk about eroticism, could no more be isolated from the reflection of the universe in the mind than the latter could be isolated from eroticism; but this implies in the first place that reflection, thought, under these conditions, must be commensurate with its object, and not that my object, eroticism, be commensurate with the traditional thought that established the contempt for that object.[4]

24

PART TWO

The Prohibition of Incest

One

The Problem of Incest

1. The Opposition between the "Eroticism" of Men and the "Sexuality" of Animals

The desire to carry the movement of thought toward a completion, which is not a nonsensical aim but a necessary condition for the study of a crucial subject, must not distract one from a preliminary question.

In the present case, the problem of the origin is decisive. Essentially, eroticism is the sexual activity of man, as opposed to that of animals. Not all of human sexuality is erotic, but it is erotic often enough not to be simply animal sexuality. Let it be said from the outset that this book surveys an entire domain whose ethereal aspect is no less meaningful than the contrary aspect.[1] But to begin with, its object is the passage from the simple sexuality of animals to the cerebral activity of man, which is implied in eroticism. I am referring to the associations and judgments that tend to qualify sexually objects, beings, places and moments that by themselves have nothing sexual about them, nor anything contrary to sexuality: the meaning attached to nudity, for example, and the prohibition of incest. In this sense, chastity itself is one of the aspects of eroticism, that is, of properly *human* sexuality.

A priori, a study of the passage from animal to man should base itself on a minimum of objective, historical data. In the light of these data we might conjecture what occurred. We cannot think of knowing in the precise sense of knowing events, but we are not so ill equipped as it seems at first. We know, on the one hand, that men made tools and used them at various tasks to provide for their subsistence. In a word, they distinguished themselves from animals through *work*. Concurrently, they imposed a certain number of restrictions on themselves concerning sexual activity and behavior with respect to the dead. In theory, the prohibition of murder is associated with the taboos relating to dead persons (corpses). For their part, the sexual taboos are tied to the basic aspects of the human sensibility, having to do mainly with excremental emissions [−but these aspects are more complex and cannot be the object of an immediate general survey].[2] In any case, the restrictions I spoke of, *which we do not cease to observe,* all appear at the dawn of mankind. The earth preserves the traces of the attention brought to bear by the first men on the remains of their fellows. Similarly, nothing allows us to suppose that there lived beings corresponding to anthropology's definitions of *Homo sapiens* who did not observe the incest prohibition.

I will leave aside for the moment certain complementary aspects of the sexual taboo: they determine the human attitude toward various functions that are more or less closely adjacent to the organs of regeneration. The study of the incest problem is doubtless the most pressing. It is true that it draws us away at first from the *total* views to which I will give primary importance in this book. But while it is true that ultimately the partial view must be situated in the framework of a more comprehensive view, the latter could not be clear if it were composed of unfamiliar details. I cannot show anything *global* except by defining it in relation to something already seen. It is the specific − and entirely external – data relating to the incest prohibition which will form the intangible core of a more complete representation. The instability of forms, perceived in the rule of incest, will provide a means of grasping an object so mobile that it seems ungraspable. Indeed, curiously, the object of human sexual desire, the object that excites this desire, cannot be defined in a precise way. In its form it is always an arbitrary conception of the mind, a kind of cerebral caprice – yet it is universal! Only the rule of incest, universal but with variable modalities, can make it sufficiently familiar. The erotic world is imaginary in its form; it is analogous to a dream, and there is no better way to get used to this oddity than by seeing the arbitrary limits of an opposite world take form, a world *in which sexuality is forbidden*. For the fundamental prohibitions divide the forms of human life into separate domains, whose partitions seem to defy our reason and our temperament as sovereign beings. What is permitted in one place is criminal in another. Such is the rule – so arbitrary as to appear a provocation – by which we became men, and of which the incest prohibition is the type.

2. The Prohibition of Incest
I cannot better represent what it is possible to know about incest than by following the writer with the most authority in the matter.

Under the somewhat closed title of *The Elementary Structures of Kinship*,[3] it is the "problem of incest" that the work of Claude Lévi-Strauss attempts to solve.

The "problem of incest" arises in the context of the family: it is always a degree, or more exactly a form, of kinship that determines the prohibition forbidding sexual relations or the marriage of two persons. Further, the kinship determination has to do with the position of the individuals with respect to one another: some cannot marry, others can. Finally, the cousin relationship offers

29

a privileged indication concerning the possibility of marriage, often to the exclusion of all other ties.

If we consider incest we are immediately struck by the universal character of the prohibition. In one form or another, all of humanity knows it, but the persons targeted by the prohibition change from place to place. Here, one kind of kinship comes under the prohibition – for example, the cousin relationship of children born, respectively, of the father and his sister; elsewhere, this is rather the preferred condition for marriage, and the children of two brothers – or of two sisters – cannot marry. The most civilized peoples limit the prohibition to relations between children and parents, brothers and sisters. But as a general rule, among primitive peoples we find the various individuals distributed into quite distinct categories that decide which sexual relations are to be prohibited or prescribed.

Moreover, we must also consider two distinct situations. In the first, the one studied by Lévi-Strauss in *The Elementary Structures of Kinship*, the precise character of the blood ties is the basis of rules *determining* not only the illegitimacy but also the possibility of marriage. In the second, which the author labels "complex structures" but does not treat in that work, the determination of the spouse is left "to other mechanisms, economic or psychological." The categories remain unchanged, but while there are still forbidden ones, it is no longer custom that determines the category from which the spouse must be chosen (if not strictly, at least *preferentially*). This takes us far from the situation with which we are concerned, but the author thinks that the "prohibitions" cannot be considered in isolation, that their study cannot be dissociated from that of the "privileges" that complement them. This is doubtless the reason why the title of his work avoids the word *incest* and refers – although with a degree of obscurity, preferable to a misunderstanding – to the *indissociable system* of prohibitions and privileges, of oppositions and prescriptions.

3. Science's Answers to the Riddle of Incest

Lévi-Strauss opposes the state of culture to that of nature, much in the way that it is customary to contrast man with animals. This leads him to say of the incest prohibition (it being understood that he also has in mind the rules of exogamy that complement it) that "it is the fundamental step because of which, by which, but above all in which, the transition from nature to culture is accomplished."[4] There would thus be in the horror of incest an element that marks us out as *human beings*, and the resulting problem would be that of *man* himself, insofar as he adds humanity to the universe. *What we are*, hence *all* that we are, would be involved in the decision that sets us against the vague freedom of sexual contacts, against the natural and undefined life of the "beasts." It may be that this formula indicates an extreme ambition, which sees in knowledge the desire to reveal man to himself and so to bring together in the one who perceives him the totality of the real and its reflection in the mind. It may be too that, finally, in the face of such a remote exigency, Lévi-Strauss will voice a disclaimer and recall the modesty of his intention. But there is no reason to think that the exigency – or the movement – conveyed in such a burning step can be limited, and by nature the decision to solve the riddle of incest is laden with consequences: it claims to illuminate what was proposed in darkness.... Moreover, if some step, long ago, accomplished "the transition from nature to culture," how could the step that would define its meaning itself fail to have some unexpected consequences?

Indeed, unavoidably we soon have to give ourselves grounds for modesty. From the outset Lévi-Strauss is led to review, for our benefit, the missteps of those who went before. They are not encouraging.

This gives us once again a general appreciation of the super-ficialities, the blunders, with which the desire to know at little expense is satisfied.

The most painful tribute is paid to the finalist theory, which construes the prohibition as a eugenic measure: it would be a matter of shielding the species from the results of consanguineous marriages. This point of view had illustrious defenders (Lewis Morgan among them). Its diffusion is recent: "it appears nowhere," Lévi-Strauss says, "before the sixteenth century";[5] but it is still widespread, there being nothing more common nowadays than the belief in the degenerate character of the children of incest. But observation has not confirmed what is based on nothing more than the crude feeling that everything in nature has a meaning.

For some, "the prohibition of incest is no more than the social projection or reflection of natural feelings or tendencies, which can be entirely explained by human nature." An instinctive repugnance (!) it is said. Lévi-Strauss has an easy time showing that the opposite is true: psychoanalysis has shown that longing for incestuous relations is common. If this were not so, why would the prohibition be such a serious matter? As I see it, explanations of this type are fundamentally mistaken: what needs to be specified is the meaning of a reprobation that does not exist among animals, that must be given historically, that is not simply in the order of things.

As it happens, this criticism is addressed by *historical* explanations.

"McLennan and Spencer saw exogamous practices as the fixing by custom of the habits of warrior tribes among whom capture was the normal means of obtaining wives."[6] Durkheim saw the *taboo* for the members of the clan, the blood of this clan – hence the menstrual blood of the women – as the explanation for the prohibition denying these women to the men of their clan, and for the absence of a prohibition on men of another clan. Such interpretations may be logically satisfactory, but "their weakness lies in the fact that the connections so established are fragile and arbitrary...."[7] To the very sociological theory of Durkheim it would be possible to join the psychoanalytic hypothesis of Freud, who places a supposed murder of the father by the brothers at the origin of the transition from animal to man: according to Freud, the mutually jealous brothers uphold vis-à-vis one another the father's prohibition against touching their mother or their sisters. Actually, Freud's "myth" introduces the most gratuitous set of circumstances, but at least it has the advantage over the sociologist's explanation of being an expression of living obsessions. Lévi-Strauss says this in felicitous terms:

> Freud successfully accounts, not for the beginning of civilization but for its present state.... The desire for the mother or the sister, the murder of the father and the sons' repentence, undoubtedly do not correspond to any fact or group of facts occupying a given place in history. But perhaps they symbolically express an ancient and lasting dream.[8] The magic of this dream, its power to mold men's thoughts unbeknown to them, arises precisely from the fact that the acts it evokes have never been committed, because culture has opposed them at all times and in all places....[9]

4. The Morally Untenable Character of the Distinctions between the Prohibited and the Licit

So the least vacuous theory is at the same time the most absurd! It is clear that Freud meant to respond, or at least was tempted to respond, to the immense ambition I spoke of. He had a feel for the peculiar, decisive and quasi-mythological approach, befitting a "riddle solver" (how to overlook the lasting resonance of a verse appearing as an epigraph to *The Interpretation of Dreams*:

Flectere si nequeo superos, Acheronta movebo...). Freud thus gave his interventions a value situated, like myths, in the totality of the real. But Lévi-Strauss's reservations, while recognizing the breadth of the inquiry, make its failure more painful. Finally, it goes without saying that only the down-to-earth, rigorous approach is suited to an inquiry that is compromised as much by inspired conjecture as by the lack of it. One must be slow and tenacious, therefore, and not let oneself be discouraged by inextricable data, by brain-racking, "jigsaw-puzzle" terms.

It is, in fact, an enormous jigsaw puzzle, doubtless one of the toughest, one of the most complex, that has ever been solved. Interminable and, moreover, it must be said, hopelessly boring: about two thirds of Lévi-Strauss's big book is devoted to a meticulous examination of the multiple combinations imagined in order to solve a problem, the very posing of which was, after all, what had to be extracted from an arbitrary imbroglio.

> Members of the same generation are also divided into two groups: on the one hand, cousins (whatever their degree) who are kinsmen from two collaterals of the same sex, and who call each other 'brothers' and 'sisters' (parallel cousins) and, on the other hand, cousins descended from collaterals of different sex (whatever their degree), who are called by special terms and between whom marriage is possible (cross-cousins).

This is, to start with, the definition of the *simple* type, the one that proves fundamental, but whose numerous variants raise endless questions. The theme given in this basic structure is moreover a riddle in itself. "Why set up a barrier," the author says,

> between cousins descended from collaterals of the same sex, and cousins from collaterals of different sex, when in respect to prox-

imity both cases are the same? Nevertheless, to pass from one to the other makes all the difference between clearly marked incest (parallel cousins being likened to brothers and sisters) and unions which are not only possible but even those which are enjoined upon everybody (since cross-cousins are designated by the term for potential spouses). The distinction is incompatible with our biological criterion for incest....[10]

Of course, things become complicated in every way, and it often seems to be a matter of arbitrary and insignificant choices; yet, among the multitude of variants, one more discrimination assumes a privileged value. There is not only a rather common privilege of the *cross*-cousin over the *parallel* cousin, but also of the *matrilinear* cross-cousin over the *patrilinear* cross-cousin. I will put this as simply as I can. The daughter of my paternal uncle is my parallel cousin; in this world of "elementary structures" with which we are concerned, there is a good chance that I will not be able to marry her, or know her sexually in any way: I regard her as the analogue of my sister, and I give her the name "sister." But the daughter of my paternal aunt (of my father's sister), who is my cross-cousin, is different from the daughter of my maternal aunt, who is also a cross-cousin: it is the first that I call patrilinear, the second being matrilinear. Obviously, there is a chance that I can freely marry either one; this is done in many primitive societies. (It may be, too, in this case that the first, the daughter of my paternal aunt, is also the daughter of my maternal uncle; indeed, this maternal uncle may very well have married my paternal aunt. In a society where marriage between cross-cousins is not subject to some secondary discrimination, this is what ordinarily takes place. Then I say of my cross-cousin that she is *bilateral*.) But it may also be the case that marriage with one of these cross-cousins is forbidden to me as being incestuous. Some "societies prescribe

35

marriage with the father's sister's daughter and prohibit it with the mother's brother's daughter, whereas in other places still, it is the contrary which occurs."[11] But the situation of my two cousins is not the same; I am likely to see the prohibition rise up between the first and myself, much less likely if I wish to marry the second. "If the distribution of these two forms of marriage is considered," says Lévi-Strauss, "it will be noted that the second type is much the more common."[12]

So, in the first analysis, these are the essential forms of consanguinity on which the prohibition or prescription of marriage is based.

It is obvious that when the terms are defined in this way the mystery is, if anything, deepened. Not only is the difference between these distinct forms of kinship a formal one, devoid of meaning for us, not only are we far from the clear specificity that counterposes our sisters or relatives to the rest of humanity, but this specificity often has a contrary – or *the* contrary – result, depending on the place. We are generally led to look to the specificity of the individuals concerned – to their respective situation, to their *relations*, in the sense of moral behavior – for the reasons behind the prohibition that affects them. But this invites us to look elsewhere. Lévi-Strauss himself notes how disarming this degree of arbitrariness is for sociologists.[13] They "find it hard to excuse cross-cousin marriage for having raised the problem of the difference between children of collaterals of different sexes, and then adding the further problem of the difference between the mother's brother's daughter and the father's sister's daughter...."

But if the author does such a good job of showing the closed nature of the riddle, this is really in order to solve it more convincingly.

It was simply a matter of finding the domain in which such distinctions, untenable in theory, have consequences nonetheless.

If certain effects differ according to whether one or another of these categories comes into play, the meaning of the distinctions will appear. Lévi-Strauss has shown the role of a distributive system of exchange in the archaic institution of marriage. The acquisition of a wife was that of a precious article of wealth, the value of which was even sacred: the distribution of this wealth raised vital problems, which had to be dealt with by rules. Apparently an anarchy like that reigning today could not have solved such problems. Only circuits of exchange in which the rights are predetermined can bring about, often poorly no doubt, but rather well on the whole, a balanced distribution of women among the various men to be provided.

TWO

Lévi-Strauss's Answer

1. The Rules of Exogamy, the Gift of Women and Their Distribution

We cannot easily submit to the logic of this situation. Given the extreme relaxation in which we live, in the world of numerous and indefinite possibilities, we cannot envisage the tension that is inherent in life in small groups often separated by hostility. It takes an effort to imagine the difficulty to which the guarantee of the rule responds. Moreover, we have to take into account the general conditions of life in these archaic societies.

Thus, it is essential that we do not picture transactions analogous to those in our time, in which material wealth is the object. Even in the worst cases, the idea suggested by a formula such as "marriage by purchase" is far removed from a primitive reality in which exchange did not have the character of a narrow operation, subject only to the rule of self-interest, that it has in our day.

Lévi-Strauss has duly placed the structure of an institution such as marriage back in the overall movement of exchanges that animates the primitive population. He refers to the "conclusions of the famous *Essai sur le don* (1923)."[14] "In this study, which today is regarded as a classic," he writes,

Mauss sought to show that exchange in primitive societies consists not so much in economic transactions as in reciprocal gifts, that these reciprocal gifts have a far more important function in these societies than in our own, and that this primitive form of exchange is not merely nor essentially of an economic nature but is what he aptly calls "a total social fact," that is, an event which has a significance that is at once social and religious, magic and economic, utilitarian and sentimental, juridical and moral.[15]

A principle of generosity always presides over these kinds of exchanges, which always have a ceremonial character: certain goods cannot be consigned to a drab or utilitarian consumption. These are generally luxury goods. Even in our day, luxury products are devoted, in a fundamental way, to ceremonial life. They are reserved for gift-giving, receptions, parties: *champagne*, for example, is treated this way. Champagne is drunk on certain occasions, where, according to the rule, it is *offered*. Of course, all the champagne that is drunk is an object of transactions: the bottles are purchased from the producer. But at the moment it is drunk, it is drunk only in part by the one who paid for it; at any rate, this is the principle governing the consumption of a good whose nature is festive, whose mere presence denotes a moment different from another, *altogether different* from just any moment – moreover, a good that, in response to a deep expectation, "must" or "should" flow abundantly, in fact *without measure*.

Readers of the first volume of this work will recognize the principles and facts that I presented there a first time. I am now resuming that exposition in the form – or very nearly – that Lévi-Strauss has given it. I cannot regret the repetition, which has this value in my view: it calls attention to a fundamental discovery. Unfortunately, I was the first – and doubtless am still the only one – to take it into account from the standpoint of economic theory. But, on the one hand, I consider the economy in *general* terms: I would not have been able to reflect on the "gift" as an "archaic mode of exchange" had I confined myself to the partial operations that political economy examines. On the other hand, the "gift," the "potlatch" analyzed by Marcel Mauss is, as Lévi-Strauss points out, a "total social fact." As such, it is situated at the same time in two domains often isolated from one another. As I begin to consider – in the context of general economy – the by no means isolable figure of eroticism, it should come as no surprise to us that the principle of the *gift*, which propels the movement of general activity, is at the basis of sexual activity. This is true of its simplest form: physically, the sexual act is the gift of an exuberant energy. This is true of its more complex forms, of marriage and of the laws of distribution of women among men.

Let us go back to the image of the champagne, itself animated by the movement of general exuberance and clearly symbolic of an overflowing energy. One sees Lévi-Strauss's thesis then: the father who would marry his daughter, or the brother who would marry his sister, would be like the owner of champagne who would never invite any friends, who would drink up his stock by himself. The father must bring the wealth that is his daughter, or the brother the wealth that is his sister, into the circuit of ceremonial exchanges: he must give her as a present, but the circuit presupposes a set of rules accepted in a given milieu as the rules of a game are.

Lévi-Strauss has explained in depth the rules that preside over this system of exchanges, which is largely free of self-interest. "These gifts," he writes, "are either exchanged immediately for equivalent gifts or are received by the beneficiaries on condition that at a later date they will give counter-gifts often exceeding the original goods in value, but which in their turn bring about a subsequent right to receive new gifts surpassing the original ones in sumptuousness."[16] What we should keep in mind here is the fact that the avowed goal of these operations is not "to receive a profit or advantage of an economic nature." Sometimes the show of generosity goes to the point of destroying the offered objects. Pure and simple destruction evidently commands great prestige. Moreover, the production of luxury goods, whose real meaning is the honor of the one who possesses them, receives them or gives them, is itself a destruction of useful labor, of the labor that could have been devoted to something useful (this is the contrary of capitalism, which accumulates useful product-making forces): the dedication of objects to glorious exchanges withdraws them from productive consumption.

This opposition to the mercantile spirit, to haggling and self-interested calculation, must be stressed if one wishes to speak of "marriage by exchange." Not even marriage by purchase fails to participate in the same movement: "it is only a modality of that basic system analyzed by Mauss...," says Lévi-Strauss.[17] These forms of marriage are unquestionably dissimilar to those in which we see the *humanity* of unions, where we assume a free choice on both sides, and yet they do not place women in the domain of commerce and calculation, but assimilate them to festivity, to *champagne*.... In this system "women are not primarily a sign of social value, but a natural stimulant."[18] "Malinowski has shown that in the Trobriand Islands, even after marriage, the payment of *mapula* represents on the man's part a counter-prestation intended to compensate for services provided by the wife in terms of sexual gratification."[19]

Thus, women are essentially pledged to *communication*, which is to say, they must be an object of generosity on the part of those who have them at their immediate disposal. The latter must give them away, but in a world where every generous act contrib-

utes to the circuit of general generosity. I will receive, if I give
my daughter, another woman for my son (or my nephew). What
we have, in sum, throughout a limited ensemble, is generosity,
organic communication. The forms of exchange are settled on in
advance, as are the manifold movements of a dance or an orches-
tration. What is denied in the incest prohibition is only the result
of an affirmation. The brother giving his sister does not so much
deny the value of sexual union with his close kinswoman as he
affirms the greater value of marriage that would join this sister
with another man, and himself with another woman. There is a
more intense communication in exchange based on generosity
than there would be in immediate gratification. More exactly, festivity assumes the introduction of movement – the negation of
withdrawal into self, hence a denial of the supreme value of avarice. The sexual relation is itself communication and movement;
it has the nature of a festival. Being essentially a communication,
it requires an outward movement from the beginning.

If the tumultuous movement of the senses is to be carried out,
it needs a drawing-back, a renunciation, a backward step without which no one could leap so far. But the drawing-back itself
requires the rule, which organizes the round and ensures its indefinite recurrence.

2. The Propitiousness of the Various, Seemingly Arbitrary, Forms of the Prohibition to the Gift-exchange

This calls for explanation, of course. Furthermore, I need to make
clear the extent to which I have gone beyond (in one respect) the
thinking of Lévi-Strauss, who only speaks implicitly and doubtless would not go so far as to say what I say: that a dialectical process of *development* is involved. . . .

He limits himself essentially to the following:

The prohibition of incest is less a rule prohibiting marriage with the mother, sister or daughter, than a rule obliging the mother, sister or daughter to be given to others. It is the supreme rule of the gift, and it is clearly this aspect, too often unrecognized, which allows its nature to be understood.... The reasons why marriage with the mother, daughter or sister can be prevented are sought in a quality intrinsic to these women. One is therefore drawn infallibly towards biological considerations, since it is only from a biological, certainly not social, point of view that motherhood, sisterhood or daughter-hood are properties of the individuals considered. However, from a social viewpoint, these terms cannot be regarded as defining iso-lated individuals, but relationships between these individuals and everyone else.[20]

Further, he emphasizes another, perhaps reconcilable but clearly opposed aspect of the value of women: their material utility. I need to specify this trait in turn: I believe it to be sec-ondary, but if it were not taken into account one would not be able to measure the scope of the exchanges that are effected, and Lévi-Strauss's theory would remain suspended. Up to this point it is a brilliant, captivating hypothesis, but we still have to find the meaning of this mosaic of varied prohibitions, the possible meaning of the choice among forms of kinship whose opposition seems insignificant. Lévi-Strauss has rightly applied himself to sorting out the effects of the various forms of kinship on the *exchanges*; in this way he has given his hypothesis a solid founda-tion, focusing on the most tangible aspect of the exchanges whose interplay he follows.

In contrast to the alluring aspect of the value of women, to which I have called attention (and which Lévi-Strauss himself mentions – without emphasis), there is in fact the material inter-est which the possession of a wife represents for the husband.

44

This interest cannot be denied and, once again, I do not think that one can correctly trace the movement of the exchanges of women without taking note of it. Later I will attempt to resolve the manifest contradiction of these two viewpoints. This is not the least bit incompatible with Lévi-Strauss's interpretation, on the contrary; but first I must insist on the aspect which he underscores himself: "But, as often noted," he says,

> in most primitive societies (and also, but to a lesser extent, in the rural classes of our own society) marriage is of an entirely different importance, not erotic, but economic. In our society, the difference between the economic status of the married man and the unmarried man amounts almost solely to the fact that the bachelor has to replace his wardrobe more frequently.[21]

The situation is altogether different in groups where the satisfaction of economic needs rests entirely on the marriage partnership and the sexual division of labor. Not only do the man and the woman not have the same technical specialization, and so depend on one another for the making of the objects needed for daily tasks, but they devote themselves to producing different types of food. A complete, and above all regular diet thus depends on this veritable "production cooperative" that a household constitutes. In a sense, this necessity for a man to marry holds a sanction in store. If a society misorganizes the exchange of women, a real disorder ensues. That is why a part of the operation must not be left to chance; it implies rules ensuring reciprocity. But however perfect a system of exchanges may be, it cannot suit every case; variations and frequent alterations result.

The basic situation is always the same and it defines the function that the system must everywhere carry out.

Of course, "the negative aspect is only the superficial aspect

THE PROHIBITION OF INCEST

of the prohibition."[22] It is important everywhere to define a set
of obligations that gets the movements of reciprocity or circulation started.

> A group within which marriage is prohibited immediately conjures
> up the idea of another group...within which marriage is merely
> possible, or inevitable, according to circumstances. The prohibi-
> tion on the sexual use of a daughter or sister compels them to be
> given in marriage to another man, and at the same time it estab-
> lishes a right to the daughter or sister of this other man. In this
> way, every negative stipulation of the prohibition has its positive
> counterpart.[23]

Consequently, "from the moment I forgo a woman, who then
becomes...available for another man, there is, somewhere, a
man who gives up a woman who becomes, from this fact, available for me."[24]

Frazer had already been the first to note that "the marriage of
cross-cousins was the direct consequence of the interchange of
sisters in marriage."[25] But he had not made this the basis of a
general explanation, and the sociologists had not taken up ideas
that were nevertheless satisfactory. While in the marriage of parallel cousins the group neither loses nor acquires, the marriage
of cross-cousins results in an exchange from one group to the
other: indeed, in ordinary circumstances the female cousin does
not belong to the same group as her male cousin. In this way, "a
structure of reciprocity is built up, according to which the group
which has given can demand...."[26] "Parallel cousins come from
families in the same formal position, which is a position of static
disequilibrium, while cross-cousins come from families in conflicting formal positions, i.e., in relationship to one another they
are in a dynamic disequilibrium...."[27]

Thus, the mystery of the difference between parallel and cross-cousins resolves into the difference between a solution favorable to exchange and another where stagnation would tend to prevail. But in this simple opposition we only have a dual organization and the exchange is said to be *restricted*. If more than two groups come into play, we pass to *generalized exchange*.

In *generalized exchange*, a man A marries a woman B; a man B, a woman C, a man C, a woman A. (And these forms may be expanded.) Under these different conditions, just as the crossing of cousins provided the privileged form of exchange, the marriage of matrilineal cousins offers, for structural reasons, open possibilities for indefinite linkage. "A human group," says Lévi-Strauss, "need only proclaim the law of marriage with the mother's brother's daughter for a vast cycle of reciprocity between all generations and lineages to be organized, as harmonious and ineluctable as any physical or biological law, whereas marriage with the father's sister's daughter" cannot extend the chain of matrimonial transactions; it cannot, in any vital way, reach a goal always tied to the need for exchange, the extension of alliances and of power.

3. The Vicissitudes of Eroticism Considered As a History

We shouldn't wonder at the ambiguous character of Lévi-Strauss's theory. On the one hand, the exchange, or rather the giving of women brings into play the interest of the one who gives – who gives only on condition of a return gift. On the other hand, it is a function of his generosity. This corresponds to the double aspect of the "gift-exchange," of the institution often given the name "potlatch": potlatch is at once a surpassing of calculation and the height of calculation. But perhaps it is unfortunate that Lévi-Strauss dwelled so little on the relation of the potlatch of women with the structure of eroticism.

47

We shall see in fact that the formation of eroticism implies an alternation of repulsion and attraction, of negation and the affirmation that follows it, which differs from the first, immediate alternation in that it is human (erotic) and not simply sexual, animal. It is true that marriage often seems contrary to eroticism. But we think of it in this way because of an aspect that is perhaps secondary. Might we not suppose that at the moment when the rules were established, which decreed these barriers and the lifting of them, they truly determined the conditions of sexual activity? Marriage appears to be a vestige from a time when sexual relations depended on them in a fundamental way. Would an institution of prohibitions and liftings of prohibition *that essentially concern sexuality* have been formed rigorously if it had no other purpose at first than the establishment of a home? Everything indicates, it seems to me, that the problem of intimate relations is addressed in these regulations. How to explain, otherwise, that the unnatural movement of renunciation of one's kin is given in them? This was an extraordinary movement, a kind of inner revolution whose intensity must have been excessive since the most terrible dread was ordinary in response to the mere idea of a lapse. It was this movement, no doubt, that was at the origin of the potlatch of women (exogamy), of that paradoxical gift of the coveted object. It seems implausible that a sanction, that of prohibition, would have been imposed so strongly – and everywhere – if it had not concerned genesial violence. Conversely, it seems to me that the object of the prohibition was first marked out for coveting by the prohibition itself: if the prohibition was essentially of a sexual nature it must have drawn attention to the sexual value of its object (or rather, its erotic value). This is precisely what distinguishes man from animals: the limit set on free sexual activity gave a new value to what was, for animals, only an irresistible, fleeting impulse, destitute of meaning.

48

This twofold movement seems to me to be the essence of eroticism and it also seems to me, following Lévi-Strauss's theory, to be that of the rules of exchange that are linked to the incest prohibition. The connection between eroticism and these rules is often difficult to perceive due to the fact that the latter have marriage as their essential object and marriage and eroticism are usually opposed to one another. Economic association with a view to reproduction became the dominant aspect of marriage. Where the rules of marriage do come into play, they may *have had* as their object the whole course of sexual life, but it is as if, finally, their only purpose were the distribution of useful wealth. Women came to be understood in terms of their fecundity and their labor.

This contradictory evolution was itself predetermined. It is certain that erotic life cannot be *settled* [reglée]. It was given rules, but these rules could only assign it a domain outside the rules. And once eroticism was dismissed from marriage, the latter tended to assume a chiefly material aspect, the importance of which Lévi-Strauss was right to underscore: the rules ensuring the sharing out of women as coveted objects did in fact ensure the sharing out of women as labor power.

It is quite clear, then, that man's sexual life cannot be considered as a simple datum, but rather as a history. It is first of all the negation of animal freedom, but the rules that it takes on are provisional: its destiny is the ceaseless overturning whose detours I will attempt to trace.

The Transition from Animal to Man

1. The Limits of Lévi-Strauss's Theory and the Transition from Animal to Man

Lévi-Strauss's work seems to provide good – and uncommonly exact – answers to the main questions raised by the strange consequences of the incest prohibition. If I thought it necessary, at the end of my analysis, to introduce a two-phase movement, this movement was nonetheless implicit in the author's exposition.

Yet, to a certain extent, the general design of the work limits, if not its import, then at least its immediate sense, which is essentially situated in a cycle of exchanges, in a "total social fact" where the whole of life takes form. This principle notwithstanding, the economic explanation is pursued almost from start to finish, as if it had to stand by itself. Not a word can be said against this, except insofar as the author himself states the necessary reservations. There remains a need to look, from rather far away, at the whole taking form. Lévi-Strauss felt this need, of course, and at the end, in the last pages of the book, he gives the expected overview. These last pages are remarkable, essential, but they represent more of an indication than a construction. The analysis of an isolated aspect is conducted to perfection, but the global aspect in which this isolated aspect is embedded remains roughly outlined. Apparently this is owing to the horror of philosophy that dominates – and doubtless for good reasons – the scholarly world. However, I think it is difficult to deal with the transition from nature to culture while staying within the limits of the science that isolates, that abstracts its views. The desire for these limits is discernible, no doubt, in the fact of speaking not of animality but of nature, not of man but of culture. This is to go from one abstract view to another, and to exclude the moment when the whole of being is engaged in a change. I think it is difficult to grasp this whole in one, or more, of its states and the change evidenced in the advent of man cannot be isolated from *all* that man's becoming is, from all that is involved if man and animality are set against one another in a laceration that exposes the whole of divided being. In other words, we can grasp being only in history: in changes, transitions from one state to another, not in the sequence of states. In speaking of nature, of culture, Lévi-Strauss has juxtaposed abstractions, whereas the transition from animal to man involves not just the formal states but the drama in which they opposed one another.

2. The Human Specificity

Understandable historical prohibitions, the advent of labor and, subjectively, of lasting repulsions and an insurmountable disgust are so characteristic of the opposition between animal and man that, in spite of the remote date of the *event*, I can say that nothing is better known. I submit as a principle the incontestable fact that man is an animal who does not simply accept the natural given, who negates it. In this way, he changes the natural external world; he derives from it tools and manufactured objects that form a new world, the *human* world. Concurrently, man negates himself; he trains himself; he refuses, for example, to give to the satisfaction of his animal needs that *free* course on which the animal placed no restraint. It still must be granted that the two negations by man — of the given world and of his own animality — are linked. It is not for us to give a priority to one or the other, to try to determine whether the training (which appears in the form of religious prohibitions) is the consequence of labor, or the labor is the consequence of moral mutation. But insofar as there is man, on the one hand there is labor and on the other a negation, through prohibitions, of man's animal nature.

Man essentially denies his animal needs, and this is the point on which his basic prohibitions were brought to bear, some of which are so universal and seemingly so self-evident that there is never any question of them. Only the Bible, if we must find an example, gives a particular form (the prohibition on nudity) to the general prohibition on the sexual instinct, saying of Adam and Eve that they knew they were naked. But one doesn't even speak of the horror of *excreta*, which is a uniquely human trait. The prescriptions that generally concern our foul aspects are not the object of any focused attention and are not even classed among the taboos. So there exists a mode of the transition from animal to man so radically negative that it is not even spoken of. It is not even regarded as one of man's religious reactions, whereas the most insignificant taboos are so regarded. The negation is so completely successful on this point that merely to note and affirm that something is there is deemed less than human.

In order to simplify, I will not speak now of the third aspect of the human specificity, which concerns the awareness of death. In this connection I will merely point out that this unarguable conception of the transition from animal to man is theoretically that of Hegel. Yet Hegel, who stresses the first and third aspects, shuns the second, thus submitting (through silence) to the universal prohibitions that we are examining. This is less important than it first appears, in the sense that these elementary forms of the negation of animality show up again in more complex forms. But where incest is the specific concern, one may doubt that it is possible to neglect the elementary prohibition on obscenity.[28]

3. The Variability of Incest Rules and the Generally Variable Character of the Objects of Sexual Prohibition

How in fact could we define incest in any other terms? We cannot say: "this" is obscene. Obscenity is a relation. There is no "obscenity" in the way there is "fire" or "blood," but only in the way there is, for example, "indecent behavior." This is obscene if some person sees it and says it is; it is not exactly an object, but rather a relation between an object and the mind of a person. In this sense, one can define situations such that given aspects of them are, or at least appear to be, obscene. Moreover, these situations are unstable; they always include ill-defined elements, or if they have some stability, this involves a degree of arbitrariness. And further, the compromises with the necessities of life are numerous. Incest is one of these situations, defined arbitrarily.

This perception is so necessary, so unavoidable, that if we could not allege the universality of incest, we could not easily show the universally human character of the prohibition of obscenity. Incest is the first evidence of the basic connection between man and the denial of sensuality, of sensual animality.

Of course man has never managed to deny sensuality, except in a superficial way (or by default). Even the saints at least have temptations. It is only a matter of setting aside domains where sexual activity cannot enter. Thus there are places, circumstances and persons that are off-limits: the aspects of naked sensuality are obscene in these places, in these circumstances or in regard to these persons. These aspects, places, circumstances and persons are variable and always arbitrarily defined. Thus, nudity is not in itself obscene: it has become so nearly everywhere, but unevenly.

54

It is nudity that, because of a misstep, Genesis speaks of, expressing the transition, through the consciousness of obscenity, from animal to man. But what offended people's sense of decency at the beginning of the century no longer offends or offends less. The relative nudity of women bathers is still obscene on a Spanish beach, not on a French one; but in a city, even in France, the woman's bathing suit upsets a great many people. In the same way, a low-cut gown, incorrect at noon, is correct in the evening. And the most intimate nudity is not the least bit obscene in a doctor's office.

Under the same conditions, the restrictions with regard to people are changeable. In theory, they limit the sexual contacts of persons who live together to relations between the father and the mother, to the inevitable conjugal life. But like the prohibitions concerning appearances, circumstances or places, these limits are quite uncertain, quite variable. In the first place, the expression "who live together" is admissible only on one condition: that it not be specified. We find just as much arbitrariness in this area – and just as many compromises – as there is in connection with the meaning of nudity. The influence of convenience is especially important here. Lévi-Strauss's exposition makes the part it plays rather clear. The arbitrary boundary between permitted and prohibited kin is a function of the need to ensure circuits of exchange. When these organized circuits cease to be useful the incestuous situation is reduced. If utility no longer enters in, one tends to remove obstacles whose arbitrariness becomes blatant. On the other hand, the meaning of the prohibition is enhanced by a stabilization; its intrinsic value is more keenly felt. Whenever it is convenient, moreover, the boundary can be extended anew, as in the divorce proceedings of the Middle Ages.... No matter, it is always a question of countering animal disorderliness with the principle of perfect humanity, for which the flesh and animality

55

do not exist. Full social humanity radically excludes the disorder of the senses; it negates its natural principle; it rejects this given and allows only the clean space of a house, of polished floors, furniture, window panes, a space inhabited by venerable persons, at once naive and inviolable, tender and inaccessible. This symbol does not just manifest the limit denying the mother to the son or the daughter to the father; in general it is the image – or the sanctuary – of that asexual humanity, which shelters its values from the violence and dirtiness of passion.

4. Man's Essence Is Found in the Prohibition of Incest, and in the Gift of Women, Which Is the Prohibition's Consequence

This does not go against Lévi-Strauss's theory in the least. The idea of an extreme negation (as extreme as possible) of carnal animality is placed at the meeting point of the two paths that Lévi-Strauss has taken, or more exactly, that marriage itself takes.

In a sense, marriage combines self-interest and purity, sensuality and the prohibition of sensuality, generosity and avarice. In its initial movement it is the contrary of animality; it is the *gift*. There is no question that Lévi-Strauss has fully illuminated this point. And he has analyzed these movements so well that in his conceptions we glimpse what constitutes the essence of the *gift*: the gift is itself the renunciation, the prohibition of immediate, unreserved, animal gratification. Marriage is not so much the act of the betrothed couple as it is that of the woman's "giver," of the man (the father or the brother) who could have freely enjoyed this woman (his daughter, his sister) and who gives her away. The gift he makes of her is perhaps a substitute for the sexual act; the exuberance of giving, in any case, has the same meaning – that of an expenditure of resources – as this act itself. But the renunciation that permits this form of expenditure, and that the prohibition established, has alone made the *gift* possible. Even if the gift relieves, as does the sexual act, this is not at all in the way that animality achieves a release, and the essence of *humanity* emerges from this excess [*dépassement*]. The renunciation of one's close kin – the *reserve* of the one who forbids himself the very thing that belongs to him – defines the *human* attitude that is contrary to animal voracity. *Reciprocally,* as I said, it underscores the alluring value of its object. But it helps to create the climate of a human world, in which respect, difficulty and restraint prevail over violence. It is the complement of eroticism, in which the object destined for coveting acquires a higher value. There would be no eroticism if there was not also a respect for forbidden values. But there would be no complete respect if the erotic deviation was neither possible nor tempting.

Of course, respect is only the *detour* that violence takes. On the one hand, respect regulates the *humanized* world, where violence is forbidden; on the other, respect opens up the possibility for violence to erupt in the domain where it is inadmissible. The prohibition does not change the violence of sexual activity, but by founding the *human* milieu it makes of that violence something that animality did not know: the transgression of the rule.

The moment of transgression (or of unbridled eroticism), on the one hand, and the existence of a milieu in which sexuality is not allowable, on the other, are only the extreme points of a reality in which intermediate forms abound. The sexual act generally does not have the meaning of a crime, and the locality where only men coming from outside can touch the local women corresponds to a very archaic situation. Most often, moderate eroticism meets with tolerance, and the exclusion of sexuality, even where it seems severe, affects little more than the façade. But it is the extremes that are the most meaningful. What matters essentially is that there exists a milieu, however limited, in which the erotic aspect is unthinkable, and moments of transgression when eroticism reaches the highest potential for reversal.

This extreme opposition is conceivable, moreover, only if one thinks of the ceaseless variability of situations. It is then that the involvement of *gift-giving* in marriage – since gift-giving is linked to festivity and the object of the gift-giving always concerns luxury, exuberance and excess – can reveal marriage, linked to the tumult of the festival, as a moment of transgression. But the transgressive aspect of marriage is blurred of course. In the end, marriage, the *transition*, has kept, but vaguely, something of the transgression that it was in the beginning (this aspect remained perceptible in an archaic tradition like that of the *droit de jambage*, which signified less the abuse of the strongest than the desire to entrust the initial operation to men who had a power of transgression: in a distant time, these were the priests). But married life absorbs into the world of prohibition, into a world comparable in part to that of mothers and sisters, is adjoined to it in any case (contaminated by it, so to speak), the whole overflowing of sexual activity. In this movement, humanity's *purity*, which the prohibition establishes – the *purity* of the mother, of the sister – slowly passes, in part, to the spouse who has become a mother. Thus, the *condition* of marriage reserves the possibility of a properly human life, pursued in the *respect* of prohibitions opposed to the free satisfaction of animal needs.

PART THREE

The Natural Objects of Prohibitions

Sexuality and Dejecta

1. The Negation of Nature

I wanted to grasp, in the movements that determined the incest prohibition, the origin of the distinctly human modes of sexuality. But it is clear that while incest is linked to that origin, it was not itself the cause of the new forms that sexuality took among human beings: it was rather their consequence. If I spoke of it first, this was because it is the surest sign of the strong aversions that opposed the free course of sexuality in the beginning. Apparently there was an oppressive feeling about the sexual act of regeneration, which animals do not experience, that brought our first ancestors to exclude it from properly human life (or, if one prefers, from life in groups).

I have already posited that the abhorrence of animal needs, together with the repugnance for death and dead persons, on the one hand, and the experience of work, on the other, marked the "transition from animal to man." Man is the animal that negates nature: he negates it through labor, which destroys it and changes it into an artificial world; he negates it in the case of life-creating activity; he negates it in the case of death. The incest prohibition is one of the effects of the repugnance felt for his condition by the animal that became human. The forms of animality were excluded from a bright world which signified humanity.

These forms, however, could only be denied fictitiously. Men were able to enclose the world of animal activity within strict limits – where it was, precisely, *in its place* – but they never sought to do away with it. They could not even have intended to do so; they had to subtilize it, withdrawing it from the light and confining it in darkness where it is hidden from notice. The place for filth is in the dark, where looks cannot reach it. Secrecy is the condition for sexual activity, just as it is the condition for the performance of the natural functions.

Darkness thus surrounds two worlds that are distinct but always associated. The same horror banishes the sexual function and excretion to the same darkness. The association is given in nature, which brings together and even in part mingles the organs. Of course we cannot determine the essential component of the aversion provoking the nausea we feel for both kinds of "filth." We cannot even know if excrement smells bad because of our disgust for it, or if its bad smell is what causes that disgust. In the matter of smell, animals do not show any repugnance. Man appears to be the only animal to be *ashamed* of that nature whence he comes, and from which he does not cease to have departed. This is a sore point for us. We have fashioned this humanized world in our image by obliterating the very traces of nature; above all we have removed from it everything that might recall the way in which we come out of it. Mankind as a whole resembles those parvenus who are ashamed of their humble origin. They rid themselves of anything suggesting it. What are the "noble" and "good" families, moreover, if not those in which their filthy birth is the most carefully concealed? This is how Saint Augustine expressed the unavowable character of the flesh that is anonymously at our source: *inter faeces et urinam nascimur,* he said, we are born between feces and urine. But we can never know if this filth, out of which we come, is itself ignoble in our eyes, or if it appears so for the reason that we come out of it. It is clear that we are sorry we came from life, from meat, from a whole bloody mess. We might think, if need be, that living matter *on the very level at which we separate ourselves from it* is the privileged object of our disgust. We take our children out of the muck, then we do our best to wipe out the traces of that origin. We busy ourselves in terrifying them as soon as they are old enough to take part (little by little) in our disgust for excrement, for everything that emanates from warm and living flesh.

At first they are insensitive to our perturbations. How to keep from thinking that these sights, these foul odors, are not in themselves so upsetting? Infants tolerate them without any reaction. We have arranged the world around us in such a way that if the "filth" were not constantly thrown out of it, the edifice would rot. But the horror that demands from us this constant movement of rejection is not *natural*. It bespeaks rather a negation of *nature*. We have to set ourselves against the natural impulses of our children if we want them to be like us. We must *artificially* deform them in our image and, as our most precious possessions, instill in them the horror of that which is only natural. We tear them away from nature by washing them, then by dressing them. But we will not rest until they share the impulse that made us clean them and clothe them, until they share our horror of the life of the flesh, of life naked, undisguised, a horror without which we would resemble the animals.

2. Menstrual Blood

We have a completely mistaken notion of primitive peoples on the question of separation from nature. They don't seem to share our aversion. So they themselves are repulsive to us, appearing to be closer than we to the object of our hatred. As to acting on their disgust, it is true that they don't have the same powerful means that we have. We are better able to obliterate the traces of any natural corruption – it's even become simple, easy, and nowadays we are very exacting. Yet, in the midst of ease, we are definitely less eager than they to deepen the gulf separating man from animality. This gulf, for *cannibals*, is always a question of life and death; for *vegetarians*, on the other hand, it is more an excuse for morbid manias, for distresses worthy of a treatment.

It is always difficult to say which of the many phobias are primordial. As concerns primitive people, ethnologists have always been struck by those behaviors whose object is menstrual blood and childbirth. Primitives have a terror of menstrual blood so great that we can hardly imagine its intensity. Prohibitions tending to preserve the collectivity from the least contact – aimed at menstruating women or girls and applying only to the women who are authorized to feed these unfortunate ones – are often sanctioned by the death penalty. The blood of women in labor is no less distressing. These kinds of behavior with respect to vaginal blood were so universally determined that they are still operative in our Western societies. As a rule they are limited to a repugnance whose irrational character is inconspicuous. We are inclined to believe that this discharge is *impure* because the organ from which it issues is thought to be so. The blood of childbirth is no longer the object of so great a horror on account of the painful and touching aspects of maternity. But, in any case, the menstrual flow seems to be a kind of infirmity, even a curse bearing on women. This is not just owing to the inconvenience it causes. Our anxious behavior shows rather clearly that at the very point where humanity removes itself from nature in disgust, there is no profound difference between the successive phases of societies, from the poorest culture to the most complex (to be precise, these reactions differ with individuals, at times even with

64

social classes). But the greatest repugnance has an archaic character nonetheless.[1]

3. Intestinal Dejecta

Menstrual blood seems to have condensed the abhorrence and the fear. The behaviors relative to the other excretions are striking, but there are no prohibitions dealing with them like those aimed at preserving humanity from the least contamination by blood. Of course, when one thinks of the distancing so frequent, or the obligatory confinement, of menstruating women, it is clear that general nature, shared alike by all human beings of all ages and both sexes, and the incessant character of intestinal evacuations, could not permit such awkward measures. What is possible in the case of periodic accidents cannot be applied to the normal state. Moreover, children, with whom our contacts are unavoidable, would destroy a priori the hope of eliminating the contamination entirely. Nothing can be demanded of the young child, whereas a pubescent girl regularly observes the prescriptions. It was necessary to get used to bearing with this infantile waste, which explains the mildness of the disgust it provokes: nothing more extreme than the reaction to animal waste. Besides, what are children if not animals becoming human – but this is not on their own initiative, and their simple clumsiness invites laughter or is considered charming. But the horror that gives rise to prohibition (to religious behavior) is not consistent with a "more or less." Familiar contact with children's excrement does not accord with an utter horror concerning that of adults, similar to the horror of menstrual blood. A horror so sick does not tolerate any degree. It is based on "all or nothing," and one may think that if women were not the only ones to be tainted, men could not have conceived of the taint in the way they did initially. In order to be taken, the distance that is observed in terror demanded the possibility

65

of a complete absence of contact, at least for half of humanity.

However, there is no reason to think, on the contrary, that the earliest humanity was more indifferent than ours to the need to dispose of waste matter and to conceal anything having to do with it (defecation and, to a decidedly lesser extent, urination). The operations necessary for cleanliness are more perfect in civilized societies, but nothing can be concluded from this. The young children of primitives have the same sort of training as ours. In this respect, nothing is more unwarranted than to believe we are further from animality, further from natural defilements. What counts is the effort, the concern; the result is secondary. If it is more perfect in the end, there is nothing to marvel at. Insofar as they bear witness to an early culture, we might rather admire these primitives for whom the eagerness to be *human* and the horror of *nature* have such force. We look down on them from our sanitary installations, and we give ourselves the impression of an unassailable purity. We are quick to overlook an immense rubbish heap, the grossness and refuse of our slums, our "lower parts"; quick to forget the disgust with being *human*, which increased from the contact with a civilization so meticulous that it often seems sick.

Two

Cleanliness Prohibitions and the

Self-creation of Man

1. The Connection of the Degree of Civilization, Race and
Wealth or Social Standing with the Cleanliness Prohibitions
In reality, there is no profound difference between the reactions
peculiar to rudimentary civilization and those of advanced civilization. The basic distinction is not in the degree of development
but in the particular traits of groups, classes or individuals. What
misleads us is simply the established fallacy that first associates
the "uncivilized" peoples with the lower classes – or with fallen
individuals. It is certain that refinement of manners and the observance of prohibitions plays a part in the continual rivalry that generally opposes men to one another. Indeed, refinement is one of
the most efficient factors operating in social classification. To a
certain extent, the observance of prohibitions is a question of
material resources. It takes a lot of money to be refined. (And it
is important, secondarily, that in return the men who have the
most resources are also those who have the most means – material or moral – for transgressing the prohibitions....) The essential thing is that a punctual observance qualifies socially. The
person who protects himself the most anxiously from the various forms of defilement is also the person who enjoys the greatest
prestige and who has the advantage over others. If a man's anxious-

ness is commensurate with the means he possesses (let us suppose that he has *the means* to live anxiously — for example, in
regard to dirt), he nonetheless stands *morally* above the man who'
is careless about safeguarding himself and who lives like an animal, in filth. But if the richest man was not any more concerned
about filth than a barefoot tramp, he could not be honored and
his standing could not rise.

Needless to say, in the society in which we live these aspects
of the matter are not clear. Things are positively blurred. Traces
remain: as a general rule, a parvenu cannot have a high standing; a poorer man often has a greater prestige; a parvenu will
never be initiated into a small number of refinements, *contrary
to nature,* opposing, to voraciousness conventional behaviors, and
to plainness of vocabulary agreed-upon formulas (obscure but all
all *agreed-upon*) suitable for expressing a fundamental anxiousness, the anxiety that *humanizes*. It is always a matter of marking
between oneself and brutish nature a strange distance, unthinkable at first and so all the greater: the distance between a man
eating in a delicate way, according to the aristocratic code, and
one who naively drinks the coffee that has fallen into the saucer
(it is significant, as I see it, that coffee intentionally spilled into
a saucer is called a "foot bath"). The second way is itself human,
but not when compared to a more anxious way. Each way of eating has different meanings according to the circumstances and
the character of the eater, but I chose the "foot bath" example
because in a particular case at least, it implies a certain indifference, a complete lack of anxiety and little abhorrence of the
animal condition of bodies. It will be said that my judgment is
arbitrary, but I deliberately put forward the case of a man taking
the liberty I speak of in a milieu where he is the only one to do
so and for no other reason than indifference.[2] Nothing is more
different from the ways of a primitive. A Kanaka might seem to

68

us to be much coarser than the "foot bath" drinker. Yet it is not the Kanaka who is beastly. He maintains *the greatest distance he can* between animal behavior and his own, so that actually the Kanaka is akin to the aristocrat, not to the boor that I have chosen to depict.

From what I have tried to show, it becomes rather clear that the horror of being animalistic operates unevenly among humans, and that primitives are no less subject to it than we are. It is not a question of more civilization or less, but rather of individual choice and social classification. It is certain that a more scrupulous observance of prohibitions tends *to distinguish* men from one another. And while it is true that wealth makes this observance easier, it is not so much wealth – beyond physical strength, or the power to command – that *distinguishes,* that qualifies socially, as it is the greatest distance from animality. Our double mistake is to think that differences of race, or differences of wealth, ensure this qualification. But this mistake is so deep-rooted that it tends to modify the real order: as a rule, one strives on all sides to reduce the differences between beings to external difference, separate and apart from an active intention to surpass and destroy animal nature within us. On all sides, one strives to deny *human* value, because this value is essentially difference – between animals and man, or between men; for this reason, one strives to reduce every difference to the insignificance of a material datum. Racism, being too intent on serving it, has betrayed the cause of difference: the privileges of race and wealth are indefensible, and they are the only ones that find defenders!

Needless to say, my intention is not to defend (to argue for the survival of) these differences that *humanize*. But, lacking knowledge of them and being unable to discern their precise meaning, we could not know anything about eroticism; we could not even know anything about human specificity....

Eroticism is a closed book to us so long as we do not see man's beginning in the repugnance he felt for a nature that was filthy in his eyes. We generally do not see it for the reason that, in our day, nature attracts men supersaturated with a civilization that is nature's complete opposite.

2. Wasn't the First Object of Repugnance Sexual?

The formation of an artificial civilized world, tied to an extreme horror of nature, became the least understandable thing in the world for us, especially since we began to protest against the "alleged" filthiness of sexual life. Filthiness — the domain of filth — is no less meaningful for all that. No one would say that excrement (or decaying matter) is a substance like any other. It is such, however, for animals: those animals that eat neither excrement nor decaying matter do not show any more repugnance toward it than those that feed on fetid substances show for fresh ones. Rationalism cannot alter this fact, and there remains an area of *irreducible* horror to which we are well adapted. The progressive and very slow lifting of prohibitions concerning things sexual, if not things obscene, changes nothing in this regard. In any case, the continuity of functions leaves sexually regenerative activity with a foulness that does not appear easily surmountable. Even if in the end ordinary sexuality no longer had any shameful associations (which would not reach the point where copulation would no longer be concealed), the shame connected with the excremental orifices or functions would still testify to the divorce between man and nature. Further, it is quite evident that nothing will prevent this indelible shame from rubbing off its mark onto the adjacent domain of the reproductive organs.

It should be unnecessary to state such obvious facts. All this went so well without saying, but the naive questioning of what was once beyond question now obliges one to speak and, at the same time, provides an occasion to clarify what was at first accepted in obscurity. The strangest thing is that when presented in this way, a current aspect of the accursed domain emerges in an unexpected light. If we judge by primitives, in times past the weakest reactions were those relating to the dejecta. The prescriptions concerning them did not have the terrible, and sacred, character of the prohibitions that concerned menstrual blood. The Australian aborigines appear less anxious, less mindful, when it comes to observing the prescribed secrecy in the evacuation of waste. We have long since ceased to believe that the Australians are the living image of the earliest men. (Only the archaic character of their material culture is accepted.) Nothing can be concluded from this behavior, then; but the primacy of the sexual, in the modesty of primitives, regarding the lower part of the abdomen is probable at the least.

In our day, menstrual blood is no longer an object of special horror. In time, the terrified feelings of archaic humanity grew less intense; moreover, their extravagant character produced, along with extraordinary consequences, a kind of frailty. In a more rational world, such reactions ceased to appear tenable. Something of them persisted, no doubt, but in a diminished state. Gradually attention slackened and, while it remained rare, contact with an impurity ceased to terrify. Finally, the various human phobias reached the same level. There is no longer any one of them that is privileged over the others. All of them continue to exist, but the world has ceased to be *absolutely* protected from the defilements; it is protected, no doubt, but *more or less* so (in an approximate way).

Further, if we grant the primacy of sexuality in matters of repugnance, we have to think a priori that an inversion of this primacy could not be avoided in the development of individuals. (Ontogeny, on this point, could not repeat phylogeny.) Indeed,

71

we teach our children to be ashamed of filth; we never tell them to be ashamed of their sexual functions. That would be very hard, and if we chance to say it, we cannot justify the prohibition we declare except in one way: the mother simply says to the child: "It's dirty," and she often even uses the childish word denoting both excrement and the forbidding of contact.

3. That the Transition from Animal to Man Must Be Grasped in a Comprehensive View

I do not intend to dwell on the problem of anteriority. It is not certain that the earlier character of sexual taboos makes much sense. I have only tried to account for the changes occurring between the time when the revulsion was occasioned by realities of a sexual nature and the present time, when it is justified by the undiscussed foulness of the dejecta.

I imagine that our disgust for excrement is secondary (that it appears foul to us because of something other than its objective reality). But my impression is contrary to the one that generally prevails, and I don't feel obliged to be convincing on this point. The result that I aim for is a view of the whole – which embraces not only all of space but the different times in succession. This being so, chronology loses at least some of its importance. That which succession brought about in a certain order may be perceived, erroneously, in a different order. The survey of the whole is what matters; the meaning of the parts is then drawn from the overall view. So what is important is the total change, the transition, in the present case, from animal to man, not the point where things began.

Moreover, it is certainly worth noting that the transition seems to have occurred all at once. The *sum* appears to be given from the start (the principle of the development that unfolded in time was given at the start in the form of change). Let there be no mis-

understanding: the operation may have taken centuries and, however improbable that may be, we will never be able to prove that
the contrary is true. In any event, we will never be able to speak
of the various phases of the transition unless it be with the desired
certainty. Whether the occurrences, the changes, are measured
in centuries or years, we can only imagine a time when things
happened fast. The only way we have to envisage the event is to
do so as if things had taken place within the limits of a very short,
virtually indivisible time span.

Man is always given whole, in an image of his creation that
he cannot situate in time's passing. Of necessity, this image is
total: man has tools, he works, he imposes sexual restrictions on
himself; he has a horror of sexually derived or excremental defilements which is hard to express, just as he has a horror of death
and the dead. We shall see, moreover, that his aversions are ambiguous, that they allow for reversals. In theory, we must envisage
the transition from animal to man as a drama, which we can take
as having lasted and as having had ups and downs, but whose unity
we must grant. In the beginning there is necessarily, if not a quick
drama, then a set of coherent peripeteia; we will never be able
to say what happened, but we know the outcome of this drama
had the value of an irrevocable decision. This is true in the sense
of a lasting effect, which extends through time to us, and is still
the motive of the activity we pursue.

4. The Decisive Importance of the First Step

It is true that, somehow, we go beyond a first step. We no longer
have to cross the distance separating animals from man..., but
this much remains clear: since that time, humanity has never had
a more astounding, more glorious moment. We doubt this, for
to the extent that we take part in being *human*, we want to have
something to do with a more important and more fascinating

moment than any other before it. Sometimes this way of think-ing relates to the achievement of an epoch, thought to be partic-ularly enlightened. Sometimes the destiny of a single individual is involved. Believers think of the moment when the words of a messiah or prophet were heard. Others cannot even conceive of the world except on the understanding that it began anew with them: their life will be the decisive affair on which the existence of true man, consolidated at last, will have depended.

André Breton speaks rather strangely of a "heroic need" that Sade would have had "to create an order of things which was not as it were dependent upon *everything* that had come before him."[3] Breton formulates in these words the seldom recognized need some men have to respond to the deepest feeling: the need to *create* authentic humanity, starting from inauthentic humanity, which alone has prevailed heretofore. Thus, for the Christians, the world prior to the coming of Jesus Christ. It must be said that this deceptive feeling cannot easily be dispelled. It involves, for the one experiencing it, what is most important, what matters so much that one would have lived for nothing had one failed to respond to it. Breton apparently attributed to Sade what he him-self felt: no one seems to have been more concerned than he with changing life from top to bottom. Following Breton, however, we have to think that life is never changed enough, that after Sade it was necessary to start afresh.... Indeed, it is as if life might be nothing more, in sum, than a continual re-creation, which more often than not implies a disregard for that which others have created before us: it seems that man lives only from renewed cre-ation, that the result of creation wears out, that without the *crea-tors*, and even very soon after their death, humanity sags, falls asleep, and it is necessary to emerge once more from darkness. Should the moral creation of man be renewed less often than his physical birth? To the destiny that requires the death of the old

74

generation, which perpetually awakens a fresher one to childhood, there corresponds the destiny that endlessly demands the rebirth of human life from nothing, or at least from profound darkness. But would this be a reason not to see that it is a way of repeating and magnifying the glorious moment when man set himself apart from the animals? And instead of preventing us from seeing, as it sometimes does, might not the feeling that Breton attributes to Sade help us rather to understand the significance of the first man, *who must have been the first in response to just such a feeling?* Stage by stage, we may have traveled an immeasurable distance since then, without ceasing to take leave of ourselves (to leave the slumber that had overtaken us each time) in ceaseless, repeated movements of creation, once the dance had begun whose first figures were already those of *self-consciousness.* What makes us incapable of understanding in this way the first advances of human life is the blind contempt in which we hold primitive peoples. True, we may believe that often a certain coarseness preceded refinement, that blind and formal attitudes, more hieratic than human, preceded sentiments that are both autonomous and complex. But such beliefs are tied to the notion that the development of spiritual life occurs in direct proportion to material culture. Yet this would-be law often proved false in the cluster of periods that are known to us. It is confirmed, albeit vaguely, only where it is a question of knowledge! We grant too much importance, I believe, to this complexity that makes all things more difficult, and so demands more efforts, more autonomous initiatives. And above all, we accept a very questionable chronology of the various spiritual forms, which assigns the crudest forms to the earliest periods, whereas the crudeness could as well be due to a somnolence as to a still incomplete awakening.[4]

75

5. Eroticism Is Essentially, from the First Step, the Scandal of "Reversed Alliances"

Many people think of the stammerings of humanity as if they had little (or no) meaning in themselves. They imagine the most groping steps at the origin of humanity's development, whereas in fact language and consciousness were linked to them. These steps scarcely resemble those of a child, and supposing that the arbitrary parallels could be established, one would still have to account for a difference between them: in the steps of the child, those of the adult are already given, and the behaviors of childhood, which have no meaning in themselves, are meaningful relative to the future person the baby will become. But the stammerings of the first men would have had a meaning relative to fully developed man – and no meaning in themselves – only if providence had arranged everything from the start; thus, as with the actual future, the full development of children of the past would likewise prefigure, as it were, and prearrange the future of today's children. But there is no reason for thinking that it happened this way: present-day humanity, it appears, could not be heralded, nor its future be prearranged, unless the actions of the first men had in themselves, owing to a leap they made, opened up the possibility of the complete development that extends at least to us: from the start, the differentiation from animals and from nature, labor and the awareness of death, or of suspended possibility, created that domain which all of history down to us was to explore relentlessly, always going further.

Even if my hypothesis cannot be established in detail, I will now give the reason why I wished to use it to introduce an explanation that makes a decisive description clearer (or less obscure). It goes without saying, in any case, that history was the exploration (perhaps unfinished) of all man's possibilities, *which the negation of nature establishes.* It is the negation of the given, of all the

76

given, whose consequences are explored down to the last one. A revolt, a refusal of the offered condition, is evinced in man's attitude at the very beginning. This is what is signified by the endlessly resumed quest for the totality of the possible – for each man, or at least for every solidary group, beyond what was possible before it. This effort is so bold, it is above all so exhausting that history consists essentially of periods when people tried to hold its first results as immutable, when they earnestly sought to *immobilize and preserve movements of profound revolution.*

It is time to go back to a principle that I have spoken of vaguely thus far. I presented as being decisive the process that established humanity, and I implied that this process heralded, in an elemental way, the totality of the possible. This assumed, as I said, that the horror of nature, which was the first movement of the process, was ambiguous, and that it anticipated a nearly simultaneous return movement. In fact, as soon as nature, which a spirit of revolt had rejected as the *given*, ceased to appear as such, the very spirit that had rejected it no longer considered it as the given (as what compelled and alienated the spirit's independence); it then regarded nature's antithesis, prohibition, as the given – that prohibition to which at first it submitted, as a way of denying its subordination to nature. At first sight this "reversal of alliances" is perhaps difficult to follow, but the basic duplicity of eroticism is unintelligible so long as this twofold movement, of negation and return, is not grasped as a *whole.* We have seen that the first aspect of the movement is rejection: the whole is developed only when that which was denied to the point of nausea, which held an ambiguous value, is remembered as desirable. If it is true that man is first of all that autonomous existence which refuses to be simply subjected to the limits of the past, it can be disconcerting to see him return so quickly to his vomit. It has been said sententiously: *"chassez le naturel, il revient au galop."*[5]

But it cannot long seem that the "return" to nature is such a commonplace. A profound difference results from the fact that the "nature" that is desired after being rejected is not desired in submission to the given, as it may have been in the first instance, in the *fleeting* movement of animal excitation: it is nature transfigured by the *curse*, to which the spirit then accedes only through a new movement of refusal, of insubordination, of revolt. Moreover, this second movement has the effect of maintaining the fervor, the delirium if you will, of the first: the temperature falls insofar as the first continues in a unilateral way (if the nausea only results in a prudent life, well protected from everything that might give rise to it). It can be maintained only on the condition that one discover what was alluring in the fact that an object is horrible – or shameful – and, in the face of shameful nakedness, make shame and desire a single, violent convulsion.

I will come back to this crucial moment of course, but first I want to stress the fact that this dual movement does not even involve distinct phases. I can, for ease of exposition, speak of it in two stages. But it is an integral ensemble and one cannot really speak of one stage without implying the other: only the comprehensive view is meaningful (just as, when we look at tides, we cannot separate the ebb from the flow except arbitrarily...).

But before connecting the "return" with the *total* image of the erotic disturbance, I need to try to describe more extensively the forms of sensibility with which the disturbance is associated.

Death

1. The Corpse and Decay

The natural domain of the prohibitions is not just that of sexuality and filth; it also includes death.

The prohibitions concerning death have two aspects: the first forbids murder and the second limits contact with corpses.

Like the prohibitions whose objects are dejecta, incestuous union, menstrual blood and obscenity, those applying to dead bodies and to murder have not ceased being generally observed (but the prohibition against murder is just about the only one to be sanctioned by laws, and, at least within well-defined limits, the demands of anatomy have ultimately opened up a margin of infraction in behavior toward the dead).

Since it goes without saying, I will not linger over the possible anteriority of the horror of death. This horror is perhaps at the root of our repugnance (the loathing of nothingness would then be at the origin of the loathing of decay, which is not physical since it is not shared by animals). It is clear, in any event, that the nature of excrement is analogous to that of corpses and that the places of its emission are close to the sexual parts; more often than not, this complex of prohibitions appears inextricable. Death might seem to be the complete opposite of a function whose purpose is birth..., but we shall see further on that this opposition is reducible, and that the death of some is correlative with the birth of others, of which it is finally the precondition and the announcement. Moreover, life is a product of putrefaction, and it depends on both death and the dungheap.

In any case, the "denial" of death is given in the original complex, not only as it relates to the horror of annihilation, but insofar as it restores us to the power of nature, of which the universal ferment of life is the *repulsive* sign.

Apparently, this aspect is not compatible with the noble and solemn representation of death. But the latter opposes, *through a secondary reaction,* the cruder representation which anguish, or rather terror, controls, and which is nonetheless primordial: death is that putrefaction, that stench...which is at once the source and the repulsive condition of *life.*

For primitives, the extreme dread of death – above all a dread of the distressing phenomenon for the survivor, more than of personal annihilation – is linked to the phase of decay: for them, whitened bones no longer have the intolerable look of decomposing flesh. In the confusion of their minds they attribute their loathing of putrefaction to the cruel rancor and hatred visited upon them by death, which the mourning rites are meant to appease. But they think that the whitened bones signify an appeasement: these bones are venerable for them; they finally have the look of death's solemn grandeur: it is to their form, still fearsome, dreadful, but without the excess of decay's active virulence, that the worship of ancestors, becoming guardians at last, is addressed.

2. Shamefully, We Get Life from Putrefaction, and Death, Which Reduces Us to Putrefaction, Is No Less Ignoble Than Birth

At least those bleached bones no longer have that sticky movement that is the privileged object of our disgust. In that movement, nascent life is not distinct from the putrefaction of life which death is, and we are inclined to see in this unavoidable comparison a basic characteristic, if not of nature, at least of the notion we have been led to conceive of it. For Aristotle himself, these animals that formed spontaneously in the earth or in the water seemed to be born of corruption. The procreative power of decay is perhaps a naive idea expressing at the same time the insurmountable repugnance and the attraction it awakens in us. But it is undoubtedly the *source* of the idea that men are nature's offspring: as if decay finally summed up this world from which we emerge and into which we return, so that the shame – and the repugnance – is linked both to death and to birth.

We have no greater aversion than the aversion we feel toward those unstable, fetid and lukewarm substances where life ferments ignobly. Those substances where the eggs, germs and maggots swarm not only make our hearts sink, but also turn our stomachs. Death does not come down to the bitter annihilation of being – of all that I am, which expects to be once more, the very meaning of which, rather than to be, is to expect to be (as if we never received *being* authentically, but only the anticipation of being, which will be and is not, as if we were not the presence that we are, but the future that we will be and are not); it is also that shipwreck in the nauseous. I will rejoin abject nature and the purulence of anonymous, infinite life, which stretches forth like the night, which is death. One day this living world will pullulate in my dead mouth. Thus, the inevitable disappointment of the expectation is itself, at the same time, the inevitable horror that I deny, that I should deny at all costs.

3. The Knowledge of Death
This vision coincides and is associated with our mortifying perceptions of obscenity, of sexual reproduction, of stench. And it

has this effect: it holds in the background of every thought the anticipation of the outcome, which is the final disappointment of expectations, silence without appeal and that ignominious putrefaction whose shameful appearance our next of kin will take care to conceal from the survivors. What marks us so severely is the *knowledge* of death, which animals fear but do not *know*. Later I will show that in tandem with this prior *knowledge* of death there is the knowledge of sexuality, to which contribute, on the one hand, the abhorrence of sexuality or the sense that it is filthy, and on the other, the practice of *eroticism*, which is the consequence of such sentiments. But the two awarenesses differ profoundly in this respect: having a positive object, consciousness of the sexual domain cannot be manifested simply in repulsion, which in fact turns us away from sexuality; so it is necessary for eroticism, which is not immediate, to bring us back from repulsion to desire. However, the repulsion of death, having immediately a negative object, is first of all a consciousness of the positive counterpart of that object, that is, a consciousness of life, or more exactly, of self: it is easy to understand that consciousness of death is essentially self-consciousness – but that, reciprocally, consciousness of self required that of death.

This should be added at once: in that maze of reactions where humanity originated, it is natural to look for one decisive reaction of which the others would only be consequences. Thus, the consciousness of death – or self-consciousness – might appear primordial.... But in my judgment it will always be possible to show that whichever primordial fact gets priority presupposes the existence of another one....

Might we not imagine – just as well – that work – and the anticipation of its result – are at the basis of the knowledge of death? The sequence is quite perceptible. It is in work that the expectation takes shape. How, if I had not begun a project, a task, unsatisfying in itself, perhaps arduous, but whose result I look forward to, how could I continue, as I do, to anticipate the authentic being which I never am in the present time and which I place in the time to come? But the fact is that death threatens to forestall me, and to steal away the object of my anticipation. In the immediacy of the animal impulse, the object of desire is already given: there is no voluntary patience or waiting; the waiting, the patience, are always unavoidable and the possession of the object is not separate from the vehement desire, which cannot be contained. Think of the voracity of animals, as against the composure of a cook. Animals lack an elementary operation of the intellect, which distinguishes between action and result, present and future, and which, subordinating the present to the result, tends to substitute the anticipation of something else for that which is given in the moment, without waiting. But the human intellect represents both the possibility of the operation and the precariousness of the one who reckons on its outcome: one may die too soon and so one's expectation will remain forever disappointed.[6] Thus, work could well be the activity in which mankind's evolution originated, the source of the disgusts and prohibitions that determined its course.

4. On the Primary Meaning of a Complex of Movements
It is possible and yet it seems useless to isolate a particular aspect when a radical change involved every element of the system.

There wasn't so much a determining element as a coincidence of the various movements which the development of humanity composed. As we shall see, work goes against erotic freedom, hampers it; and, conversely, erotic excess develops to the detriment of work. But the lags on both sides do not prevent a reciprocal acceleration of movements. The consciousness of death is itself opposed to the return of eroticism, which is likely to reintroduce avidity, fever and violence that will not wait. But anguish, which lays us open to annihilation and death, is always linked to eroticism; our sexual activity finally rivets us to the distressing image of death, and the knowledge of death deepens the abyss of eroticism. The curse of decay constantly recoils on sexuality, which it tends to eroticize: in sexual anguish there is a sadness of death, an apprehension of death which is rather vague but which we will never be able to shake off.

If need be, it is possible to reduce the complexity of reactions to a constant pursuit of autonomy (or of sovereignty). But this way of looking at things results in an abstract view, where the immediate abhorrence of, and half-physical disgust for nature – that is, nature as putrefaction – are given arbitrarily as the consequence of a calculation, of a presumed politics of autonomy. As a matter of fact, nothing proves that the struggle for autonomy is not, materially, the consequence of the disgust.

5. *Death Is Finally the Most Luxurious Form of Life*
What is disconcerting about these movements where opposed forms are interdependent is due to the common misappreciation of death. It calls for us to despise the link associating death with eroticism, regarded as a promise of life. It is easy, but, all in all, it is dishonorable (a lack of intellectual virility) to turn away from the luxurious truth of death: there is no doubt that death is the youth of the world. We don't admit this, we don't want to admit it, for a rather sad reason: we are perhaps young at heart, but this doesn't mean we are more alert. Otherwise, how could we not be aware that death, and death alone, constantly ensures the renewal of life? The worst is that, in a sense, we know this very well, but we are just as quick to forget it. The law given in nature is so simple as to defy ignorance. According to this law, life is effusion; it is contrary to equilibrium, to stability. It is the tumultuous

movement that bursts forth and consumes itself. Its perpetual explosion is possible on one condition: that the spent organisms give way to new ones, which enter the dance with new forces.[7]

We could really not imagine a more costly process. Life is possible at much less expense: compared to that of an infusorian, the individual organism of a mammal, especially a carnivore, is an abyss where enormous quantities of energy are swallowed up, are *destroyed*. The growth of plants presupposes the amassing of decayed substances. Plant-eaters consume tons of living (plant) substance before a small amount of meat allows a carnivore its great releases, its great nervous expenditures. It even appears that the more costly the life-generating processes are, the more squander the production of organisms has required, the more satisfactory the operation is. The principle of producing at the least expense is not so much a human idea as a narrowly capitalist one (it makes sense only from the viewpoint of the incorporated company). The movement of human life even tends toward anguish, as the sign of expenditures that are finally excessive, that go beyond what we can bear. Everything within us demands that death lay waste to us: we anticipate these multiple trials, these new beginnings, unproductive from the standpoint of reason, this wholesale destruction of effective force accomplished in the transfer of one individual's life to other, younger, individuals. Deep down, we even assent to the condition that results, that is almot intolerable, in this condition of individuals destined for suffering and inevitable annihilation. Or rather, were it not for this intolerable condition, so harsh that the will constantly wavers, we would not be satisfied. (How significant at present that a book[8] is entitled, ludicrously, *Afin que nul ne meure!*...) Today our judgments are formed in disappointing circumstances: those among us who best make themselves heard are unaware (and want *at all cost* to be unaware) that life is the luxury of which death is the highest

85

degree, that of all the luxuries of life, human life is the most extravagantly expensive, that, finally, an increased apprehension of death, when life's security wears thin, is at the highest level of ruinous refinement.... But oblivious of this, they only add to the anguish without which a life devoted entirely to luxury would be less boldly luxurious. For if it is human to be luxurious, what to say of a luxury of which anguish is the product and which anguish does not moderate?

PART FOUR

Transgression

ONE

The Festival, or the

Transgression of Prohibitions

1. The Death of the King, the Festival, and the Transgression of Prohibitions

Sometimes, in the face of death, of the failure of human ambition, a boundless despair takes hold. Then it seems that those heavy storms and those rumblings of nature to which man is ordinarily ashamed to yield get the upper hand. In this sense the death of a king is apt to produce the most pronounced affects of horror and frenzy. The nature of the sovereign demands that this sentiment of defeat, of humiliation, always provoked by death, attain such a degree that nothing, it seems, can stand firm against the fury of animality. No sooner is the event announced than men rush in from all quarters, killing everything in front of them, raping and pillaging to beat the devil. "Ritual license," says Roger Caillois, "then assumes a character corresponding strictly to the catastrophe that has occurred.... Popular frenzy is never resisted in the least way. In the Hawaiian islands, the populace, upon learning of the king's death, commits every act ordinarily regarded as criminal. It burns, pillages and kills, and the women are required to prostitute themselves publicly...." The disorder "ends only with the complete elimination of the putrescent substance of the royal cadaver, when nothing more is left of the royal remains but a hard, sound, and incorruptible skeleton...."[1]

2. The Festival Is Not Just a Return to One's Vomit

Looking at this second movement, we might imagine that, the first having failed, man returns, without the least change, to the animality from which he started. But the explosion that follows death is in no way the abandonment of that world which the prohibitions *humanize*: it is the festival, it is of course, for a moment, the cessation of work, the unrestrained consumption of its products and the deliberate violation of the most hallowed laws, but the excess consecrates and completes an order of things based on rules; it goes against that order only temporarily.

Moreover, we should not be misled by the appearance of a return by man to nature. It is such a return, no doubt, but only in one sense. Since man has uprooted himself from nature, that being who returns to it is still uprooted, he is an uprooted being who suddenly goes back toward that from which he is uprooted, from which he has not ceased to uproot himself.[2] The first uprooting is not obliterated: when men, in the course of the festival, give free play to the impulses they refuse in profane times, these impulses have a meaning in the context of the human world: they are meaningful only in that context. In any case, these impulses cannot be mistaken for those of animals.

I can't give a better idea of the gulf separating the two kinds of free play than by drawing attention to the connection between laughter and the festival. Laughter is not the festival by itself, yet in its own way it indicates the festival's meaning – indeed, laughter is always the whole movement of the festival in a nutshell – but there is nothing more contrary to animality than laughter....[3]

I will go further: not only is the festival not, as one might think, a return by man to his vomit, but it *ultimately* has the opposite meaning. I said that the initial human negation, which created the *human* in contrast to the *animal*, had to do with the being's *dependence* on the natural given, on the body which it did not choose, but the break constituted by the festival is not at all a way of renouncing independence; it is rather the culmination of a movement toward autonomy, which is, forevermore, the same thing as man himself.

3. *The Failure of the Denial of Animality*

What then is the essential meaning of our horror of nature? Not wanting to depend on anything, abandoning the place of our carnal birth, revolting intimately against the fact of *dying*, generally mistrusting the body, that is, having a deep mistrust of what is accidental, natural, perishable – this appears to be *for each one of us* the sense of the movement that leads us *to represent* man independently of filth, of the sexual functions and of death. I have no objection, this clear and distinct way of looking at things is that of man in our time; it is assuredly not that of the first men. In fact, it assumes a discriminating consciousness and the articulated language on which that consciousness is founded. But I can start by envisaging the way of feeling and reacting that determined the first prohibitions. Everything suggests that these feelings and these early reactions respond obscurely to the fact that we now have the ability to think discursively. I won't labor this point: I am referring to the entire history of religions that I must only allude to, not wishing to review it in detail. The line of development from taboos on incest or menstrual blood to the religions of purity and of the soul's immortality is quite clear: it is always a matter of denying the human being's dependence on the natural given, of setting our dignity, our spiritual nature, our detachment, against animal avidity.

But obviously I cannot limit myself to this first perception. I know that that initial movement failed. If I look for the integral meaning of my will to act and of the earliest fears that I share, I cannot help but note the futility of an effort so wrongly placed.

I can deny my dependence, denying sexuality, filth, death, and insisting that the world submit to my action. But this negation is fictitious. I finally have to tell myself that the carnal origin of which I am ashamed is my origin nonetheless. And however great my horror of death may be, how can I escape the fatal appointment? I know that I will die and that I will rot. Work, for its part, finally marks the limits of my means: so limited is the extent to which I can respond to the threats of misfortune.

4. What the Festival Liberates Is Not Merely Animality but Also the Divine

Of course, in their own way men recognized long ago the failure of the negation of nature: it could not fail to appear inevitable from the beginning. But from the beginning there must have been two feelings about it. According to the second of these, it was neither possible nor desirable for man to be *truly* protected, to be so protected that the accursed element would permanently cease to matter. That element was denied, but this denial was the means of giving it a *different* value. Something unfamiliar and disconcerting came into being, something that was no longer simply nature, but nature transfigured, the *sacred*.

In a basic sense, what is *sacred* is precisely what is *prohibited*. But if the *sacred*, the *prohibited*, is cast out of the sphere of profane life (inasmuch as it denotes a disruption of that life), it nevertheless has a greater value than this profane that excludes it. It is no longer the despised bestiality; often it has retained an animal form, but the latter has become *divine*. As such, relative to profane life this *sacred* animality has *the same meaning* that the negation of nature (hence profane life) has relative to pure animality. What is denied in profane life (through prohibitions and through work) is a dependent state of the animal, subject to death and to utterly *blind* needs. What is denied by means of *divine* life

92

is still *dependence*, but this time it is the profane world whose *lucid* and *voluntary* servility is contested. In a sense, the second contestation appeals to forces that the first had denied, but insofar as they cannot truly be confined within the limits of the first. Drawing on their input, the movement of the festival *liberates* these animal forces, but now their explosive liberation interrupts the course of an existence subordinated to ordinary ends. There is a breakdown – an interruption – of the rules; the regular course of things ceases: what originally had the meaning of limit has that of shattering limits. Thus, the *sacred* announces a new possibility: it is a leap into the unknown, with animality as its impetus.

What came to pass can be summed up in a simple statement: the force of a movement, which repression increased tenfold, projected life into a richer world.

5. *The Negation of the Profane World and the Divine (or Sacred) World*

I emphasized earlier[4] that "the 'nature' that is desired after being rejected is not desired in submission to the given...: it is nature transfigured by the *curse*, to which the spirit then accedes only through a new movement of refusal, of insubordination, of revolt." This is the basic difference between ordinary and divine animality. Of course, it would not be possible to say that simple animality is analogous to the profane sphere. I only meant to point out that relative to profane life sacred animality had the same meaning that the horror of nature had relative to the first animality. For there was negation and overcoming each time. But now I will have to describe in detail, and discursively, a system of oppositions that is familiar to us, but unconsciously so, in an obscurity that favors confusion.

The negation of nature has two clearly and distinctly opposed aspects: that of horror or repugnance, which implies fever and passion, and that of profane life, which assumes the fever has subsided. I have already spoken[5] of those movements that we strive to make immutable, immobile, of those revolutions that we regard as a state, a lasting entity, that we naively preserve, as if their essence were not change. This is not necessarily the absurdity that one imagines it to be: we can neither preserve nor abolish change, yet we cannot always be changing. But we should not confuse change with the stable state that results from it, that ultimately resumes the course of the previous state, which the change had ended.

Profane life is easy to distinguish from mere animal life; it is very different from the latter. Taking it as a whole, animal life is nonetheless the model of life without history. And profane life is an extension of it in the sense that it knows nothing of destructive and violent changes: if such changes befall it, they befall it from the outside.[6]

If I return now to a characteristic thrust and counterthrust, ebb and flow of a twofold movement, the unity in the violent agitation of prohibition and transgression will be evident: it is the unity of the sacred world, contrasting with the calm regularity of the profane world.[7]

Two

The Phaedra Complex

1. The Connection of Horror and Desire

It is obviously the combination of abhorrence and desire that gives the sacred world a paradoxical character, holding the one who considers it without cheating in a state of anxious fascination.

What is sacred undoubtedly corresponds to the object of horror I have spoken of, a fetid, sticky object without boundaries, which teems with life and yet is the sign of death. It is nature at the point where its effervescence closely joins life and death, where it is death gorging life with decomposed substance.

It is hard to imagine that a human individual would not withdraw from such an object in disgust. But would he withdraw if he were not tempted? Would the object nauseate if it offered him nothing desirable? Am I wrong, then, to think the following: it often seems that, by overcoming a resistance, desire becomes more meaningful; resistance is the test that assures us of desire's authenticity and thus gives it a force that comes of the certainty of its dominion. If our desire had not had so much difficulty overcoming our undeniable repugnance we would not have thought it so strong, we would not have seen in its object that which was capable of inciting desire to such a degree. So it was that Phaedra's love increased in proportion to the fear that arose from the possibility of a crime. But on the other hand, how would the repugnance maintain itself, or more simply, to what would it respond if its object did not present anything dangerous? Pure and simple danger frightens one away, while only the horror of prohibition keeps one in the anguish of temptation.

If I consider from this standpoint any repugnant object, a decomposing corpse for instance, it is true that my argument seems no longer to hold. However, I can bring specific considerations to bear. I will take for granted the assertion that every horror conceals a possibility of enticement. I can then assume the operation of a relatively simple mechanism. An object that is repugnant presents a force of repulsion more or less great. I will add that, following my hypothesis, it should also present a force of attraction; like the force of repulsion, its opposite, the force of attraction will be more or less great. But I didn't say that the repulsion and the attraction were always directly proportional to one another. Things are far from being so simple. Indeed, instead of increasing desire, *excessive* horror paralyzes it, shuts it off.

Of course, the *excessiveness* of the horror brings in the subjective element. Instead of the Hippolytus of the story, I imagine a parricide, who would not have just satisfied an incestuous desire but would have killed Theseus. I am free to picture a Phaedra overcome by the crime she would have unintentionally provoked, refusing to see her lover again. I might also, miles away from the classical theme, imagine her burning with renewed passion for the abominable Hippolytus. Or, finding another instance of the game that Racine delighted in, I can even see her overcome, lacerated, but all the more ardent despite – or because of – her horror of Hippolytus and of herself.

If the horror is in fact more or less great, this is not merely because of the object that gives rise to it; the individual who feels it is himself more or less inclined to feel it. This doesn't in any way alter the situation most favorable to desire: it is both the situation of Racine's Phaedra and the one that I proposed last, that I gave prominence to, placing it in the setting it requires — the situation that calls for the cries, the sighs and the silences of tragedy. The more difficult the horror is to bear, the more desirable it is — but one must be able to bear it!

But the Phaedra example relates to sexual desire, and to the incest prohibition that makes it criminal, but in a clearly defined case. A rotting carcass, it seems, still has nothing desirable about it; apparently, the prohibition on contact with decayed matter, dejecta, corpses, couldn't protect these objects from a nonexistent desire!

2. The Allurement Linked to the Corpse's Putrefaction
Apparently and in principle, the prohibition concerning the dead is not designed to protect them from the *desire* of the living. The horror we have of them does not seem to correspond to any attraction. Freud, it is true, thought that their obvious defenselessness justified the forbidding of contact. But other subsidiary hypotheses of Freud's are groundless.... It is not at all the same with corpses as with kinsmen who can't have sexual relations with us: the *forbidden*, criminal character may add an allurement to the horrible significance they have been given. But the horror of putrefaction, it would seem, will never be coupled with any desire. The value of what I said in reference to Phaedra would thus be limited to the narrow domain of objects of sexual desire. It would be wrong to suppose as I did that horror always conceals a possibility of desire.

Here I need to point out that, as concerns death, I spoke of the dead, with whom it is criminal to have contact; I only alluded briefly to the living, whom it is criminal to kill.

97

Now, while it is true that men seldom want *to have disrespect-ful contact with the dead* (which is after all only a venial crime), it is certain that sometimes they desire *to kill the living*. It may be, however, that the two prohibitions are connected. I have delayed speaking thus far of the universal law that forbids (in principle) the killing of human beings. Nevertheless, respect for the dead might be a corollary of respect for the living. Mightn't the pro-hibition on corpses turn out to be an extension of the prohibi-tion on murder? Isn't a dead person, in the belief of primitives, the presumed victim of a murder? Primitives are inclined to tell themselves, in fact, that death cannot be natural: face to face with a dead person, one must suppose that a spell or some act of witch-craft is responsible for the death; one must set out in search of the culprit. We may suppose that, in a dead body, an attraction, a hidden response to our desire, doesn't relate to the very object that has filled us with horror, but rather to murder.

We shouldn't be surprised, if this is so, at our lack of con-sciousness of it. We don't much like to think that we might kill, and even less that we might enjoy killing.

Undoubtedly, if any desire is mixed with the horror of the dead, the lure of murder contributed to it. And yet this way of looking at things strikes me as being very incomplete; at most it gives us the beginning of an explanation. There is more in the hor-rible attraction of the dead than the desire to kill can bring into play. Going back to the festival I spoke of, which is rudimentary, shapeless, we can embrace the complex that combines death, eroticism and murder: perhaps that is the comprehensive view we must adhere to....

Sexual activity is ordinarily limited by rules, and murder is regarded as awful, unthinkable. This regular order of things means that the movement of life is restrained, controlled the way a horse is by a good rider. It is the prolonged life of old people that stabilizes the course of social activity. It is the stagnation, or at least the slowing down, that keeps this course under the sway of work. Conversely, the death of old people, and indeed death in general, accelerate the effusion and exuberance of life, with the best effect resulting from an alternation of arrest and sudden release of motion.

In the end, we don't know anything, or scarcely anything, if we isolate it from this movement that death liberates, from the immense seductive power that generally belongs to life and gives a response to the depressing look of corpses bearing no makeup. This passage from authority to impotence, from the uprightness of being to absence, from the negative, [word illegible] position of the living to the endless denial of limits heralds the return, the triumph even, of neglectful, reckless, capricious life, full of tender abandon and obscure disorder. Violence responds to decay, which calls it forth; the nothingness of decomposition, relative to the enormous abandon of disorderly passions, is analogous to that aura of sacred terror that tragedy radiates.

The crux of a convulsion as complete as this comes at the moment when life, assuming in death the look of impotence, appears, *at that cost,* in its endless breaking-loose. A power of annihilation, underlying a power of proliferation, of renewal, of freshness, is announced by a putrefaction inevitably full of life: would there be a young generation if the cemeteries did not fill up to make room for it?

3. *The Secret of Desire*
There is, however, a gulf between the decaying of flesh, given in nature, and the link associating youth with the dismal operations that the landscape of graves covers up. It is characteristic of man to obliterate or hide the traces of so black an alchemy; and, just as they are buried in the ground, so they are buried in the inac-

cessible parts of memory. Moreover, the most difficult job of recovery has to do with the *whole* of a vast movement. It may be possible to rediscover the connection between prescriptions of respect for the dead and the desire to kill. But, detached from the rest, this view is superficial. And however complete a picture the "festival of the king" may be, linking the decay of the royal corpse to sexual licentiousness and the frenzy of murder, it is still only a schema whose meaning must be constructed.

What I have already shown enables us to grasp what links the horror of the dead and the desire that relates to the total movement of life. This is already an improvement over the theoretical connection exhibited in a festival tableau. But I must go further and show finally that, on the other hand, the sexual life of human beings, eroticism, would not be intelligible without this connection. It is possible no doubt to imagine eroticism independently of the horror of the dead. But actually this independence is not given. I can imagine passion independently of Phaedra's circumstances: nothing is more common than the *innocent* love a woman has for a man she is entitled to love (in our day, moreover, Phaedra's passion for Hippolytus ceases to appear criminal to us...). But leaving aside an extreme case, which is the efficient desire to kill, sexual desire – responsive to the pull of a movement that unceasingly casts a part of humanity into the grave – is stirred, as it were, by the horror we nonetheless have of this movement. Just as the crime, which horrifies her, secretly raises and fuels Phaedra's ardor, sexuality's fragrance of death ensures all its power. This is the meaning of anguish, without which sexuality would be only an animal activity, and would not be *erotic*. If we wish to clearly represent this extraordinary effect, we have to compare it to vertigo, where fear does not paralyze but increases an involuntary desire to fall; and to uncontrollable laughter, where the laughter increases in proportion to our anguish if some dangerous element supervenes and if we laugh even though at all costs we should stop laughing.

In each of these situations, a feeling of danger — yet not so pressing as to preclude any delay — places us before a nauseating void. A void in the face of which our being is a plenum, threatened with losing its plenitude, both desiring and fearing to lose it. As if the consciousness of plenitude demanded a state of uncertainty, of suspension. As if being itself were this exploration of all possibility, always going to the extreme and always hazardous. And so, to such a stubborn defiance of impossibility, to such a full desire for emptiness, there is no end but the definitive emptiness of death.

THREE

Desire Horrified at Losing and

at Losing Oneself

1. Joy Demands That We Consume Our Resources of Energy
Horror associated with desire and the poverty of a desire not
enhanced by any horror cannot, however, prevent us from seeing
that desire has the *desirable* as its object. Anguish, when desire
opens onto the void – and, sometimes, onto death – is perhaps
a reason for desiring more strongly and for finding the desired
object more attractive, but in the last instance the object of desire
always has the meaning of delight, and this object, whatever one
might say of it, is not inaccessible. It would be inexcusable to
speak of eroticism without saying essentially that it centers on
joy. A joy, moreover, that is excessive. In speaking of their raptures, mystics wish to give the impression of a pleasure so great
that the pleasure of human love does not compare. It is hard to
assess the degree of intensity of states that may not be incom-
municable, perhaps, but that can never be compared with any
exactness, for lack of familiarity with other states than those we
personally experience. But it does seem allowable to think that
we may experience, in the related domains of eroticism and religious meditation, joys so great that we are led to consider them
exceptional, unique, surpassing the bounds of any joy imaginable.

Be this as it may, there can be no doubt about the excessive, exorbitant character of the transports of joy that eroticism gives us. I believe that the skepticism shown by a small number of blasé individuals is a response either to the affectedness of statements, or to the awkwardness or bad conditions of an experience. It remains to be seen how the pursuit of such great joys must go via that of horrors and repugnant objects of every sort.

What I said earlier tended to show that horror was present and played a part in erotic attraction. I furnished what might be considered sufficient evidence of this paradoxical fact, but I still have not given a clear enough account of its peculiarities. To this end, I will put forward a hypothesis that is perhaps fundamental.

I think that the feeling of horror (I am not talking about fear) does not correspond, as most people believe, to what is bad for us, to what jeopardizes their interests. On the contrary, if they horrify us, objects that otherwise would have no meaning take on the highest present value in our eyes. Erotic activity can be disgusting; it can also be noble, ethereal, excluding sexual contact, but it illustrates a principle of human behavior in the clearest way: what we want is what uses up our strength and our resources and, if necessary, places our life in danger.

Actually, we don't always have the means to want it; our resources run out and our desire fails us (it is quite simply inhibited) as soon as we are faced with a danger that is all too unavoidable. If, however, we are blessed with enough courage and luck, the object we desire most is in principle the one most likely to endanger or destroy us. Individuals differ in their ability to sustain great losses of energy or money – or serious threats of death. But insofar as they are able (once again it is a question of strength, a quantitative matter), men risk the greatest losses and go to meet the most serious threats. If we generally believe the contrary, this is because they generally have little strength; but within their

personal limits they have nonetheless been willing to spend and
to expose themselves to danger. In any event, whoever has the
strength and of course the means for it, indulges in continual
spending and repeatedly exposes himself to danger. Through examples, and through detailed analysis of the operation of contrary
factors, which is most clearly apparent in eroticism, I will attempt
to show the significance and scope of this law; further, I will not
neglect to come back to the theoretical aspect of the problem. I
have presented its general lines in the first part of this work. What
I first explained starting from the movement of production, I will
now show at work in the individual fever, thus in a more concrete
way, contributing to a fuller view by way of a detour. What cannot change in any case is a way of looking at things that is radically opposed to the correct judgment of thought.

Everything that "justifies" our behavior needs to be reexam-
ined *and overturned:* how to keep from saying simply that thought
is an enterprise of enslavement; it is the subordination of the
heart, of passion, to incomplete economic calculations. Humanity
is letting itself be led the way a child submits to a professor; a
feeling of poverty paralyzes it. But those general interests that it
alleges are valid to the extent that fear prevails, or energy is lacking. They make sense only in the short view that obtains in official discourse; but energy abounds and fear doesn't stop anything.
Between an indolent thinking and a violent course of things, dis-
cord is sovereign; and our wars are the measure of those impotent and reasonable professors that lead us.

2. Literature and Anguish; Sacrifice and Horror
For the time being, in order to illustrate the law by which we
seek the greatest loss or the greatest danger, I will limit myself
to two references, the first being fictional literature. For the
charm of a novel is linked to the misfortunes of a hero, to the

threats that hang over him. Without troubles, without anguish, his life would have nothing that captivates us, nothing that excites us and compels us to live it with him. Yet the fictional nature of the novel helps us bear what, if it were real, might exceed our strength and depress us.[8] We do well to live vicariously what we don't dare live ourselves. Not that it is a question of bearing misfortune without weakening: on the contrary, enduring it without too much anguish, we should *take pleasure* in the feeling of loss or endangerment it gives us.

But literature only continues the game of religions, of which it is the principal heir. Above all, it has received sacrifice as a legacy: at the start, this longing to lose, to lose ourselves and to look death in the face, found in the ritual of sacrifice a satisfaction it still gets from the reading of novels. In a sense, sacrifice was a novel, a fictional tale illustrated in a bloody manner. A sacrifice is no less fictional than a novel; it is not a truly dangerous, or culpable, killing; it is not a crime but rather the enactment of one; it is a game. At its beginning it is the narrative of a crime whose final episode is *performed* for the spectators by the priest and the victim. Of course, the victim is the unnamed animal – or man – that *plays* the role of the god – in other cases, of the king – whom the priest is meant to kill: the ritual is connected with a myth of which it is the periodical reenactment. Sacrifice is no less meaningful for that: as a rule, it even seems to have reached, in horror, the limit of anguish which the spectators could bear: otherwise, how to account for excesses that confound the imagination? And how many times was it required by softened conditions to adapt to a greater sensitivity?[9] That it was of a game's nature reduced its gravity, but it always involved plunging the spectators into anguish tied to a feeling of vertiginous, contagious destruction, which fascinated while it appalled.

What matters, in any case, is not the horror itself; nor does the anguish that is maintained in literature count purely as anguish. The fondness for literature is not a vice, where anguish would be morbidly sought after. An object fascinates in sacrifice – or in literature – which is not ordinarily present in horror or anguish. In the most common circumstances, horror may only have a putrescence as its object; or anguish, a kind of void. But the object that fascinates in sacrifice is not only horrible, it is *divine*, it is the god *who agrees* to the sacrifice – who exerts an attraction and yet has only one meaning: losing oneself in death. The horror is there only to accentuate an attraction that would seem less great if he did not offer himself up to a painful agony.

The novel seldom achieves the rigor of this movement. Yet it's the same with the basic narrative as with classical tragedy: it is most engaging when the character of the hero leads him, of his own accord, to his destruction. The closer the hero gets to divinity, the greater are the losses he incurs, and the greater are the dangers he willingly faces. Only divinity verifies, in an excessive way, the principle according to which desire has loss and danger as its object. But literature is closer to us, and what it loses in the way of excess is gained in the way of verisimilitude.

3. Life, "on the Level of Death," Founded the Riches of Religion and Art

The kind of panic followed by a prolonged explosion that might respond to the death of a king shows the strength of a monstrous temptation that draws us to ruination. We are constantly tempted to abandon work, patience and the slow accumulation of resources for a contrary movement, where suddenly we squander the accumulated riches, where we waste and lose as much as we can. The enormous loss that the death of the sovereign constitutes does not necessarily give the idea of counterbalancing its effect: better, since the mischief is done, to plunge furiously into mischief.

In a sense the death of a king is like looking into a void from which we are not separated by any guardrail: the view may cause us to step back, but the image of the possible fall, which is connected with it, may also suggest that we jump, in spite or because of the death that we will find there. This depends on the sum of available energy which remains in us, under pressure, but in a certain disequilibrium.

What is certain is that the lure of the void and of ruination does not in any way correspond to a diminished vitality, and that this vertigo, instead of bringing about our destruction, ordinarily is a prelude to the *happy* explosion which is the festival. Actually, trickery and failure are the rule of these movements: in the first instance, the prohibitions prepared for the transgression of the festival, and the measureless character of the festival observes the *happy* measure nonetheless, holding in store the return of life governed by the prohibitions. But when the prohibitions corresponded to the negation of nature and to the intention men had to do away with their dependence on the natural given, the failure was intentional. Men had to cheat to avoid recognizing the impossibility for them to reduce themselves to pure mind. Their failure was thus unintentional. If they brought measure into a movement that called for measurelessness, then, on the contrary, they intentionally failed. We generally don't consent to the definitive ruin and death where measurelessness would lead us. The festival is perhaps no less fictitious than the negation of nature, but whether it has the form of literature or of ritual this time, the fiction is purposely invented. It is intentional at least, even if it puts consciousness to sleep. The desire is perhaps fooled, but with the half-complicity of children who are deluded by the playthings we give them. Only the available resources are squandered. In principle, there is no collective festival that cuts into a basic wealth, without which the coming of the next festival – measureless and measured at the same time, like the first – could not be assured. And ultimately it is not ruination, let alone death, it is joy that the pursuit of ruination attains in the festival. We draw near to the void, but not in order to fall into it. We want to be intoxicated with vertigo, and the image of the fall suffices for this.

One might say rather precisely that true joy would require a movement to the point of death, but death would put an end to it! We will never know authentic joy.... Moreover, death itself is not necessary. I believe that our strength fails us before life does: the moment death approaches it creates a void in us that incapacitates us in advance. So not only is trickery necessary in order not to die, we must avoid dying if we wish to attain joy. Thus, only the fictitious approach of death, through literature or sacrifice, points to the joy that would fully gratify us, if its object were real – that would gratify us at least in theory, since if we were dead we would no longer be in a condition to be gratified.

Further, why rebel too stubbornly against a definitive difficulty? Not that we should turn away from death, on the contrary: stare at it, look it straight in the face, that is the most we can do. Lasting gentleness, irony and cunning are worth more than that protest about which we can predict that if it's maintained it will turn, like all literature, to trickery. In fact, protest would soon be out of the question. Ought we not in a sense aim for a joy that involves the totality of being, setting ourselves against the interests of the egoist that, albeit in spite of ourselves, we never cease to be? In this connection, to the extent that they reflected, in the dazzling play of their facets, the changing multiplicity of life, didn't tragedy and comedy, and likewise the authentic novel, respond in the best way possible to the desire to lose ourselves – tragically, comically – in the vast movement where beings endlessly lose themselves? And if it is true that trickery presides over literature, that an excess of reality would break the momentum that carries us toward the point of resolution where literature aims us, it is also true that only a real daring has enabled us to find, in the anguish of figurative death or downfall, that singularly excessive joy that engages being in its destruction. *Without this daring we cannot oppose the riches of religion and art to the poverty of animal life.*

Four

The Object of Desire and the

Totality of the Real

1. The Object of Desire Is the Universe, or the Totality of Being

Rather strangely, I describe what is hardest to comprehend, but at the same time it is the most familiar thing. Spectators of tragedy and readers of novels get the meaning of it without fully understanding it; and in their own way those who attend mass religiously do nothing but contemplate its essence. But if from the world of passion, where without difficulty tragedy and the novel or the sacrifice of mass form recognizable signs, I pass to the world of thought, everything shuts off: in deciding to bring the movement of tragedy, that "sacred horror" which fascinates, into the intelligible world, I am aware that, disconcerted, the reader will have some trouble in following me.

In reality, what fascinates in this way speaks to passion but has nothing to say to the intellect. Thus it appears, in many cases, that the latter is less lucid than a simpler reaction. In point of fact, the intellect cannot justify the power of passion, and yet it naively considers itself obliged to deny that power. But in choosing to hear no other reasons but its own, the intellect errs; for it can go into the reasons of the heart if it so chooses, provided it does not insist on reducing them first to the calculation of reason. Once it has made this concession it can define a domain in which it is no longer the sole rule of conduct: it does so if it speaks of the *sacred*, of what surpasses it by nature. The most remarkable thing is that it is quite capable of speaking of what surpasses it; indeed, it cannot conceive that it might finally be able to justify itself without abandoning its own calculations.

The intellect fails, in fact, in that with its first impulse it *abstracts*, separating the objects of reflection from the concrete totality of the real. It constructs, under the name of science, a world of abstract things, copied from the things of the profane world, a partial world dominated by utility. Nothing is stranger, once we have surpassed it, than this world of the intellect where each thing must answer the question "What is the use of that?" We then realize that the mental process of abstraction never gets out of a cycle in which one thing is related to another, for which the first is useful; the other thing in turn must be useful...for something else. The scythe is there for the harvest, the harvest for food, the food for labor, the labor for the factory where scythes are made. If, beyond the labor necessary for the manufacture of as many new scythes as are needed to replace the old ones, there is a surplus, its utility is defined in advance: it will serve to improve the standard of living. Nowhere do we find a *totality* that is an end in itself, that is meaningful as such, that doesn't need to justify itself by pleading its usefulness for some other thing. We escape this empty and sterile movement, this sum of objects and abstract functions that is the world of the intellect, only by entering a very different world where objects are on the same plane as the subject, where they form, together with the subject, a sovereign totality which is not divided by any abstraction and is commensurate with the entire universe.

To make this radical difference between two worlds perceptible, there is no finer example than the domain of erotic life, where the object is rarely situated on another plane than the subject.

The object of sensual desire is by nature another desire. The desire of the senses is the desire, if not to destroy oneself, at least to be consumed and to lose oneself without reservation. Now, the object of my desire does not truly respond to it except on one condition: that I awaken in it a desire equal to mine. Love in its essence is so clearly the coincidence of two desires that there is nothing more meaningful in love, even in the purest love. But the other's desire is desirable insofar as it is not known as a profane object is, from the outside (as an analyzed substance is known in a laboratory). The two desires fully respond to one another only when perceived in the transparence of an intimate comprehension.

Of course, a deep repulsion underlies this comprehension: without repulsion the desire would not be boundless, as it is when it does not give way to repulsion. If it were not so great, would it have that convincing force of the lover answering her lover, in darkness and silence, that nothing, absolutely nothing separates them now? But it doesn't matter: now the object is no longer anything but that immense and anguished desire for the other desire. Of course, the object is first known by the subject as *other*, as different from it, but at the moment it reduces itself to desire, the object, in a tremor that is no less anguished, is not distinct from it: the two desires meet, intermingle and merge into one. Without doubt, the intellect remains behind and, looking at things from the outside, distinguishes two solitary desires that are basically ignorant of one another. We only know our own sensations, not those of the other. Let us say that the distinction of the intellect is so clearly contrary to the operation that it would paralyze the latter's movement if it were compelled to fade from awareness. But the intellect is not wrong merely because the illusion denounced is efficacious, because it works and no purpose would be served by depriving the deluded partners of their contentment. It is wrong in that *this is not an illusion.*

To be sure, illusion is always possible in any domain whatever. We thus fool ourselves if some incomplete perception is interpreted by us as being that of a bottle: it is not a bottle; a simple reflection gave me the impression it was, and I thought I was going to touch it. But the example proves nothing. For an error of this kind is verifiable and other times it is indeed a bottle that my hand grasps. It is true that a bottle in the hand, a correct proof, is something certain, solid. Whereas, in the most favorable case, the possibility of attaining the desire or the existence of the other and not just its external signs is generally disputed. Yet an infant is not able, the first time at least, to deduce the presence of another, *internally* similar to it, from external signs. On the contrary, it can finally infer a presence on the basis of external signs only after having learned to associate the signs with that presence, which it must first have recognized in a *total* contact, without any prior analysis.

It is not easy to isolate this contact – an internal thing on both sides – when we are talking about the embrace of adults: it occurs under conditions in which the differentiated sensations and the complex associations can never be set aside (as they are for the very young child). We are always entitled to adopt the reasoning of science: this complex of definable sensations is associated by the subject with a belief in the desire of his partner. Possibly so. But it would be futile, in my opinion, to advance further on the path of isolation. This goes without saying: we will never find in this way an *isolable* moment in which it will be certain that these conventionally isolated elements are not sufficient. Better to take the opposite approach, focusing on the *total* appearance manifested in the embrace.

This is because in the embrace *everything* is revealed anew, everything appears in a new way, and we have every reason from

114

the start for denying the interest, and even the possibility, of abstract mental operations that would follow this unfolding. Besides, no one has attempted these operations.... Who would presume to delineate from ponderous analyses what appeared to him at that moment? This appearance might even be defined by showing that it cannot be grasped through treatises like those published in the journals of psychology.

What strikes one from the first is a "recession" of discernible elements, a kind of drowning in which there is nothing drowned nor any depth of water that would drown. It would be easy to say to the contrary: not at all...and to cite distinct impressions. These impressions do in fact remain, despite the feeling of being drowned to which I refer.

This feeling is so strange that, as a rule, one gives up the idea of describing it. Actually, we have only one way to do so. When we describe a state we ordinarily do this by singling out aspects that distinguish it, whereas here we merely have to say:

> It seems to me that the totality of what is (the universe) swallows me (physically), and if it swallows me, or since it swallows me, I can't distinguish myself from it; nothing remains, except this or that, which are less meaningful than this nothing. In a sense it is unbearable and I seem to be dying. It is at this cost, no doubt, that I am no longer myself, but an infinity in which I am lost....
>
> No doubt this is not entirely true; in fact, on the contrary, never have I been closer to the one who...but it's like an aspiration followed by an expiration: suddenly the intensity of her desire, which destroys her, terrifies me; she succumbs to it, and then, as if she were returning from the underworld, I find her again, I embrace her....
>
> This too is quite strange: she is no longer the one who prepared meals, washed herself, or bought small articles. She is vast, she is distant like that darkness in which she has trouble breathing, and

she is so truly the vastness of the universe in her cries, her silences are so truly the emptiness of death, that I embrace her inasmuch as anguish and fever throw me into a place of death, which is the absence of bounds to the universe. But between her and me there is a kind of appeasement which, denoting rebellion and apathy at the same time, eliminates the distance that separated us from each other, and the one that separated us both from the universe.

It is painful to dwell on the inadequacy of a description, necessarily awkward and literary, whose final meaning refers to the denial of any distinct meaning. We can keep this much in mind: that in the embrace the object of desire is always the totality of being, just as it is the object of religion or art, the totality in which we lose ourselves insofar as we take ourselves for a strictly separate entity (for the pure abstraction that the isolated individual is, or thinks he is). In a word, the object of desire is the *universe*, in the form of she who in the embrace is its mirror, where we ourselves are reflected. At the most intense moment of fusion, the pure blaze of light, like a sudden flash, illuminates the immense field of possibility, on which these lovers are subtilized, annihilated, submissive in their excitement to a rarefaction which they desired.

2. The Analytical Representation of Nature and the Vague Totality, Which Is Both Horrible and Desirable

In speaking of a totality, the problem is that we usually speak of it lightly, without being able to fix our attention on that total object we speak of (when in fact it would need to be considered with the exasperated attention of the lover...).

The totality is truly alien to ordinary reflection in that it includes at the same time objective reality and the subject who perceives the objective reality. Neither the object nor the sub-

OBJECT OF DESIRE, TOTALITY OF THE REAL

ject can form by themselves a totality that involves the whole. In particular, what the totality, called "nature," is for the scientific mind is a simple caricature; it is the complete opposite of a conception according to which, in the case of an unlimited sexual desire (a desire not hindered by any reservation, not contradicted by any plan, not curbed by any work), its object is precisely *the concrete totality of the real;* and this implies that fusion with the subject which I clumsily attempted to describe.

I am obliged to linger over the analytical representation of nature, as opposed to an accurate representation of the totality, since I myself have spoken of *nature*, in a very different sense of the word. Here I must look for a terminological exactness without which I will have spoken to no purpose.

Theistic philosophy contrasts nature with the totality: for it, there is God on the one hand, and nature on the other. (In this there is even an embryo of dualism, which theology prefers not to develop.) I don't mean to defend the theistic conception of the world; on the contrary, I would like to distance myself from a representation of nature that makes it, like the scientific spirit, a substitute for God. My intention is at all costs to protect the totality from the colorations that taint it; it is neither God nor nature; it is not anything that answers to the multiple meanings of these words, nor even to any one meaning among them. Insofar as such meanings do not deceive us, what they denote is in fact only an abstract part of it. And likewise, the nature of which I speak in this book, a part of the totality, cannot be envisaged in a concrete way except insofar as it is included in the totality. As I said, it is foul and repugnant: the object that I designate in this manner does not refer to anything abstract that one might isolate and stabilize, the way I isolate and stabilize in my thought some useful object – a piece of bread, for example. This detached piece of bread is an abstraction. But the moment I eat it, it reenters the unstable totality, with which I connect it by eating, insofar as I connect myself with the concrete totality of the real. This becomes clearer if I come back to "foul nature": it is the animality that I can grasp in the totality which the embrace constitutes.

The moment comes when my attention in the embrace has as its object the animality of the being I embrace. I am then gripped with horror. If the being that I embrace has taken on the meaning of the totality, in that fusion which takes the place of the subject and the object, of the lover and the beloved, I experience the horror without whose possibility I cannot experience the movement of the totality. There is horror in being: this horror is repugnant animality, whose presence I discover at the very point where the totality of being takes form. But the horror I experience does not repel me, the disgust I feel does not nauseate me. Were I more naive I might even imagine, and moreover I might even claim, that I did not experience this horror and this disgust. But I may, on the contrary, *thirst for it;* far from escaping, I may resolutely quench my thirst with this horror that makes me press closer, with this disgust that has become my delight. For this I have *filthy* words at my disposal, words that sharpen the feeling I have of touching on the *intolerable* secret of being. I may say these words in order to cry out the uncovered secret, wanting to be sure I am not the only one to know it; at this moment I no longer doubt that I am embracing the totality without which I was only *outside*: I reach orgasm.

Such moments require the growing intensity of sensations that inform us of the totality and braid together its objective and subjective elements inextricably: this is the complex of sensations that proclaims at the same time the other and oneself — that is not in any way reducible to an analysis where nothing ever appears but abstract elements, colors, sounds and so on, whose ground is always the totality.... If the sensations do not have their greatest intensity, it is possible for us to isolate specific objects on the field of the totality; whereupon we no longer know anything but those objects; we know them clearly and distinctly, but the presence of the totality escapes us. The sense of the totality demands an extreme intensity of *the vaguest sensations, which reveal to us nothing clear or distinct:* these are essentially animal sensations, which are not merely rudimentary, which bring back our animality, effecting the reversal without which we could not reach the totality. Their high-pitched intensity overruns us, and they suffocate us at the very moment they overthrow us morally. The negation of nature (of animality) is what separates us from the concrete totality: it inserts us in the abstractions of a human order — where, like so many artful fairies, work, science and bureaucracy change us into abstract entities. But the embrace restores us, not to nature (which is itself, if it is not reintegrated, only a detached part), but rather to the totality in which man has his share by *losing himself.* For an embrace is not just a fall into the animal muck, but the anticipation of death, and of the putrefaction that follows it. Here eroticism is analogous to a tragedy, where the hecatomb at the end brings together all the characters. The point is that the totality reached (yet indefinitely out of reach) is reached only at the price of a sacrifice: eroticism reaches it precisely inasmuch as love is a kind of immolation.[10]

PART FIVE

The History of Eroticism

One

Marriage

1. Eroticism Developed out of Illicit Sexuality

The subject of this book is the *history* of eroticism, and thus far I
have only talked about the elements that constitute eroticism. But
it is really a matter of the *first, historic steps* that led to the different forms of man's sexuality, as they evolved in time. It will easily be granted that these *first steps* had a decisive importance.
A history of eroticism that did not consider them first and foremost would make little sense.

This is all the more important seeing that while eroticism
subsequently developed varied forms, these always take up its
basic themes: the "reversal of alliances," the Phaedra complex and
the desire to consume oneself do not cease to exert their force
in a movement whose end is always the totality. The repetition
of these themes is carried out whenever all at once a human being
behaves in an astounding way, in violent contrast with his ordinary behaviors and judgments – revealing an unavowable reverse
side matching the pleasant, correct side, the only one we show.
It is always a question of revealing feelings, parts of the body and
ways of being that we are *ashamed of* at any other time. It is a
matter of showing what at any other time it is impossible to show,
and what we show precisely because it is impossible to show it.

Further, I need to make this *normal* aspect of eroticism clearer in one regard.

The status of man's sexual activity is surprising: it is not at all forbidden in principle. It is subject to restrictions, of course, but these restrictions leave open an extensive field of possibilities. Whereas the history of eroticism is by no means that of sexual activity allowed within the limits defined by the rules: indeed, eroticism only includes a domain marked off by the *violation of rules*. It is always a matter of going beyond the limits allowed: there is nothing erotic in a sexual game like that of animals. And perhaps eroticism is relatively rare (it is hard to say anything definite on this point due to the paucity of reliable data): it consists in the fact that accepted forms of sexual agitation occur in such a way that they are no longer allowable. So it is a matter of passing from the licit to the forbidden. Man's sexual life developed out of the accursed, *prohibited* domain, not the licit domain.

2. The Dubious Character of Marriage

This brings me to reconsider the initial form of properly human sexuality, in which the prohibition is clearly limited and the transgression of the prohibition takes place according to rules. Among the diverse forms of human sexuality, marriage occupies an ambiguous position which is quite unsettling.

I asserted that in the beginning it was the transgression of a prohibition. Actually, this is a very difficult thing to prove. It even conflicts with a conspicuous aspect of the institution, which is essentially licit. But there are other examples of transgressions *that comply with the transgressed law.* If one bears in mind the fact that sacrifice is a crime,[1] one recognizes the paradox of a lawful crime – an infraction of the rule allowed by the rule itself! This poses a problem. If one follows me, just as the act of killing as performed in sacrifice is forbidden from the very first, the sexual act performed in marriage would have been, at its origin, the object of a prohibition: the prohibition would be the rule – and marriage the violation. This is more tenable than it appears. I cannot offer any convincing proof, but it isn't necessary for such a prohibition to have actually had a value as effective as the prohibition of murder. It is enough that a prohibition *in principle*, derived from the one bearing on close kin, may have corresponded in the beginning to the general feeling. The Judaic commandment, which goes far beyond the prohibition on incest, is perhaps the trace of this feeling. In the original situation close kinsmen had an exclusive claim on their daughters and sisters, their nieces and female cousins. But the prohibition laid on them induced them to transfer their claim to other men. Those who had a claim on women could agree on a transgression of the prohibition in favor of those who had no claim (as we have seen, on condition that the gift be reciprocated). This way of looking at the problem has something arbitrary about it, no doubt, yet it has the merit of indicating the coherence of a whole tableau (I believe it alone can do so). This amounts to saying that the power of transgression implies in theory *an existence outside the rule connected with right*. This could have been the only solution to a problem that resulted from the general prohibition on the sexual act. This sort of trickery would be consistent with the inordinate decisions and halting practices that are normal in the human species. The idea of entrusting the deflowering of new brides to men who generally possess a power of transgression, such as priests, seems to have been common: apparently, the *droit de cuissage*,[2] which was still operative in France in the Middle Ages, had no other origin. The main thing was not to hand girls over to men who, owing precisely to their right, were particularly linked to the prohibition.

It is natural, moreover, that the right to avail oneself of women would have been given, transferred, to men tied to a clan by a practice of reciprocity of ritual gifts. We know that the meaning of these gifts is similar to that of sacrifice. And we must not forget that they mainly involve *sacred* or sumptuary goods and not products that are simply useful, the reason being that there is generally an element of transgression connected with them, as there is with sacrifice. The destruction, breaking or burning of the offered objects is the most striking form of it, but their luxurious use always confers on them the value that loss has in the sphere of productive wealth. There is always a transgression with regard to profane life, to an order of utilitarian things, where the rule of utility dominates.

In a sense, marriage in which the father or brother gives a woman with a view to transgression associates the father or brother with this transgression. But by *giving* his daughter or sister, he averts the danger (the curse) hanging over the immediate author of the transgression. The incest prohibition would thus indicate rather clearly the general meaning of the malaise related to sexuality. Sexuality appeared to contain something so foul and so dangerous, so equivocal, that one could not approach it without taking multiple precautions and detours. This is what the rules of marriage were designed for. But an attention of this kind cannot be ascribed to indifference and we have to conclude that scandal had, in this privileged case, the entirely opposite effect, which morality fears. Nothing could have given more meaning to the curse that was laid on it. In a profound way, eroticism is the meaning of the horror man had of sexuality: these reactions resemble those of a girl who flees a man because of love and flees him only to love him in spite of herself, moved by a passion stronger than the will.

3. Marriage and Habit

Usually we are at a loss to understand the erotic character of marriage, owing to the fact that, in the end, we only see the state: we forget the transition. Actually, we have every reason for this. The transition is not lasting, and in the sequel the licit aspect overshadows the regular irregularity of the transition. We direct our attention to sexual activities outside marriage, reserving the word eroticism for them, and we neglect the first forms in which the giving of a woman by her close kin to relative strangers represented a kind of break. In actual fact, more often than not the economic value of the transferred woman tends to minimize the erotic aspect of the transition and, from this viewpoint, marriage has taken on the meaning of habit, dulling desire and reducing pleasure to nothing.

Habit is not necessarily inimical to the intensity of sexual activity. It is favorable to the harmony, to the secret understanding of one by the other, without which the embrace would be superficial. It is even possible to think that only habit sometimes has the value of a deep exploration, in opposition to the misunderstandings that turn continual change into a life of renewed frustration. I am even inclined to think that the anxiety that makes us desire change is often only impatience, a tendency to shift the responsibility for failure onto another, onto a partner's lack of charm – an incapacity for the intuition without which we cannot discover a path that is often hidden. What nonetheless justifies our suspicion of marriage is the very structure of eroticism, which would not have been able, in the framework of habit, to compose the figures and signs that come into play in its outbursts. Aren't these figures, these signs – from nudity to orgy, from prostitution to violence – supported by habit? Recall that eroticism developed out of illicit sexuality, outside marriage. It cannot help but shatter the framework within which the

127

strict rule was intended to maintain a fundamental irregularity.

Sexual life would have been poor, it would have stayed within the bounds of habit very near the animal level, if it had not developed freely in response to those uncontrollable explosions that impel it forward. Indeed, if it is true that habit spreads it forth, can we ever say to what extent a given habit, which we know was favorable, did not depend on those capricious forms that the movements of irregularity gave rise to?

Two

Unlimited Fusion, the Orgy

1. The Ritual Orgy

We don't know anything about the exact conditions under which eroticism, beyond the forms of marriage, accentuated the transgressiveness that is its foundation. But it is certain that the regular framework of marriage could not give an outlet to all the feverish energies that kept individuals under pressure, expressed first by a suffocating sexual anguish, then by violent and uncontrolled explosions.

It should be understood that these explosions retained the transgressive character of marriage: they were, like marriage, irregularities provided for by a rule. Even the "festival of the king's death," in spite of the formless aspect it assumes, is still in a sense lawful: the rule authorizes it by the *regular* suspension of its effects, during the time when the king's corpse is rotting. Ritual orgies, which often constitute one of the episodes of a festival, are even more regularly structured. Moreover, they give themselves a pretext: they are not *intentionally* the violent reversals I have spoken of, but rites of contagious magic aimed at fertilizing the ground.... The orgy nonetheless has a characteristic meaning: it is the transgression of a prohibition. Indeed, in this respect it is a pinnacle of transgression and a kind of general – resolute and unreserved – removal of limits. Chance did not decree that at the orgies of the Saturnalia the masters should serve the slaves: the rules and structures sank under a tidal wave of crude forces, which were normally powerless. It was a matter of producing in everything the opposite of what the rules prescribed. The rules were dissolved in a vast movement of animal fury; the prohibitions that one ordinarily respected in terror were suddenly ineffectual. Monstrous couplings were formed, and there was no longer anything that wasn't an occasion for offensive behavior. These hyper-agitated men panted after the very things that usually terrified them. They revelled in a fear whose object was their dreadful license, a license that fear made exhilarating.

The effectiveness of the orgy as a practice of contagious magic cannot be accepted as an essential explanation of the orgy. An avowable motive does not prove there were not unavowable ones. But the fecundity associated with the orgy nonetheless has a deeper meaning, beyond the vulgar one: I argued that the disgust with nature has as its privileged object that decomposing matter in which we see the fundamental coincidence of life and death, whose striking contradiction is finally only the result of a super-ficial view. In theory, the sexual organs have nothing to do with the disintegration of the flesh: indeed, their function places them at the opposite pole. Yet, the look of the exposed inner mucosae makes one think of wounds about to suppurate, which manifest the connection between the life of the body and the decomposi-tion of the corpse. Moreover, the filthiness of dejecta do not cease to link these organs to death. For its part, the vegetation of the fields never looks repugnant. But it signifies nature to us: could we not say that the orgy reduces us to that nature with which it invites us to merge, whose womb it suggests that we reenter?

But here it is necessary to recall that the nature in question, into which man is invited to sink, is not the one from which he

UNLIMITED FUSION, THE ORGY

emerged: it is *deified* nature. And similarly, the orgy is not at all the return to a natural, indefinite sexuality. It is incongruous sexual behavior, tied to that feeling of topsy-turvydom which is produced by an almost general lifting of prohibitions. Efficacy never gives another meaning to the orgy. We are entitled to think that its magical value depended on transgression, which is unknown to profane nature.... But it doesn't matter, if the orgy opened up the possibility for sexual life to be obdurate – to take a resolute approach – in the pursuit of situations where the vertiginous impressions of eroticism are heightened.

2. The Witches' Sabbath

In my view, it is absurd to think that the primitive orgy had the opposite meaning of a relative indifference to indecency. Thus, obscenity would not have had the horrifying value that it has for us; more specifically, the ritual orgy is easy for men whose sense of shame is much less developed than ours. Actually, this judgment goes together with an opinion we have of ourselves, according to which our civilization, by nature, absolutely rules out the indecency of a ritual orgy. But this is a delusion, and even a rather gross one: *it took innumerable burnings at the stake to put an end to the custom.*

Of course, we don't know and will never know anything for certain about the nocturnal revelries of the Middle Ages and the beginning of modern times. The blame for this falls, moreover, on the merciless repression of which they were the object: the confessions that callous judges extracted from wretched individuals put to the rack cannot be given as sources of information that leave our minds in peace. These judges made their victims say whatever they themselves believed they knew or perhaps imagined. We may nevertheless think that the Christian repression was not able to prevent the pagan festivals from continuing, at least in areas of deserted heathland. But the worship of Satan replaced that of the old deities. That is why it is not absurd to recognize a *Dionysos redivivus* in the Devil.

At all events, the sabbaths that were dedicated in the remoteness of the night to the worship of this god who was only the reverse of God could not help but deepen the traits of a ritual that itself carried the festival's sense of reversal to extremes. No doubt, the judges in witchcraft trials prompted their victims to accuse themselves of a parody of Christian rites that worsened their case. But, supposing the judges themselves suggested these aspects, they could have done so only to the extent that the same aspects might have occurred to the witches. So we have no way of knowing whether an isolated trait relates to the judges' imagination or to the practices of those they accused; and yet we cannot believe that *sacrilege*, or the inversion of the sense of the rituals, was the principle guiding this research on the heath. In any case, there is little reason to suppose that the name *black mass*, at the end of the Middle Ages, did not correspond to anything real. In all probability, the *black mass* presented itself so seldom in the guise of a phantasm or a suggestion of torturers that it could well have been *authentically* celebrated in our time: the mass that Huysmans attended, which he described in *Là-bas*, bore no resemblance to those *profane* simulations that are still organized, I'm told, to indulge the fancy of rich hobbyists.

3. The Link between Eroticism and Evil

What makes the satanic orgy especially significant is the fact that it does not merely reverse the profane and regular order of things, as does the classical or primitive orgy, but reverses the course of the sacred world, of its *majestic* form at least.

This is possible because Christianity brings into the religious sphere a division unlike the one that existed before it. Within the limits of paganism, the sacred world always had one side that was pure and another that was impure, the first being majestic and the second accursed. Both parts of this world were equally *sacred*, were equally removed from the profane world. The gulf separating these two worlds left the impure things side by side with the pure ones; only neutral things were outside the ambiguous domain of religion.[3]

Actually, Christianity retained the divine character of the Devil, but avoided recognizing the fact. And there was, in its eyes, on one side the divine world of light, on the other the darkness in which the profane and the diabolical worlds join their miserable destinies. Moreover, this confusion is today in every mind whose training either is Christian or partakes in a religious moralism of the same order. Thus, a disciple of Durkheim, Robert Hertz, seeing the opposition of the pure and the impure, was able, in a valuable and erudite study,[4] to link together the pure, the right and the sacred, the impure, the left and the profane.

What gives importance to this paradoxical division, contrary to that of primitive forms, is the fact that it implies a change in the moral sense of eroticism. This change puts an end to the ambiguity maintained until then in the matter of reprobation. As I said, this general lifting of prohibitions was, under primitive conditions, both illicit and licit. There was a lifting of the prohibition, but on condition that it be temporary; there was nothing in the prohibition that opposed this lifting. There were then no partitions dividing humanity into fundamentally separate worlds, into so many sealed compartments. If forms were opposed to each other, there was no need for going to the limit of the opposition. The awareness of a totality of opposed forms was maintained and it seemed easy *to modulate* the discordances. But since it set up a radical opposition between the *attractive* world of the good, of majestic forms, and the world of *repulsion*, of corruption and *evil*,

133

Christianity associated eroticism unambiguously with evil. What in paganism was only the momentary reversal of the course of things became the lot of the damned, the share that came under God's eternal curse. Not only was eroticism the object of a definitive reprobation, because of the appeal to horror that precipitated its movements, but it became the inexpiable wrong, and something like an essence of evil.

Moreover, we are obliged to recognize the degree to which this way of looking at things was justified. The denial of animal sexuality and the repulsion that averted people from it never prevented desire from reclaiming its rights. In fact, these elements were an inducement, and we have seen that eroticism owes its value to the distaste we have for the animality of sex. Under such conditions, sexuality exerted an excess of agonizing attraction. Considered within the limits of the sinner's self-interest, *evil* has an excuse all the same: it is not *sovereign* evil having its reason for being in itself. Only eroticism is evil for evil's sake, where the sinner takes pleasure for the reason that, in this trespass, he attains *sovereign* existence.

4. Eroticism, or the Demon of Evil versus the God of Good

The Devil's sovereignty has two contrary aspects. For believers it is a matter of rivalry: the Devil is jealous of God; he can't accept God's precedence. But the *non serviam*, the refusal to have only a useful value, to be a tool in the world, does not always have the odious meaning that relates to a confusion. The desire to accede to authentic being, to the *sovereignty* without which an individual or an action have no value in themselves, but are merely useful.[5] The hammer is useful to the one who drives the nail. And I can likewise be useful if I shine the shoes of passersby, but between the bootblack that I am and the passerby, relations are established, at least for a while, which are those of a sovereign, or a master, to a servant. Now let us suppose that my servitude is not temporary and that the passerby, whose boots I polish, never renders me the service that I render him, that doubtless I earn my daily bread, but I never get to enjoy, as does the passerby, any useless luster. This luster does not *serve*, has no meaning outside itself, but it bespeaks the sovereignty of the passerby as well as my degradation. I am not saying that the only way not to be reduced to what my shoeshine box and my brush are is to refuse those services I render. But what if I accept without saying anything or thinking anything? But above all: What if the whole of humanity observed the same silence and the same lack of thought?

Actually, it is not often that a man sinks so low; but degradation burdens the whole of humanity. The most serious thing would be if degradation were to win out in the long run, and spread to the point where it would burden the very *meaning* that man generally has for himself. So it is important not to lose sight of man's limits or of his possibilities. No one can envisage the elimination of useful work, but man could not be reduced to it without being eliminated himself.

Now, an ambiguity is introduced if one speaks of the God of good, which is to say, the God of works, of useful action. Within the framework of the Church, an age-old struggle enacted the refusal to accept the value of works. But the sovereignty of the faithful, Jansenists included, is indirect; they participate in the sovereignty of God, provided they are on their knees. I don't mean to say that submission, even to the God of works, rules out autonomy, but in simple terms this is an autonomy of the afterworld; it is not given, it is only promised. In its establishment, Christianity took up in a renewed form the movement that set the first men against nature. Christians repudiated the pagan world in which transgression counterbalances the prohibition to form the totality. In this way, they revived within themselves the original drama that was the transition from animal to man: they did this with an efficacy all the greater because of the ignominious death on the Cross, before which they took their stand, maintaining transgression's moment of horror within themselves. But under these conditions the totality continued to exist only insofar as Christianity did not destroy what it had in view: that pagan world which it regarded, not without some justification, with the horror that the first men had of nature.

This gives meaning to the blackness that the *condemned* eroticism of the Christian ages was to assume. The sabbath was the blackest form, wherein the play of nocturnal terrors and the play of licentiousness were combined — wherein, above all, desire comes full circle and the consciousness of doing wrong, of [...].[6]

THREE

The Object of Desire

1. Of Frenzy in the Distinctly Erotic Sense of an Object

Two contrary figures make up the tableau of eroticism. In the first, pure negation is given free rein; it occurs directly and all bounds are passed at once: the humanized order of things is generally abolished. There remains an immense disorder in which the animal explosion is released blindly. This is no longer pure sexuality, and eroticism is involved, certainly, but in a completely negative way, for an orgy is a transgression of the rule, or of all the customary rules, and does not at all present itself in an alluring form. The positive, alluring aspect of eroticism is very different: there the object of desire is distinct, its nature opposes it to all others, and if it is erotic it is positively so first of all. A naked woman, young and pretty, is doubtless the exemplary form of this object. (But I speak of this now only in order to give a material image of it right away. In actual fact, a naked woman does not always have the erotic meaning that I ascribe to her. Moreover, the nakedness of the earliest times could not have had any particular meaning.)

The crucial element in the distinct constitution of erotic objects is a little disconcerting. It takes for granted that a human being can be regarded as a *thing*. In theory, he is just the oppo-

137

site of a thing. He is not a person either, but always a *subject*. I am not a thing; vis-à-vis things, objects, I am the subject that sees them, names them, and handles them. But if I consider my fellow being, I cannot place him on the side of things, which I see and handle, but rather on that of the subject *that I am*. I can say "it is" of a thing, but it could not say "I am" of itself. I can say "he is" of my fellow being, but he can say "I am" of himself, in the same way that I do. So I cannot take him for a thing and instead I should call him, a bit childishly, an "I am," to distinguish him in this way from those things that are subordinate to me and that in fact I regard as *nothing*.

The animal might in a sense but cannot actually say "I am." The same is true, moreover, of the sleeping man: the animal is perhaps a man asleep, man an animal that rouses itself from the sleep of nature.... More often than not, we don't know what to make of an animality to which, for very deep reasons, the earliest men attributed a divine life. But we easily treat animals as things. From the beginning they were at once things and beings similar to us, at times even undefinable aspects of the divine. When men reduced other men to slavery, they finally were in the presence of men who had lost human dignity and who no longer counted except as things. This extreme degradation had its limits; the life of slaves, which never became animal life, was not reduced to the absence of the thing either. Slavery was necessarily a fiction and slaves never really stopped being men. But the fiction through which our ancestors looked on their fellow men as things is full of meaning. The fiction is conveyed essentially in the fact that human beings can be useful goods, objects of ownership and transaction. But inasmuch as they also alienated part of their rights to the sovereign totality, these same beings acquired the possibility of being a function of that totality, the erotic function, for example.

Slavery aside, men generally tended to see women as things. Before marriage, women were the father's or brother's things. If the father or the brother transferred his right of ownership by means of a marriage, the husband in turn became the master of that sexual field which she would need to lend him and of the labor power which she would be able to place at his service.

The sexual rights of the husband are an object of jealous possession. Of course, since the satisfaction of sexual desire requires the possession of a precious object, eroticism does not escape a tendency that is radically contrary to the one I spoke of first. If it corresponds to the desire to lose or to risk, it nonetheless has the effect of starting us down the path of acquisition and conservation. This second desire is so conscious, so active, so strong, it appears so inconsistent with the first that it is usually the only one noticed. More often than not, we neglect to look at it a little more closely. Thus, we don't see that acquisition is the only means of losing more, and if we weren't able to conserve anything we wouldn't have anything at our disposal. Moreover, what did I say but that we want to lose as much as we can; at the same time I made clear the extent to which poverty and cowardice limited us. Jealousy is perhaps the most impoverishing of virtues and there is no doubt that it stands in the way of happiness. But eroticism's enrichment demanded this reducing of women to an object of possession. I say this in a narrow sense, but that is the only one which can count here. If women had not become objects to be possessed, they could not have become, as they did, the *objects* of erotic desire: these objects have forms, particular aspects, which the maenads doubtless did not have. The maenads would flee in disarray, whereas the object of desire adorns herself with the greatest care and offers a motionless figure to the temptation of a possessor.

The opposition is simplified but it can furnish the symbols of the two contrary worlds that make up the totality of eroticism.

139

It is necessary to contrast the courtesan's carefully arranged beauty with the disheveled animality of the maenads....

2. The Object of Desire and the Prostitute

Actually, the possession of women in the life of regular couples had only an indirect effect in this sense. It wasn't the wife who became the erotic object thus offered to the desire of all men. As a thing, both because and in spite of male jealousy, a wife is mainly the woman who bears children and works at home: this is the form in which she is objectified in the manner of a brick or a piece of furniture. The prostitute is, just as much as the married woman, an object whose value is assessable. But this object is erotic, from one end to the other and in every sense. This condensation of all the signs of eroticism into one object obviously had a decisive importance: it is at the origin of those figures that command the reactions of man's sexual life, replacing the motive signs of animal sexuality.

It would be naive, no doubt, to limit the determination of all erotic values to an overly schematic view. Experience has shown us, unambiguously, that when they mean to seduce, respectable women tend to resort to the embellishments of the harlot. But many factors entered into the formation of the signs that are apt to provoke desire. Nothing proves that nudity, which has no *sexual* meaning in itself, owes its general *erotic* value to prostitution. It gets that value more from the use of clothes.... But, unless nudity is pure (which not only is not unusual but is, after all, in the order of things), it always has a savor of animality, which accords with the fallen state of prostitutes. The allure of nudity is not the exclusive property of prostitutes, but it is the allure of a thing, of a seizable object, and venal love has the privilege of reducing a woman to that "object" which erotic nudity is.

We are far from paying prostitutes the attention that such a

140

fully determined form of *human* life warrants. This lack of attention is due to the frivolousness of the intellect, which immediately turns away from its object if it is not insignificant. There will
never be a lack of compassionate souls to protest the miseries of
prostitution, but their cries conceal a general hypocrisy. It may be
painful, humanly, to admit that the detour of prostitution played
a part in the formation of our sensibility. But this is not so serious if we stop to think that in matters of erotic reaction there is
nothing humanity has not persisted in denying. (But since we all
yield to the desire, since we *all* succumb to the desire – even
saints at the moment of their temptation – there is *nothing* that
answers better to our ineluctable demand, *nothing* that expresses
more faithfully our heart of hearts.)

We need the *shame* that is linked to prostitution and that
enters into the alchemy of eroticism from every slant. But we
could have met with shame in another way: the very *figure* of
desire could not have been traced had not the venality of women
liberated the movement that did the tracing. This figure had to
be independent; it needed to freely compose the response to
desire's burning inquiry.

Let us come back to the principle according to which desire
demands the greatest possible loss. In a sense, the orgy offered
the fullest satisfaction to this need, but the loss then had the
shortcoming of not being clearly limited, of being shapeless and
of never offering desire anything to grasp. The same is not true if
the prostitute forms a definite figure whose meaning is that of
loss. In fact, she is not just eroticism but also *loss* having taken
the form of an object. That sparkling finery and that make-up,
those jewels and those perfumes, those faces and those bodies
dripping with wealth, becoming the *objects*, the focal points of
luxury and lust, though they present themselves as goods and as
values, dissipate a part of human labor in a *useless* splendor. The

essence of loss is this intense consumption that exerts a dangerous fascination, that prefigures death and finally attracts more and
more. But in principle the loss disappears, and were it not for
these visible hotbeds whose fires condense and settle in, the
attraction of destructive consumption would not have this contagious power. But let us restate things more simply, starting from
the dual principle of loss and risk: prostitutes receive as a gift large
amounts of money; they use this money for the sumptuary expenditures that make them more desirable and increase their power
to attract gifts, a power they had from the start. The principle of
this circulation of wealth is not commercial from the start. The
money is *given*, and likewise the prostitute makes a voluntary *gift*.
What is involved is not necessarily a sale subject only to the rule
of self-interest. What circulates on both sides is surplus, that
which generally does not represent, for either party, the possibility of a productive use. Of course, the desire for a prostitute
is liable to cause ruination, but if it is true that beyond a given
limit necessities enter into circulation, this is because a *dangerous*
fascination leads to a senseless use and the principle remains,
according to which only the excess should have been spent: in
other words, the vertiginous desire defines its victim and consecrates him in that henceforth he does not just dissipate his excess
wealth, but burning *himself* up to the point of dying, he behaves
as if he were a complete superfluity, a being for whom, in his
account, duration has no meaning.

3. The Object of Desire Signifies Instantaneous Gratification
I cite this last, extreme case in order to bring out the traits of
the desirable prostitute, a figure in which death is readable in the
aspects of excessive life. Besides, the prostitute is generally the
figure of death under the mask of life in that she signifies eroticism, which is itself the locus where life and death become con-

fused with one another.... But this is true at the extreme limit, at the apex, if prostitution makes an offered woman into a dead object, or more exactly, the *dead point* of the passionate outburst.

It is necessary in fact that an individual be regarded as a thing if desire is to compose the figure that corresponds to it.

This is an essential element of eroticism, and not only must the figure have been passive in order to have received this or that form and to have been associated with particular objects, but passivity is in itself a response to desire's insistence. The object of desire must in fact restrict itself to being nothing more than this response; that is, it must no longer exist for itself but for the other's desire. In a real, always eventful, life, in which the waiting is rushed, it is clear that capricious beings, existing for themselves first of all, have at least as much allure as those static figures, those beings destroyed as ends for themselves, which prostitutes are. We usually prefer, instead of that passivity, the movements of beings more real, existing for themselves and wanting to respond first to their own desire. But if we are in the presence of such beings, even those completely intent on responding to that desire which is not ours, we cannot prevent ourselves from struggling toward a destruction. We must also bring this object equal to ourselves, to the subject, inside the purview of the dead object, of the infinitely available object, which possession [assigns[7]] precisely to the prostitute.

Let us say that desire always seeks two objects, one that is mobile and alive, another that is fixed and dead. And what characterizes eroticism is not the mobile-living but the fixed-dead, which alone is detached from the normal world. This is the end to which we want to lead the mobile-living. It is a matter of breaking the ordinary and conscious sequences in order to find the detached: what is detached exists only as an object or a fusion.

This opposition between the solid and the fluid, between the nullified, stationary thing and the elusive motion has a paradoxical meaning at first. For, in fact, the object at rest generally signifies *duration*, and motion signifies life in the *moment*. Such an opposition is found in many forms: it is the opposition between the beauty of Apollo and the orgy of Dionysus. Yet, the dialectic of opposite terms often has variable relations between them. The raid of the Maenads has the primary meaning of life limited to the moment, but the play of consciousness fascinated by the object that disturbs it has the same value in a secondary sense: the fugitive outburst of the passions has, in relation to that *object*, the meaning of infinite duration. The basic theme is given in the opposition of the Maenad devastating the world of useful objects and these objects kept safe from destruction. In the secondary theme the Maenad is not changed in herself, but she has a neutral meaning in the mind of the one fascinated by the object of desire, and she is merged, *for him,* into the aggregate of an indifferent and immutable world. All at once the response to desire denies the opacity, the very fabric, of this world; it is the sudden rent in that fabric, given to the trembling consciousness in a flash of lightning. So that what justifies the reaction in which the Dionysian world is indistinct in the general opacity of the opaque world is the intoxication or the dimming of consciousness without which the incursion of the disheveled girls is unthinkable. The positing of desire's object is the intrusion – into the world of clear and distinct objects – of the lightning stroke that left the dazzled Maenads *in darkness*. It is the lightning stroke given to consciousness.

4. Prostitution and Idleness

But things can't happen directly! What has a fulgurating character is not *directly* alluring. It's the same with the contents that desire posits as with the lightning flash whose light is blinding: the oblique way is necessary if a *final* response to desire's persistence is to be given us. The form in which the response comes in the *first* instance is beauty: to begin with, the object of desire is feminine beauty.

If we say of a woman that she is desirable, as a rule this is because she is beautiful. Many factors, some of which are variable and conventional, others relatively stable, enter into the determination of beauty. Moreover, it is the feminine aspect, the Venus-like grace — which is to say, a partial aspect of beauty — that is essential.

Idleness, which made prostitution possible, is not the same thing as beauty; often beauty coexists with work, ugliness with idleness. But work is never favorable to beauty, the very meaning of which is to be free of oppressive constraints. A beautiful body, a beautiful face convey beauty only if the utility they represent has not altered them in any way, only if they cannot suggest the idea of an existence reduced to serving and, for that reason, made ungainly. There are beautiful draft horses and admirable oxen, but their beauty is bound up inescapably with the idea of a movement of energy triumphing over the hardest physical tasks, and Venus-like grace is antipodal to it. Only figures that are slender and even a little wild correspond to what desire is seeking. The desirable form is always that which servile necessity has not subjected to its laws. By nature, the object of desire has nothing to do in this world except to respond to desire. So much so that the salient muscles of a ballerina, even though the dance is, contrary to work, a sovereign activity having no other meaning than beauty, are likely to detract from the greatest charm. The least reminder of a material servitude is always liable to thwart desire, insofar as "beauty" offers it a response.

It must be added that feminine beauty is far from being reduced to any simple element. While it is true that ugliness is often the sign of fatigue, heaviness and decline, desirable beauty always suggests – a world away – youth, flowers, springtime and an upwelling of fresh energy. I distorted things a little by stressing the baneful aspects of a renewal that is the principle if not of being then of its multiform appearance. If beauty is indeed the sign of *sovereignty*, of what is never prostrate, never reduced to the servile state, renewal (youth) like idleness signifies beauty. It also speaks of abundance, ease and the inexhaustible effusion of energy. Assuming that one is attentive to my argument, it will be clear that the adverse aspects of death, if they predominate, are to be seen first as the condition of a resurgence, and second as the greatest luxury: the greatest energy, is it not that which, beyond the immediate charms of flowers or of springtime, causes us to seek the wrenching experience of tragedy? But tragedy and in general all the splendors that anguish and death command don't mean anything different than the most beautiful flowers and the strongest upwellings of spring vigor. They don't sunder death from a youth often rich in anguish, but rich through an excess of blood.

But that surface beauty which inflames desire in the first place is not just a positive sign of the overflowing power of life; in a form where discretion has little place, it is always an accentuation of the traits of the other sex. Under the conditions of wealth, leisure and choice that prostitution reserves for women, it is a matter of using paints, jewels and finery to make them more feminine. In this perfection of femininity, idleness has a part, the most significant part perhaps, for the intensity of work reduces the contrast of the sexes. The prostitute is the only human being who logically should be idle, being what she is. A man who does nothing does not seem manly; the characteristics that distinguish him are thereby degraded. If he is not a soldier or a member of the underworld, our first thought is to suspect him of effeminacy.

THE OBJECT OF DESIRE

(I don't think we can speak of the poet's idleness because, first of all, if he doesn't have a laborious life, a poet at least has a creative life; moreover, it may be pointless to speak in a general way of the living conditions of poets....) But by living in idleness, the prostitute preserves the completely feminine qualities that work diminishes, that soft and fluid form of the voice, of the smile, of the whole body, or the childish tokens of affection demanded obsessively in the desire of a woman.

In contradistinction, women subjected to a factory job have a roughness that disappoints desire, and it's often the same with the crispness of businesswomen, or even with all those women whose dryness and sharpness of traits conflict with the profound indolence without which a beauty is not entirely feminine.

Femininity's attraction for men, and masculinity's for women, represent in eroticism an essential form of animal sexuality, but they modify the latter in a radical way. What directly excites the body of animals, in a way analogous to the motor action of light, reaches men through symbolic figures. It is no longer a secretion whose odor gives rise to another odor, but a constructed image, *signifying* in sum the essence of femininity. Moreover, femininity participates in that reduction of the erotic object to softened forms, which captivate without breaking what they touch.

FOUR

Nudity

1. Obscenity and Nudity

Nudity, about which there is agreement that it arouses to the extent that it is lovely, is also one of the softened forms that announce but do not reveal the sticky contents that horrify and seduce us. But nudity is unlike the beauty of faces and decently clothed bodies in that it draws one near the repulsive source of eroticism. Nudity is not always obscene and can appear without recalling the indecorousness of the sexual act. Possibly so, but as a general rule a woman stripping naked in a front of a man exposes herself to his most unseemly desires. Nudity thus has the meaning, if not of outright obscenity, of a slipping toward it.

Outright obscenity is not disturbing. A naked woman, if she's old and ugly, leaves most men unmoved: but if such a woman is obscene without disturbing anyone, the obscenity which the nude body of a pretty woman lets one glimpse arouses to the extent that it is obscene, that it causes anguish but does not suffocate, that its animality is repugnant yet doesn't exceed the limits of a horror which beauty makes bearable and fascinating at once.

2. The General Unfolding of the History of Eroticism

Moreover, obscenity itself is nothing but that natural animality, the horror of which establishes our humanity. Let us recall that

149

humanity stands opposed in us to the dependence of which animality is the sign, but that the calculations and labors of *profane* life, in which man hoped to find *independence* with respect to nature, soon became revolting in that they ensured man's subordination to *means*. In every case, it was the desire for autonomy, without which there is no humanity, that determined the human attitude *(but that never led us anywhere but from one dependence to another, the second dependence never having anything but the power to escape from the first)*. The *sacred* in a vague and impersonal form became the new principle of pure autonomy, but missing from this principle was consciousness. The sacred was no longer animality; its truth had, negatively, the meaning of a breach of the rational laws of work, or of effective forbearance; positively, that of an explosive release which no longer lasted. In the sphere of sexuality, marriage and the orgy corresponded to the operations of the sacred in the domain of symbolic figures. We can now be more explicit by saying that nudity and generally the positing of an *object* of desire contrast with the orgy's consciousless confusion, just as the positing of a sacred *object* in sacrifice contrasts with vaguely articulated forms of religious thought and figuration.

3. A Backward Reference and a New Reflection on Marriage

This reference back allows us to perceive finally, in a less imprecise way, the proper meaning of marriage. With nudity being posited as such, it is legitimate to think that marriage is an earlier and still confused form of sexuality. The isolated union of spouses is actually close to the diffuse union of the orgy: at an *unarticulated* stage of sexual activity, marriage is a form of reduced transgression — it is the least possible transgression; the orgy, on the contrary, is a generalized transgression and a kind of exacerbated state of transgression. But in marriage as in the orgy, there is no positing of the object. The arousal is immediate; it is that produced by the contact of bodies as sleep approaches. The principle of marriage is copulation in darkness. It is quite evident, moreover, that the union of spouses does not allow for the possibility of making the wife the consecrated object of desire. For that she would need to be withdrawn from the general movement of life, as is the prostitute. The look of a wife cannot have the meaning of eroticism: it speaks of the couple's shared life *as a whole.* So it is inconceivable that the nudity of the married woman had the value for the husband that I am trying to situate.

This doesn't at all mean that marriage could not have attained, in the second place, a complex form in which wives borrowed from prostitution the meaning of an object of desire. Moreover, marriage (or the couple united by a shared life) is finally the only form of sexual activity capable of linking all the possibilities of eroticism, going from purity to impurity, from the disorder of the senses to the making of a home, from individual desire to all that is.

4.

I will go back to the nudity that I characterized as a slipping toward obscenity. This slipping is often difficult to grasp in that nudity is the least defined thing in the world; actually, the slipping is what constitutes it, and the slipping is the reason why the object of desire, whose reality is provocative, constantly escapes distinct representation. Indeed, what disturbs one man leaves another indifferent and, what is more, the same individual that such an object lacerates one day is indifferent the next. If we reflect on nudity, the appearance if not of obscenity then of license, and hence of provocation, is always deceptive: in fact it conceals the sheer obscenity which itself has an equivocal meaning, as we have seen.

But these reflections can't prevent us from perceiving in erotic nudity the relatively stable element that is sanctioned by a general prohibition. This prohibition is not categorical. Christianity itself, which has pushed it furthest, has so loosely formulated it that it no longer forbids girls the sight of their own nudity.[8] But in our cultures, in one form or another, the prohibition of nudity has given a clear meaning to the fact of undressing. In the first place, only the sexual organs have been the object, but the custom of wearing clothes has given the same meaning to the adjacent parts which may, unlike the organs in question, have a true beauty (as for example the buttocks, the legs, or the breasts). Today these elements combine to give a nude woman that joining of feminine beauty with animal obscenity that distinguishes the *object of desire*.

5. The Conscious Sexual Act

By convention, nudity can be stripped of the character it has conventionally acquired: paintings and sculpture are proof of this. And similarly, the disturbing element that nudity gives us may shift to other objects (in the fetishism of corsets, boots, black stockings...). Moreover, a situation whose sometimes prohibited nature accords with the disarray or absence of clothing may be linked to the bodily state. Places or surrounding objects, whether by contrast or by intended purpose, can heighten the sensual emotion that the sight of nudity communicates. In any case, a multiple agreement composes in depth the unity of an erotic moment. The sensations of the sexual act themselves have a *provocative* agreement with the figures. The sensation *exhibits* the true object of desire (but the object of desire is itself an exhibit of the sensation). The tepidness of rain in the [brambles? rosebushes?[9]], the dull fulguration of the storm, evoke both the figure and the inner sensation of eroticism. The smoothness, the tumescence,

the milky flow of feminine nudity anticipate a sensation of liq-
uid outpour, which itself opens onto death *like a window onto
a courtyard.*

6.

But it is human to search, from lure to lure, for a life that is at
last autonomous and authentic.

PART SIX

The Composite Forms
of Eroticism

ONE

Individual Love

1. The Ahistorical Nature of Individual Love

In all that I've said until now – which concerns *love* – I have not spoken of those strong and obsessive feelings that attach an individual being to another whom he has chosen.

I wanted to describe a historical succession in which a few distinct forms appeared, which could not have appeared all at once. But individual love is an entirely separate matter. It has variable aspects and there is no doubt that they vary with the different forms of sexuality I speak of. They also vary with the different forms of culture.... In actual fact, individual love, precisely in that it doesn't involve society but only the individual, is the least historical thing in the world. It is not an aspect of history, and if it depends on historical conditions this is to a small extent, in a quantitative way. Harshness of life is not favorable to it, and neither are social forms in which the warring element is preponderant. In short, it presupposes resources commensurate with developed needs, resources *in excess*. A deficiency or a use of resources for other purposes are enough to deprive it of the possibility of existing, but the same is not true of the obstacles of custom, laws, or morals: clandestinity is not at all necessary to individual love, but it often increases the intensity of feelings.

What seems most clear to me is that one can't make love depend (as I believed and as is usually thought) on a particular given, on a stage in the development of historical man. If I say of individual love that it is outside history, this is insofar as what is *individual* is never manifest in history. Those men whose names fill our memories have nothing individual about them except an appearance that we lend to them: their existence is given to us only to the extent that their destiny corresponds with the general movement of history. They indeed rise up in isolation before our eyes, but it is the isolation of statues at the crossroads of history. They were not independent, they served that history which they imagined they were leading. Only their private life escaped (at least in part) the *function* that ensured their overt role. But the wall of private life, precisely if it protects individual love, marks off a space outside history.

The possibility of individual love was given from the moment when man became separate from animals. The least developed civilizations are familiar with it: it requires neither developed technical culture nor intellectual refinement. The precondition for its appearance was given in the relative abundance of resources. Now, we must assume this abundance was at the origin of a transition from animal to man. It may have resulted from labor – and a temporary scarcity may have been the primary factor in its production – but only an animal that was not bound by the constant necessity of subsistence, that generally had a surplus at its disposal, could have transcended useful procedures, creating that will to autonomy which established a vital point in nature that depended on itself alone. Such a being could not have lacked the conditions of individual attachment. At most we can imagine that the first men were so concerned about the autonomy I speak of as to be insensitive to the *individual* charm of their sexual partner. But an objection of this kind has the most limited meaning....

It is necessary to assume an immense diversity and a profusion of possibilities from the first. Only scarcity or war are capable of shrinking human life, of reducing it to that animal poverty that excludes the desire of a being distinguished from all the others.

2. The Fundamental Opposition of Individual Love and the State

The only element without which choice would make no sense is the prior existence of eroticism. I have adduced the reasons why the transition from animal to man can't be considered sensibly unless we imagine eroticism given – virtually – at one go. Consequently, I can picture man as being open from the start to the possibility of individual love, much as we are today (think of the persistent rarity of love worthy of the name when one considers numerically limited groups; could refinement of sentiments be so banal these days? What prevails is coarseness of the worst kind). But whatever form it may have had, in marriage or outside it, this love necessarily had a sense of transgression opposing it to animal sexuality. Individual love is quite different from eroticism, but it is fundamentally tied to erotic transgression. Individual love is not in itself opposed to society; yet, for lovers, what they are has no meaning unless it is transfigured in the love that joins them; otherwise, it is unavoidable meaninglessness – an unreality truer, alas, than the only reality. Lovers, in any case, tend to negate a social order that contests more often than it grants their right to live, that never yields to such a trifling thing as personal preference. Under difficult conditions, the elements of transgression essential to the sexual act, its brutally erotic character, the overturning of the given order and the silent horror that are connected with it, even if the lovers cannot bear them, take on the value in their eyes of hideous emblems of their love. Like sorcery, which is so often linked to it (in the use of potions, magic spells), love is in itself an opposition to the established sacred order. It is opposed to that order in the same way that the individual's being is at odds with social reality. Society is not universal truth, but it has that meaning for each particular being. Actually, if we love a woman nothing is further from the image of our beloved than the image of society or, a fortiori, of the State. But this doesn't have the meaning one might think, in that the concrete totality of the real, contrary to society or the State, is quite close to the loved individual. In other words, in both individual love and impersonal eroticism, a man is immediately in the universe. I am not saying exactly that his object is the universe, which would imply an opposition between subject and object. Individual love is analogous to carnal eroticism in this also, that the fusion of the object and the subject is its meaning. Of course, we may object to a way of looking at things wherein it is not the global union (fusion) of individuals in the state that represents the *universal* in us, but rather the couple, in which the object is reduced to what is most heavily *particular* in the world, the individual; where the fusion of this object with the subject always has a transitory character (whereas in the State the individuals, not their union, are transitory). But the State never means the totality to us. The State cannot in any way *use up* that part of ourselves that comes into play in eroticism or in individual love, for it cannot rise above interest (the generality of interest), and a share of ourselves (precisely the *accursed* share) cannot in any way be given within the limits of interest. We may be able, in the service of the State, to transcend the concern we have with increasing individual resources, an individual fortune, but we then escape the enclosure of individual interest only to be confined within the *general interest*. The State (at least the modern, fully developed State) cannot give free rein to a movement of destructive *consumption* without which an indefinite accumulation of resources situates us in the universe in exactly the same way as cancer is inscribed in the body, as a *negation*.

Contrariwise, the object of individual love is, from the start, the image of the universe that is presented for the measureless consumption of the subject standing before it. This object is itself consumption exerting its pull, and what the object offers to the subject who loves it is to open itself to the universe and to no longer differentiate itself from the universe. In the fixation of love there is no longer any distance between an indistinct but purely concrete totality of what is universally real and the object of this love: the beloved *in* love is always the universe itself. I admit that this may appear to be nonsense, but we cannot understand without an impression of the love object's uniqueness and exclusivity. Actually, this impression doesn't depend at all on a valorization of the individual. Far from it, in love the individual necessarily has the value of the universal. The choice of the object occurs in such a way that the subject is unable thenceforth to conceive of itself without the object and, reciprocally, the object separate from the subject becomes itself inconceivable for the latter. So the object doesn't sum up the universe by itself, but it does so for the subject, which it completes and which completes it. Needless to say, these views are not characterized by objectivity: the universe beheld in love is commensurate with the beholder; the limits of the subject are reflected in the choice of its object. But the two together must so clearly form the totality of the possible that we may speak of an error: the error consists in a choice such that the union of the subject with the chosen object gives us the impression of a mockery of the universal. But this detracts nothing from the accuracy of the feelings that are at stake: whatever error there may be in it, the beloved object is for the lover the substitute for the universe. This means that in desire nothing else counts any more, and the object gives the subject what it lacks in order to feel replete with the totality of being, so that at last it no longer lacks anything. Obviously, this implies a reciprocated love, for the object doesn't truly complete the subject except by loving it. (Unless a sense of dissatisfaction might sometimes have a deeper meaning than its opposite: at times what gets away from us reveals itself with an increased intensity compared with the moment when we possessed it....)

If I have been understood, we are not dealing with a characteristic of the object that is universal in itself (otherwise, for women no object would meet expectations better than the mind of a philosopher..., and for men mates would be quite rare...). The obscure feeling of coincidence, which determines the choice, assumes qualities such that the moral requirements of the subject will be satisfied (and often in their least acknowledged form). Further, it is necessary that a relative opposition of those brought together by affinity tend to make a complete world out of their pairing. But, above all, it is *consumption* that joins individuals most closely; the object is chosen insofar as it means consumption to the subject. This conditions the choice at any rate. But the *meaning* of consumption must always be considered relative to the subject. I am referring to *happy* consumption. *Intense* consumption, even when it is tied to an abundance of resources, can just as easily give rise to horror and fear. As a rule, for the subject the loved individual symbolizes an optimum consumption, one consistent with happiness in life but not so great as to cause anguish. Needless to say, very often the object of one's love means a consumption that is too great, as when a woman breaks the one who loves her by buying finery and giving parties: in this case, as it sometimes happens, anguish alone has the meaning of consumption to the lover. More generally, the lovers' consumption is measured *strictly*, by mutual agreement, in terms of possibility. But love joins the lovers only in order to spend, to go from pleasure to pleasure, from delight to delight: theirs is a society of consumption, as against the State, which is a society of acquisition.

3. From the Lovers' Society of Consumption to the Married Couple's Society of Acquisition

What misleads us concerning the union of lovers is its basic instability. If we fail to recognize the instability we naively consider forms in which the union I've spoken of – that fusion of a subject with an object filling up the whole universe – yields to compromise. Lovers have a social life and they also join together for show. If they form the universe in joining together they put forward that totality in which their union accedes to the recognition of others. They cannot content themselves with being the *only ones* to know that happiness whose limit is the universe. But they can themselves offer it for recognition only provided they do not appreciate it for what it is. They know this: their happiness (or rather their sovereign totality) will be recognized insofar as it is reduced to exteriority – and to failure. The others are right, moreover: if recognition of this happiness is proposed to them, they would be wrong to situate it beyond the usual limits; the lovers accredit these limits for their own part by entering the show; they submit themselves – and along with them, the universe they are – to those sets of judgments that subordinate being to useful ends, in terms of which only the State has any coherence. And they already judged other lovers as they agree to be judged themselves. The very incoherence (habitual in these perspectives) that upholds the principles of value tied to consumption (like fine clothes, wealth or social rank) finishes relegating the lovers' universe to the status of an indefensible vanity.

In a different sense, let us suppose that the union is stabilized, at least in appearance. The sexual play of the lovers has reproduction and the growth of a family as its effect, if not as its purpose.

Reproduction does ensures stability, but the union that endures in this way is not necessarily the same as the initial one. It may be a pure and simple society of acquisition. It is this in the sense that the family grows according to the number of children; and often it is this through the accumulation of wealth.

It would be foolish to judge these changes unfavorably. Besides, the birth of children is not reducible to acquisition. (I don't intend, within the limits of a book on eroticism, to describe the often contradictory aspects of the world of children, a world of consumption par excellence, but which leaves parents with the responsibility for growth – for acquisition....) But it would be absurd in any case to consider the union of lovers and that of parents as identical. The union is never stabilized except in appearance.... On the contrary, everything indicates that the love union is never given in duration. It genuinely endures, and even this is deceptive, only provided it arises again from a desire itself rising again from its ashes. What we condemn in love does not then reveal, as we too often believe, a lack of breadth: individual love is even a way of being that is supremely unbounded, but it succumbs to the impossibility of maintaining itself in its purity, or to the awkwardness of its transcriptions, whenever it moves (or gets bogged down) in a world not its own, in a world where the senses are limited. What we condemn in love is thus our own powerlessness, and never the possibility that it *opens up*.

4. Individual Love and Literature
The incompatibility of individual love and duration is so general (even if duration is its principle) that love's privileged domain is fiction.

Love does without literature (which may even be responsible for the prevailing mistrust toward it), but literature cannot avoid joining its own wealth of possibilities to that which love has in abundance but cannot realize. Few things are more meaningful to us, moreover, than adding the loves of legend to those that we live. In this way, we come to awareness of an equivalence between love and the universe; in this way, too, love comes to trace its limitless circuits in us and to reveal the precise meaning of that *universe*, detached from the world of narrow actuality, which we become if it transfigures us.

But at the same time that it shows consciousness the most distant meanings of love, literature does what it can to insert love in history, making of that ahistorical part of ourselves an element enmeshed in the great mechanism of constructions unmaking themselves that history is. No doubt this is in an incidental way, and history itself is affected thereby only insofar as it takes account of our will to escape its ruthless determinations.

Actually, the influence – historically situated – of literature on the ways of individual love is of limited interest: of the literary works that refer to the code of love, the most famous one holds all the others up to ridicule. But doubtless there are few examples of a ridicule more respectful, finally, of its object, boundless love, than the work by Cervantes; in fact, the romances it makes fun of are those that conveyed a sense of profanation. . . . If one surveys those chivalrous works of imagination, they do seem to refer to the prescriptions of initiatory societies,[1] according to which the initiates, in this case the knights, had to choose a lady to whom they would offer their feats of arms as a tribute: in the real world this would involve war exploits or those dangerous demonstrations of valor that tournaments represented. Tournaments were held during sumptuous festivals of which they were the main event. Each knight would ritually fight under the eyes of his chosen lady, to whom his jousts were dedicated, just as nowadays a matador sometimes dedicates the bull he faces to a woman spectator. Wearing provocatively opulent garments, the fair lady would watch the combat as if it were an exhibition, so that we can legitimately say of these rites that they had the meaning of a festival of individual love. These fictional feats of arms took place in a mythological world where enchanters, dragons and rescues gave the word *adventure*, expressing the initiate's destiny, its semidivine value.

We cannot fail to take note of the final lesson of these captivating displays, whose purpose seems to have been betrayed as much as it was served. From this episodic entry of individual love into history there clearly emerges the incompatibility of meanings of a historical event on the one hand, and on the other, of the lovers' absorption in the universe engendered by their embrace. On the side of the event there is the manifest need of discourse, of formulas that convey values in keeping with limited ends. On the side of the universe, secrecy and silence are essential, where nothing takes place that doesn't signify the totality of being affirmed at one go, compared with which all the rest, whose meaning is definite, has no meaning ultimately but that of the void.

Two

Divine Love

1. The Two Directions of Extreme Eroticism: Sadism, or Limitless Eroticism, and Divine Love

Individual love is an aspect of eroticism and we could not imagine it without the carnal embrace that is its consummation and in the heat of which the choice of the beloved becomes fully meaningful. Only the agitation of eroticism, its ambiguous character, is capable of lowering the barriers between individuals; conversely, the partner of an enjoyment that is all too intimate, all too cunning, offers herself from the start to the possibility of love. Yet it is certain that the inhibition of love heightens the intensity of erotic pleasure, or similarly, that love diminishes one's interest in pleasure. Two fundamental directions appear in this manner.

One extends eroticism further, closing itself to that which eroticism isn't: it is basically opposed to the concern for the partner, which limits the consumption to tolerable excesses that the object and the subject alike will have the strength to bear. It demands a boundless *energy* which, stopping at nothing, never limits the destruction. In its ordinary form, it is the vice to which physicians gave the name sadism. In its reasoned, doctrinaire form, elaborated by the Marquis de Sade himself in the interminable solitude of the Bastille, it is the pinnacle, the fulfillment of lim-

167

itless eroticism, the meaning of which I will explain in the final chapter of this description of eroticism.[2] We shall then see the extent to which eroticism responds to man's determination to merge into the universe.

Starting from individual love, and leading in the opposite direction, divine love carries on the search and finally gives it the deep meaning I have spoken of. But in order to go through with this search for the other, it rids itself of the accidental elements that always attach the real being to the world of sordid actuality. Too often the beloved is reduced under our eyes to that which she imagines herself to be, an existence subordinated to the conditions of a servile world. Hence the idea of replacing her with the imaginary object that mythology proposed to us and theology elaborated.

2. From the "Song of Songs" to the Formless and Modeless God of the Great Mystics

Already within the limits of human love, the presence of the other was given – exceptionally – apart from sexual relations. This separation corresponded to the possibility of a secondary opposition between the different pursuits of the erotic object and the beloved. But these two objects may be one and the same, and if the beloved emerges from the abyss of death where eroticism revealed her (or projected her), she immediately loses the virtue of opening up the totality of being to the subject. Only eroticism is capable, in silence and transgression, of admitting the lovers into that void where even the mumbling is stopped, where no speech is conceivable, where it is no longer just the other but rather the bottomlessness and boundlessness of the universe that is designated by the embrace. Pure love, on the contrary, is inseparable from chatter. But it sometimes happens in any case that the ponderous element of eroticism makes us want to extricate the other's purity from a natural embeddedness. Rarely do we consent to depend, at the extreme moment, on a contingency so wretched that it binds us precisely to the mire. This is the secret of alchemy nevertheless, but more often than not we are afraid.

But by freeing the beloved from the contingency of disgust, we only mire her in that of vulgar reality. So that the passage from individual love to purity has only two possible meanings: either we allow this love to be reduced to vulgarity (kept nonetheless in a halo of consumption by the birth of children or the constant threat of death); or, holding resolutely to purity, but at the same time to the desire for the *other*, for that which is missing and which alone might yield us the totality of being, we are in search of God.

What we attain in the embrace where the truth of the other is revealed we can of course find without resorting to these middle terms. If one understands what I've been saying, it is only a question of overthrowing the established order that subordinates us to some objective reality, independent of us. It is a question of living in a sovereign manner, of refusing to submit to that which remains alien to us: the natural order in the first instance, then the profane order..., ultimately it may be everything that has the appearance of contingency, in which case the whole of reality is denied on behalf of the single absolute, the logically formulated supreme being.

But we meet with a difficulty in this search. If we arrive at a logical formulation of God, we do not have His sensible presence. Nothing *burning* consumes us. And once eroticism is abandoned we have nothing within us except the poverty of language. But we are still not reduced to impotence. We only have to go back to the byways we encountered in the darkness of eroticism; we have to reencounter horror, anguish, death. The experience of God is kept alive in the throes of sacrifice and it corresponds poorly with the affirmations of positive theology, to which it opposes the silences of a negative theology. What the mystic glimpses in the laceration of his knees is a God dying on the Cross, the horror of death and suffering – a vision granted him to the very degree that his strength gives way. We shouldn't wonder, then, if the language he uses, in the hope of a more complete out-pouring of silence, is not the discourse of theology but of human love. "One knows," says a believer,

> of the part played by the *Song of Songs* in the language of the mys-
> tics. And if one considers the literal meaning of the *Song*, one can't
> help but observe that it is full of amorous expressions. Yet, the mys-
> tics saw in the *Song* the most adequate grammar of the effects of
> divine love and they never tired of annotating it, as if those pages
> had contained a prior description of their experiences.[3]

I don't intend to reduce "mystical states" in this way to a "transposition of sexual states."[4] The whole thrust of my book is contrary to these simplifications. It seems to me no more legiti-mate to reduce mysticism to sexual eroticism than to reduce the latter, as people do, even without saying it, to animal sexuality. Yet we cannot seriously deny the connections that turn two dis-tinct forms of love equally into modes of *consumption* of all the individual being's resources. I know that mystics only spend appa-rently small amounts of energy in their devotional demonstrations. But we would be mistaken not to take them at their word: their life is *aflame* and they *consume* it. It is certain that the mystics exhaust in their effusions all the energy that sustains them, and that is brought to them through the labor of others. Their asce-sis cannot be considered a modality of growth: it is a special form of consumption, in which an acquisition reduced to nothing gives the resulting preponderance of consumption a sense of extremity.

Whatever one makes of the erotic language of the mystics, it must be said that their experience, having no limitation, transcends its beginnings and that, pursued with the greatest energy, it finally retains only eroticism's transgression in a pure state, or the complete destruction of the world of common reality, the passage from the perfect Being of positive theology to that formless and modeless God of a "theopathy" akin to the "apathy" of Sade.

THREE

Limitless Eroticism

1. The Utility of God, Limit of the Experience
of the Mystics

I think that by giving a restrictive interpretation to the experience of *divine love*, we lose sight of that resolve to explore all that is possible without which all mankind abdicates. But divine love cannot by itself assign a limit to what is possible, and in any case if it is understood in its own terms it is poorly defined to say the least. The object that the mystic offers up for love's measureless consumption is itself involved in the opposite world of acquisition: so little is it the pure negation constituted by an absence of form and mode that it receives the *major* definition of a God of the State. He is the creator, the guarantor of the real world and the real order; he is the preeminent utility. Whether he transcends it or not, he is still the very reality of this world which is not *of itself* the betrayal of God but rather the expression of God. Whatever the manner in which he subjects us, we are at the same time subjected to the world that constrains us to serve history, engaged as we are in our subordinate attitudes. The final truth in this regard is that the perfect Being is just as contrary to the truths of mysticism as he is to those of an experience of eroticism. There cannot be, in the domain under God's rule, anything that goes beyond history or action, anything that *in the very moment* transcends a series of acts subordinated to their results.

2. On the Need to Go to the Limit of Seduction, at Least in Thought

I don't mean to say that by extending an experience of all that is possible in the direction of individual love, such a limitation can be avoided. These possibilities and their present limits do tempt one to begin the search anew; how can one keep from dreaming of an experience for whom nothing would constitute the object defined ahead of time? But then we would have to refer once more to an experience sought, starting from eroticism, in the opposite direction. There is no doubt that the way of individual love obliges us to limit ourselves not only to those possibilities that make allowance for the partner's interest, but also those that the partner herself can bear. From this opposition it emerges that the negation of partners opens up a last domain to eroticism. This domain was difficult of access at first, when the partner's accord seemed on the contrary to be a means of achieving an added intensity. It is assuredly inhumane, turning one's back on that accord, to search in indifference for new forms of ruination, forms that redouble the transgression, beyond complicity, through a boldness that increases in cruelty and crime.

In a single exercise, the *works* if not the life of the Marquis de Sade gave this negation its logically consistent form, so much so that one cannot dream of surpassing it. Maurice Blanchot stresses this fact: the basic trait of Sade's thought is the most indifferent denial of the partners' interests and of their very life. (Blanchot's study on Sade's thought[5] rescues its object from a night so deep that it may have been darkness for Sade himself: if Sade had a philosophy, it would be useless to look for it elsewhere than in Blanchot's book, and conversely, Blanchot's thought is consum-

mated perhaps by matching itself against that of Sade, the consummation of both having demanded what thought generally
refuses, the undeclared *community*, the collusion of minds – and
yet this accord is contrary to the unicism of Sade!) The repudiation of partners is in fact the key component of the system. For
eroticism falls short of its potential if it turns the death impulse,
which it is in principle, into a communion. Analogous to the rest
of life in this respect, sexual union is at bottom a compromise,
it is a half-measure, and the only measure to take between the
charm of life and the extreme rigor of death. Only by being separated from the communion that limits it does sexuality freely
manifest the exigency that is its basis. If no one had had the
strength, at least while writing, to absolutely deny the link that
attached him to his fellow men, we would not have the work of
Sade. Sade's life reveals an element of braggadocio, but this very
braggadocio was necessary to the elaboration of a thought that
expediency does not reduce to servile principles, to principles
such that utility, mutual aid or kindness have more force than
seduction has. We easily understand the impossibility of going to
the limit of that which seduces, if we consider the difficulties
for others that could result from a complete accord with our
desires. But when others are no longer taken into account, these
desires, even if their affirmation is literary, are manifested without any alteration.

"The ethical system [of Sade]," says Blanchot, "is based on the
primary fact of utter solitude." He

> said it and repeated it in every form: nature brought us into the world
> alone; there is not any sort of relationship between one man and
> another. The only rule of conduct, therefore, is that I prefer every-
> thing that affects me in a good way, and that I regard as inconsequen-
> tial everything that owing to my preference may be bad for another.

175

The greatest suffering of others always counts for less than my pleasure. No matter if I must purchase the smallest pleasure with an
unprecedented combination of heinous acts, because pleasure satisfies me, it is inside me, but the effect of crime does not touch me,
it is outside me.

3. *Sensual Pleasure and Crime*

Insofar as it considers the connection between destruction and
voluptuous pleasures, Maurice Blanchot's analysis adds nothing
to Sade's basic assertion. Sade is sometimes inconsistent, but not
about this: he states and restates, as an established truth, the paradox of crime's being a condition of sensual pleasure. This aspect
of Sade's work is presented in such a way that nothing could be
added to it; Sade's thought on this point is quite explicit, his consciousness quite clear. We may even say that he was sure of having made a fundamental discovery about human beings. But we
see then how narrowly cohesive the system is. If the isolation of
the individual is not laid down as a principle, the close connection between criminal destruction and sensual pleasure is dissolved; or at any rate it can play only a small role. Nothing is more
evident in reading Sade than the absurdity of a continual denial
of the value of men for one another: this denial militates against
the truth value of Sade's thought, involving it in the most banal
contradictions, and Sade's life does not bear him out, or does so
only in part. Not that isolation was never a factor in his own life;
it may even have been the greatest factor, but it was not the only
one. It is difficult to reduce to a pretense what we know about
Sade's character, which places him far above the odious heroes
he depicts. (He loved his sister-in-law; he had a humanitarian
political career; he was overcome with horror at seeing the guil-
lotine working from his prison window; and he cared so much
about his writing that he shed "tears of blood" over the loss of a

manuscript.) But the fallacy of isolation is the truth condition of a relationship between love and crime, and one cannot even imagine the work of Sade without the insistence with which he denied the value of men for one another. In other words, the true nature of the erotic stimulant can only be revealed by literary means, by bringing into play characters and scenes from the realm of the *impossible*. Otherwise it would still be unknown, the pure erotic reaction could not have been recognized under the veil of tenderness, for love is usually *communicated*, its very name has tied it to the existence of others; consequently it is ordinarily diluted.

The very vehemence with which Sade affirms his truth is not calculated to convince us. But it forces us to think. Maurice Blanchot meant to bring Sade's thought to light, but I can now add a further detail. Given Sade's representations, it is possible to observe that tenderness cannot change a fundamental operation. In using the destruction that is brought about through this operation, tenderness cannot make it the opposite of what it is. In the most general way, eroticism is contrary to customary behavior as expenditure is contrary to acquisition. If we behave according to reason we strive to increase our resources, our knowledge or, generally, our power. We are inclined, using various means, to possess more. Our self-assertion in the social sphere is always tied to behavior aimed at growth. But in the fever of sexual passion we behave in a contrary fashion: we expend our forces without counting, and we lose substantial amounts of energy without restraint and without gain. Sensual pleasure is so closely connected with ruination that we have named the moment of its paroxysm "*la petite mort*." Consequently, the objects that evoke sexual activity for us are always linked to some sort of disorder. Thus, nudity itself signifies a downfall, and even a kind of betrayal of the appearance that we give ourselves in our clothing. But in this sense we are never satisfied with little. In general, only passionate destruction and reckless betrayal are capable of showing us into the world of eroticism. To nudity we add the peculiarity of half-dressed bodies, which may be cunningly nuder than nude. Sadistically inflicted suffering and death are situated further along on this vector that slides toward ruination. In like manner, prostitution, the erotic vocabulary and the unavoidable link between sexuality and filth contribute to making the world of love a world of downfall and death. The truth is that we have no real happiness except by spending to no purpose, and we always want to be sure of the uselessness of our expenditure, to feel as far away as possible from a serious world, where the increase of resources is the rule. But it is not enough to say far away, we want to be opposed to that world: in eroticism there is ordinarily an impulse of aggressive hatred, an urge to betray. That is why a feeling of anguish is connected with it, and also why, on the other hand, when the hatred is a powerlessness and the betrayal an abortive act, the erotic element is ludicrous.

4. Apathy, the Negation of Others and of Oneself, and "Sovereignty"

Sade's system in this regard is only the most consistent, and most costly, form of erotic activity. Moral isolation signifies the removal of constraints and, moreover, it alone manifests the deep meaning of expenditure. Anyone who believes in the worth of others is necessarily limited; he is restricted by this respect for others, which prevents him from knowing the meaning of the only aspiration that is not subordinated within him to the desire to increase his material or moral resources. There is nothing more common than a momentary incursion into the world of sexual truths, followed, all the rest of the time, by a fundamental denial of those truths. The fact is that solidarity keeps man from occupying the place that is indicated by the word "sovereignty": human beings'

178

respect for one another draws them into a cycle of servitude where subordinate moments are all that remains, and where in the end we betray that respect, since we deprive man in general of his sovereign moments (of his most valuable asset).

In opposition to this, "the center of the sadistic world" is, according to Blanchot, "the demand for sovereignty affirming itself through an immense negation." At this point, the essential bond that subjugates man in a general way is revealed, the bond that robs him of the strength to reach that place where sovereignty would be achieved. For, in fact, the essence of the erotic world is not just the expenditure of energy, but also negation pushed to the extreme; or, if one prefers, the expenditure of energy is itself necessarily this negation. Sade applies the term "apathy" to this supreme moment. "Apathy," says Blanchot, "is the spirit of negation attributed to the man who has chosen to be sovereign. It is in a sense the cause and the source of energy." Sade seems to reason more or less as follows: The individual of today represents a certain quantity of force; in most cases he dissipates his strength by giving it over to those simulacra that are called others, God, ideals; he is wrong to exhaust his possibilities by squandering them in this way, but even more so to base his conduct on weakness, for if he expends himself for others this is because he thinks he relies on their support. Fatal weakness: He weakens himself by spending his strength in vain, and he spends his strength because he thinks he is weak. But the true man knows he is alone and he accepts being so; everything within him relating to others, the legacy of seventeen centuries of cowardice, he rejects; for example, pity, gratitude and love are sentiments that he destroys; in destroying them he reclaims all the strength he would have needed to devote to these debilitating impulses, and more important, from this work of destruction he derives the beginning of a true energy. – It must be understood in fact that

179

apathy doesn't consist merely in doing away with "parasitic" affections, but also in resisting the spontaneity of any passion. The degenerate who surrenders immediately to his vice is nothing more than a weakling who will ruin himself. If they merely follow their inclinations, even brilliant profligates, with everything it takes to become monsters, are doomed to catastrophe. Sade insists on this: In order for passion to become energy it must be held in check, it must be mediated by going through a moment of coldness; only then will it be as great as possible. In the first stage of her career, Juliette hears herself reproached constantly by Clairwill about this: she commits crime only when inflamed by the passions; she places lust, the effervescence of pleasure above all else. Dangerous indulgences. Crime is more important than lust; cold-blooded crime is greater than crime carried out in the fervor of emotion, but crime "committed in the callousness of the sensitive part," sinister and secret crime, matters more than anything, because it is the act of a spirit that, having destroyed everything within it, has accumulated an enormous force which will identify itself completely with the total destruction that it is working toward. All those great libertines, who live only for pleasure, are great only because they have annihilated any capacity for pleasure in themselves. This is why they engage in dreadful aberrations; otherwise the mediocrity of normal pleasures would be enough for them. But they have made themselves callous: they claim to delight in their callousness, in that denied, annihilated sensitivity, and they become ferocious. Cruelty is only the negation of oneself, carried so far that it is transformed into a destructive explosion; callousness becomes a throbbing of one's whole being, says Sade: "the soul passes to a kind of apathy that is soon transmuted into pleasures a thousand times more divine than those which their weaknesses got them before."

5. The Perfect Moment, or the Identity of Theopathy and Apathy

This passage should have been cited in full, because it clarifies the central point. The negation cannot be separated from those ways in which voluptuousness is not manifested sensually but in which its mental mechanism is disassembled. And likewise, voluptuousness apart from this negation remains furtive, contemptible, powerless to hold its place – the supreme place – in the light of consciousness. "I would like," says Clairwill, Juliette's companion in debauchery,

> to find a crime whose perpetual effect would be exerted even when I no longer acted, so that there would never be a single moment of my life, even when asleep, that I was not the cause of some disorder and that this disorder might spread to a degree where it would induce a general corruption or a derangement so absolute that even beyond my lifetime the effect of it would still continue.

Who would dare remain ignorant of the fact that within him there is a tendency toward voluptuousness that would reach its outer limit only at this point? Who would refuse to admit finally that voluptuousness, in its abasements, has a value incomparable to the interests of reason? Who would refuse to see in voluptuousness, from the angle of an eternal instant, the rapture without which the agonizing and cruel and man-denying divine could not even have been imagined?

This enormous negation has two aspects. First of all it divinely denies the separate being, the precarious individual, faced with the vastness of the universe. It denies him perhaps on behalf of another who is no less precarious, but who, because of his universal negation, even though he affirms himself to the extreme degree of affirmation, does so only in order to deny. So that being logically, from the start, the spirit of annihilation, there is nothing within him that does not lay itself open, beforehand, to blows like those he delivers on all sides. This affinity with cruel destruction is not ordinarily manifested by Sade's heroes, but one of his most perfect characters, Amélie, expresses it as fully as one could wish.

> She lives in Sweden. One day she goes and sees Borchamps.... Hoping for a huge execution, the latter has just handed over to the sovereign all the members of a plot (which he himself has hatched), and the betrayal has fired the young woman with enthusiasm. "I love your ferocity," she tells him. "Swear to me that one day I too will be your victim. Ever since I was fifteen years old, my head has been inflamed by one idea: to perish a victim of the cruel passions of libertinage. I don't want to die tomorrow, mind you – my extravagance does not go that far – but I want to die only in that manner; to become the occasion of a crime by expiring is the idea that makes my head spin." A strange head, well deserving of this reply: "I love your head madly, and I believe that we'll do some outrageous things together." "It is rotten, putrefied, I admit." Thus "for the complete man, who is mankind's all in all, no evil is possible." If he injures others, what a pleasure! If others injure him, what a delight! Virtue pleases him, because it is weak, and he crushes it, and vice because he draws satisfaction from the disorder that results therefrom, be it at his expense. If he lives, there is no event in his existence that he can't experience as a happy one. If he dies, he finds an even greater happiness in his death, and in the consciousness of his destruction, the consummation of a life that only the need to destroy justifies. Thus the denier is in the universe as an extreme denial of all the rest, and this denial cannot leave him safe from harm himself. Doubtless the force of denial bestows a privilege as long as it lasts, but the negative action it exerts with a superhuman energy is the only protection against the intensity of an immense negation.

At this point it should be clear that the effects envisaged go
beyond the human sphere in any case. This kind of completion
has never been conceived except in the mythical form that places
it if not outside the world then at least in the domain of dreams.
The same holds true in Sade's work, but – this is the second
aspect of the negation – what is denied here is not denied for
the benefit of some transcendent affirmation. Sade speaks with
an extraordinary vehemence against the idea of God. Actually, the
only profound difference between his system and that of the theologians is that the negation of isolated beings, which no theology accomplishes less cruelly, save in appearance, leaves nothing
existing above it, nothing that consoles, not even an immanence
of the world. There is this negation at the top, and that is all. It
is quite suspended, quite disconcerting, and it is no less so for
one who sees this single possibility out of reach. (Sade's representations are so perfect in fact that in their way they leave the
ground, and whoever grasps them insofar as they can be grasped
places them beyond his personal possibilities with the first step
he takes.) In the end, this ultimate and inaccessible movement,
the mere idea of which leaves one breathless, replaces the image
of God with an impossible human authority, the need for which is
nonetheless compelling, more logically compelling than the need
for God once was. For the idea of God was a pause, a moment of
stasis in the vertiginous movement that we follow; whereas Sade's
negation signifies the strength a man would have not to stop but
to speed up this movement.

It is more than a little strange that such a passage to the apa-
thetic sovereignty of the universe differs from the limited negation
of the mystics only in being a limitless negation. Like theopathy,
the apathy of Sade required a contempt for raptures and sen-
sory joys, experiences that leave the supreme profligate and the
supreme mystic equally unaffected. In the region where the

autonomy of the subject breaks away from all restraints, where the categories of good and evil, of pleasure and pain, are infinitely surpassed, where nothing is connected with anything any more, where there is no longer any form or mode that means anything but the instantaneous annihilation of whatever might claim to be a form or mode, so great a spiritual energy is needed that it is all but inconceivable. On this scale, the chain releases of atomic energy are nothing. Of course this domain cannot have definite boundaries, and the least consumption situates us *on the scale of the universe,* but we want to control it, we harbor the anguish which says that soon it will overpower us. This doesn't matter if we have realized, once, that the universe is the only limit of our revolt, that an unlimited energy engages one in a limitless revolt – in that autonomy without which we do not agree to live – but that in our weakness we want to know without dying, at least from the death that "apathy" reserves for us.

PART SEVEN

Epilogue

In the universe as a whole, energy is available without limit, but *on the human scale* which is ours, we are led to take account of the quantity of energy we have at our disposal. We do this spontaneously, but in return we should recognize the need to consider another fact: *we have quantities of energy that we are obliged to spend in any case.* We can always dry up its source; we would only have to work less and be idle, at least in part. But then leisure is one way among others of squandering – of destroying – the surplus energy, or, to simplify, the surplus available resources. Twenty-four hours of leisure activities cost, in positive terms, the energy necessary for the production of a day's supply of necessary provisions; or negatively, if one prefers, a nonproduction of everything a worker would have produced in this lapse of time. Pure leisure (and of course labor strikes) is merely added to the outlets that the available energy has beyond what is required for basic necessities. These outlets are essentially eroticism, luxury products (whose energy value is calculable in labor time) and amusements, which are the small change of the holiday; then there is work, which in some way increases the amount of production we will have at our disposal; and lastly, wars. . . .

Of course, what we spend in one category is in principle lost for the others. There are many possibilities of slippage: alcohol, war and holidays involve us in eroticism, but this means simply that the possible expenditures in one category are ultimately reduced by those we make in the others, so that only the profits found in war truly alter this principle; even so, in most cases these profits correspond to the losses of the vanquished.... We need to make a principle of the fact that sooner or later the sum of excess energy that is managed for us by a labor so great that it limits the share available for erotic purposes will be spent in a catastrophic war.

Of course, it would be childish to conclude right away that if we relaxed more and gave the erotic game a larger share of energy the danger of war would decrease. It would decrease only if the easing off occurred in such a way that the world did lose an already precarious equilibrium.

Indeed, this picture is so clear that we can immediately draw a different conclusion: we will not be able to decrease the risk of war before we have reduced, or begun to reduce, the general disparity of standards of living, that is, the general disequilibrium. This way of looking at things leads to a judgment that is clearly only theoretical at present: it is necessary to produce with a view to raising the global standard of living. So here I am reduced to repeating what every rational man already knows. To the common opinion I only need to add one particular: if nothing along such lines were to take place, war would soon be unavoidable.

Yet I don't wish to dwell on such a gloomy prospect. If the standard of living is prevented from rising, this is insofar as there exists in the world what is called a state of Cold War, accentuated at one point by actual war. We can say, consequently, that there exists for the time being a third solution, which is the present solution or Cold War. It is not very reassuring, but it affords us the time to think that barring war or extreme military tension a general raising of the standard of living might occur.

So there remains in the world a chance for peace connected with this resolve: to affirm, against all opposition, the unconditional value of a politics that would level individual resources, adding that such a politics can be pursued, exactly insofar as possible, without ceasing to respond to the immediate necessities imposed by the Cold War.

Once again, I cannot contribute anything here but these banalities, which will appear quite empty to most. It was not necessary to formulate a theory of eroticism for the purpose. Indeed, their relation with a theory of this kind ends up reducing the significance of these political considerations. In appearance at least, for the theory in question is essentially a historical exposition of the forms of eroticism, but an element is missing from the exposition.

Eroticism is in any case, even to the small extent that it has a history itself, on the fringe of history properly speaking, that is, military or political history. As it happens, this aspect of the matter carries a meaning that allows me to broach the conclusion of the historical account this book constitutes. For there remains, under the conditions I have laid out, the possibility of an episode of eroticism's history. We have known eroticism on the fringe of history, but if history finally came to a close, even if it drew near its close, eroticism would no longer be *on the fringe of history*. It would thus cease to be a minor truth, whose importance is overshadowed now, as it has been for a long time, by the factors that make up history. It might receive the full light of day and appear clearly to consciousness. True, the idea that history may end is shocking, but I can put it forward as a hypothesis. To my way of thinking, history would be ended if the disparity of rights and of living standards was reduced: this would be the precondition of an ahistorical mode of existence of which erotic activity is the expressive form. From this necessarily hypothetical point of view, consciousness of erotic truth anticipates the end of history; this consciousness brings profound indifference into the present time, the "apathy" of an ahistorical judgment, of a judgment tied to perspectives that are very different from those of men totally engaged in struggle. This does not in any way mean that the perspectives of those who join battle are senseless from my point of view. But neither do they have the sense that the opposed parties ascribe to them. We know beforehand that the resolution of the combat lies beyond its internal perspectives: the two camps are both wrong in the sense that the defenders are protecting indefensible positions, and the attackers are attacking unassailable positions. We can't do anything, on the contrary, that goes against the leveling of living standards. Neither can we reduce the meaning of productive activity to its usefulness. The meaning of any activity is situated beyond its useful value, but we cannot grasp it so long as we insist on remaining confined to the perspective of the battle.

Actually, the circumstances we are experiencing open up precise possibilities in this regard. The battle cannot truly be decisive except on one condition, that it fail, that it not go to the limit. If the end of history is to emerge from these current convulsions, this is conditional on a détente, for nothing else is capable of bringing it about. A victory inevitably won on a heap of rubble would sanction the insensibility on which a victorious party would have based itself. If the vicissitudes of men come to an end, if the gross stupidity of a definitive victory is spared them, history might have the only end it can reach... in a fizzling-out [en queue de poisson].

We cannot by struggling find a truth on which to base anything: in struggling we never see more than a part of things, even if the movement opposing the will to remain where we are has its privileged value. On the contrary, it is by distancing ourselves from every reason for fighting, by achieving perfect moments, which we know we can't surpass, that we have the power to assign to the movement of history that end which can only be insofar as it escapes us.

This much that is clear might finally emerge from my book – and from the epilogue that follows it.

Men committed to political struggle will never be able to yield to the truth of eroticism. Erotic activity always takes place at the expense of the forces committed to their combat. But what is one to think of men so blinded as to be ignorant of the motives for the cruelty they unleash? At least we can be certain they are lying. But by no means can we try to replace their directives with our own. We don't expect anything from a *direction*. We cannot base our hopes on anything but a détente, in which a wisdom coming from the outside might make itself heard. Of course this kind of wisdom is a challenge. But how could we not challenge the world by offering it the appeasement it needs? This can only be done rashly, in defiance of violent language, and far from prophetic agitation; it can only be done in defiance of politics.

Moreover, it is time in any case to oppose this mendacious world with the resources of an irony, a shrewdness, a serenity without illusions. For, supposing we were to lose, we would be able to lose cheerfully, without condemning, without prophesying. We are not looking for a rest. If the world insists on blowing up, we may be the only ones to grant it the right to do so, while giving ourselves the right to have spoken in vain.

VOLUME THREE

Sovereignty

PART ONE

What I Understand
by Sovereignty
(Theoretical Introduction)

ONE

Knowledge of Sovereignty

1. The General and Immediate Aspect of Sovereignty

The sovereignty I speak of has little to do with the sovereignty
of States, as international law defines it. I speak in general of an
aspect that is opposed to the servile and the subordinate. In the
past, sovereignty belonged to those who, bearing the names of
chieftain, pharaoh, king, king of kings, played a leading role in
the formation of that being with which we identify ourselves, the
human being of today. But it also belonged to various divinities,
of which the supreme god was one of the forms, as well as to the
priests who served and incarnated them, and who were sometimes
indistinguishable from the kings; it belonged, finally, to a whole
feudal and priestly hierarchy that was different only in degree
from those who occupied its pinnacle. But further, it belongs
essentially to *all men* who possess and have never entirely lost the
value that is attributed to gods and "dignitaries." I will speak at
length about the latter because they *display* that value with an
ostentation that sometimes goes with a profound baseness. I will
also show that they *cheapen* it by displaying it. For I shall always
be concerned, however it may seem, with the apparently lost
sovereignty to which the beggar can sometimes be as close as
the great nobleman, and from which, as a rule, the bourgeois is

voluntarily the most far removed. Sometimes the bourgeois has resources at his disposal that would allow him to enjoy the possibilities of this world in a sovereign manner, but then it is in his nature to enjoy them in a furtive manner, to which he strives to give the appearance of servile utility.

2. The Basic Elements: Consumption beyond Utility, the Divine, the Miraculous, the Sacred

What distinguishes sovereignty is the consumption of wealth, as against labor and servitude, which produce wealth without consuming it. The sovereign individual consumes and doesn't labor, whereas at the antipodes of sovereignty the slave and the man without means labor and reduce their consumption to the necessities, to the products without which they could neither subsist nor labor.

In theory, a man compelled to work consumes the products without which production would not be possible, while the sovereign consumes rather the surplus of production. The sovereign, if he is not imaginary, truly enjoys the products of this world – beyond his needs. His sovereignty resides in this. Let us say that the sovereign (or the sovereign life) begins when, with the necessities ensured, the possibility of life opens up without limit.

Conversely, we may call sovereign the enjoyment of possibilities that utility doesn't justify (utility being that whose end is productive activity). Life *beyond utility* is the domain of sovereignty.

We may say, in other words, that it is *servile* to consider duration first, to employ the *present time* for the sake of the *future*, which is what we do when we work. The worker produces the machine bolt with a view to the moment when this bolt will itself be used to assemble the automobile, which another will enjoy in a sovereign fashion, in contemplative drives. The worker does not personally have in view the sovereign pleasure of the future car owner, but this pleasure will justify the payment that the factory owner anticipates, which authorizes him to give a wage to the worker without waiting. The worker turns the bolt in order to obtain this wage. In principle, the wage will enable him to meet his needs. Thus, in no way does he escape the circle of constraint. He works in order to eat, and he eats in order to work. We don't see the sovereign moment arrive, when nothing counts but the moment itself. What is sovereign in fact is to enjoy the present time without having anything else in view but this present time.

I know: These statements are theoretical; they account for the facts only vaguely. If I consider the real world, the worker's wage enables him to drink a glass of wine: he may do so, as he says, to give him strength, but he really drinks in the hope of escaping the necessity that is the principle of labor.

As I see it, if the worker treats himself to the drink, this is *essentially* because into the wine he swallows there enters a *miraculous* element of savor, which is precisely the essence of sovereignty. It's not much, but at least the glass of wine gives him, for *a brief moment,* the *miraculous* sensation of having the world at his disposal. The wine is downed mechanically (no sooner swallowed than the worker forgets it), and yet it is the source of intoxication, whose *miraculous* value no one can dispute. On the one hand, to freely take advantage of the world, of the world's resources, as does the worker drinking the wine, partakes in some degree of the *miraculous*. On the other, it is the substance of our aspirations. We must satisfy our needs, and we suffer if we fail, but where the necessities are at stake we are only obeying the animal injunction within us. Beyond need, the object of desire is, *humanly,* the *miracle*; it is sovereign life, beyond the necessary that suffering defines. This *miraculous* element *which delights us* may be simply the brilliance of the sun, which on a spring morning transfigures

199

a desolate street. (Something that the poorest individual, hardened by necessity, sometimes feels.) It may be wine, from the first glass to the intoxication that drowns. More generally, this miracle to which the whole of humanity aspires is manifested among us in the form of beauty, of wealth – in the form, moreover, of violence, of funereal and sacred sadness; in the form of glory. What is the meaning of art, architecture, music, painting or poetry if not the anticipation of a suspended, wonder-struck moment, a miraculous moment? The Gospel says that "man does not live by bread alone," that he lives by what is *divine*. This expression has such clear evidence in its favor that it must be seen as a first principle. "Man does not live by bread alone" is a truth that sticks in the mind; if there is a truth that counts before the others, it has to be this one.[1]

The divine is doubtless but one aspect of the *miraculous*. There is nothing *miraculous* that is not in a sense *divine*. The question is difficult, moreover. The category of the *miraculous*, though not so narrow as that of the *divine*, is awkward nonetheless. I may say that the object of laughter is *divine*, but at first this is just my feeling; nowadays it is not that of everyone. If I am right, if my feeling is justified, I will still have to prove it. I may also say of this impure and repugnant thing that it is *divine*, but granting this assertion implies that one has understood the principle of the ambiguity of the divine, which is no different in principle from the ambiguity of the sacred.[2] The extreme aspects of eroticism, the obsessive desire in eroticism for a miraculous element, are doubtless more familiar, easier to grasp. (The difference, however, is not such that we would not also find in this domain the ludicrous and the repugnant in their murkiest form.) It is more than a little strange, certainly, that death and birth communicate to us the clearest sensation of the miracle of the sacred.

200

3. Considerations on Method

The domain that we shall survey fully, but only in its general lines, is so complex that one feels the need for a coherent description. If the sovereign partakes at once of the divine, of the sacred, of the ludicrous or the erotic, of the repugnant or the funereal, shouldn't I consider the general morphology of these aspects? It seems useless to go any further in our exploration of sovereignty without accounting for the underlying unity of aspects whose appearance is so varied. Nevertheless, it would seem to me untimely, at the outset, to pursue that course.[3] A morphology describing complex domains could only come after a posing of fundamental problems. It might be a final result, which would come at the end. I prefer to examine what is essential, without lingering over the question of method. I shall save for another volume the coherent exposition of the method I've followed. For the present I shall only make a few quick remarks about it. My "labors," if I may speak in that way, only tend to continue the effort of "researchers" who pursued various disciplines. I have not been overly concerned about the legitimacy of the results that I borrowed, as judiciously as I could, from the history of religions, from sociology, from political economy or from psychoanalysis.... Moreover, my inquiries were made with shameful casualness (that of too long a patience, a bit wearily), but neither am I a stranger to the demands of phenomenology. On one point I contribute a new element.

I grant, in a fundamental way, that we know nothing beyond what is taught by action with a view to satisfying our needs. What action teaches undoubtedly goes beyond the purposes of the action: we may even say of science, acquired in practice, by means of practice, that it is, or at least can be, *disinterested*. But science is always subject to the primacy of the future over the present. To do science is to disregard the present time with a view to subsequent results. And the most surprising thing, no doubt, is that the situation doesn't change when, once the results are obtained, we have access to the knowledge itself, when, the science done, the knowledge is given us seemingly in the present time. Hegel saw very well that, were it acquired in a thorough and definitive way, knowledge is never given to us except by *unfolding in time*. It is not given in a sudden illumination of the mind but in a *discourse*, which is necessarily deployed in duration. Knowledge, and the most profound knowledge, never appears to us in full except, finally, as the result of a calculated effort, an operation useful to some end. Knowledge can't in any way be confused with the last moment or the *end* of the operation; it is the entire operation. The end of a useful operation may be an object devoid of utility, for example an automobile employed, as I said, for contemplative drives. By becoming useless, that automobile detaches itself rather clearly in thought (if not in mechanical reality) from the operation that produced it. This detachment is not in any way possible if one considers the operation of knowledge in its homogeneity. Knowledge is always comparable to what the enjoyment of an automobile would be if driving it were just that *and nothing more,* without any other essential and new aspect, a homogeneous extension of the work of the shop that made it.

To know is always to strive, to work; it is always a servile operation, indefinitely resumed, indefinitely repeated. Knowledge is never sovereign: to be *sovereign* it would have to occur in a moment. But the moment remains outside, short of or beyond, all knowledge. We know regular sequences in time, constants; we know nothing, absolutely, of what is not in the image of an operation, a servile modality of being, subordinate to the future, to its concatenation in time. We know nothing absolutely, of the moment. In short, we know nothing about what ultimately concerns us, what *is supremely* [souverainement] *important to us.* The operation leaves off as soon as sovereignty is its object.

Yet we are in fact conscious of the moment. (Indeed, we are conscious of nothing but the moment.) But this consciousness is at the same time a slipping-away of the moment, insofar as it might be clear and distinct, insofar as it is not a vague knowledge of oneself but knowledge of an object: knowledge of an object needs to apprehend that object caught up in duration, beyond the present moment. Consciousness of the moment is not truly such, is not sovereign, except in *unknowing*. Only by canceling, or at least neutralizing, every operation of knowledge within ourselves are we in the moment, without fleeing it. This is possible in the grip of strong emotions that shut off, interrupt or override the flow of thought.

This is the case if we weep, if we sob, if we laugh till we gasp. It's not so much that the burst of laughter or tears stops thought. It's really the *object* of the laughter, or the *object* of the tears, that suppresses thought, that takes all knowledge away from us. The laughter or the tears break out in the vacuum of thought created by their object in the mind. But these moments, like the deeply rhythmed movements of poetry, of music, of love, of dance, have the power to capture and endlessly recapture the moment that counts, the moment of rupture, of fissure. As if we were trying to arrest the *moment* and freeze it in the constantly renewed gasps of our laughter or our sobs.[4] The miraculous moment when anticipation dissolves into NOTHING, detaching us from the ground on which we were groveling, in the concatenation of useful activity.

So there are — at rare, privileged moments — objects of thought whose conditions can be known in the same way as the other objects of knowledge; thus the object of laughter, the object of tears.... But what is peculiar to these objects is, at least hypothetically, that the thought that conceives them dissociates them, and thereby dissolves itself as thought. The content prior to this dissolution, even the conditions under which it dissolves, can be known: these conditions can be known, for example, if the object in question provokes a laughter that won't stop. Consequently, we shall stop speaking of the NOTHING into which the object dissolves; we shall speak rather of what the dissolved object was, and of what determined the dissolution. In this way it will be possible for us, perhaps, *to speak* of what is sovereign. The thought that comes to a halt in the face of what is sovereign rightfully pursues its operation to the point where its object dissolves into NOTHING, because, ceasing to be useful, or subordinate, it becomes *sovereign* in ceasing to be.

4. The Paradox of Happy Tears (Further Consideration on Method)

In principle there is no need, in an essay that considers the movement of sovereignty only in a general way, for us to linger over the specific aspect of laughter or tears to which the preceding suggestion refers in particular. I will merely remark that as concerns laughter this conception is classic. But I shall dwell longer on tears, for the reason that I derive from reflection on tears the general notion of *miraculous* that dominates this book.

It seems best to set out my thought here as it takes shape. Its final cohesion, I believe, would be less interesting (although achieving that cohesion would demand nothing more in sum than an enormous amount of time).

For many years, I was struck by the ambiguous aspect of tears, which a happy event provokes as readily as misfortune. But happy tears have not been the subject of innumerable and meticulous investigations as laughter has. This surprising lacuna, by itself, showed me the disappointing nature of the agglomeration that our psychological knowledge forms as a whole. I had observed that on occasion these tears would well up in my eyes in circumstances that left me disconcerted. I am not inclined to record these kinds of facts in succession, but one of them has stuck in my memory. One of my cousins by marriage is an officer in the British Navy; he served during the war on board the *Hood*. Just a few hours before the *Hood* was to sink, and the whole crew with it, my cousin was assigned a separate mission and sent on board a smaller boat. The admiralty officially reported his death to his mother. This was logical, since he was part of the crew of the *Hood*, which had perished almost to the last man. But some days after, my mother received a letter from him relating the circumstances in which he had, "by a miracle," escaped death. I didn't become acquainted with my cousin until much later, so these were events that had not affected me personally at first. But, without dwelling on it otherwise, I had the opportunity to tell the story to friends, and every time I did so, to my great surprise tears came to my eyes. I didn't see the reason for this, but I am in the habit of wondering, for this thing and that, what *is known about it* (even if I only have to tell myself, rather vaguely, that it must be found in some book . . .): finally, I began to suspect that no one knew anything about this. Apparently, no one had even advanced an absurd hypothesis, having at least the merit of initiating an inquiry; probably no one had even perceived the interest of these paradoxical tears (yet, in the case of laughter the most secondary questions have been the subject of numerous studies). I am no longer sure of this lack; I should look further, I know. But I spoke of the matter in a lecture attended by some eminent philosophers and no one seemed to know any more about it than I did.

This point is unimportant in itself, but I had to try to solve by myself a problem that astonished me. I reflected at first on the relationship between such tears and good fortune. Everyone knows that one weeps for joy. But I didn't feel any joy. The fortunate

<blockquote>205</blockquote>

outcome appeared to me to correspond possibly to a set of circumstances about which I had, in spite of everything, a more general and more detailed picture than I now have. Then it dawned
on me – while I was considering the problems of this work – that
a *miracle*, that only a miracle, caused those happy tears to arise.
A miracle or, if not, something that seemed that, since in such
circumstances we cannot expect a repetition of the same fact. In
any case, we cannot expect it from our efforts. . . . This *miraculous*
quality is conveyed rather exactly by the expression: *impossible and
yet there it is,* which had once appeared to me to take on the meaning of the *sacred.* I imagined at the same time that art has no other
meaning, that art is always a response to the supreme hope for
the unanticipated, for a miracle. This is why the measure of art
is genius, while talent relates to the rational, explicable means,
whose result never has anything unanticipated about it.

I wanted to present the development of my thought, disclosing
in the course of time, little by little, unexpected relations, rather
than offer a drily theoretical statement of those relations or of
the method I followed. From the beginning, this content, the
miraculous, that I ultimately recognized where one would least
expect it, in the object of tears, seemed to me to be in basic agreement with humanity's expectation. So I was able to say to myself
with a feeling of certainty that "man needed more than bread,
that he was just as hungry for a miracle." Above all, I understood
this essential point: what I had found in happy tears was also
found in unhappy ones. This *miraculous* element that, each time
tears rose to my eyes, I recognized in amazement, was not lacking
in unhappiness. The death that deprived me of my fellow man,
of the very one in whom I had recognized being – what was it if
not, in a negative form, the unanticipated, the miracle that takes
one's breath away? *Impossible, yet there it is* – what better way to
cry out the feeling that death inspires in men? May we not say of

206

death that in it, in a sense, we discover the negative analogue of a miracle, something we find all the harder to believe as death strikes down the one we love, the one who is close to us, something we could not believe, *if it, if death were not there.*

5. The Equivalence of the Negative Miracle (Death) and the Positive Miracle (Final Considerations on Method)

The most remarkable thing is that this *negative miraculous*, manifested in death, corresponds quite clearly to the principle stated above, according to which the miraculous moment is the moment when *anticipation dissolves into* NOTHING. It is the moment when we are relieved of anticipation, man's customary misery, of the anticipation that enslaves, that subordinates the present moment to some anticipated result. Precisely in the miracle, we are thrust from our anticipation of the future into the presence of the moment, of the moment illuminated by a miraculous light, the light of the sovereignty of life delivered from its servitude.

But, as I said, the anticipation dissolves into NOTHING. So we must raise the two-part question: if this NOTHING is that of death, it is hard for us to see how the moment can be the sovereign illumination of life; if, on the other hand, what is involved is a miraculous appearance that captivates, like the extreme beauty of an authentic work of art, it is hard for us to see why the beauty would be NOTHING, why it would have no other meaning than NOTHING. I spoke of a *negative miraculous*, but in this negative the miraculous element is contrary to desire, and this manner of speaking implies the existence of a *positive miraculous*, which alone seems to justify the *value* that is ordinarily connected with the word miracle, and whose positive form corresponds with the anticipation of a blessing.

It is precisely on this point, in order to address this difficulty, that I bring out how the method I followed led me away from the usual paths of knowledge. I resolved long ago not to seek knowledge, as others do, but to seek its contrary, which is unknowing. I no longer anticipated the moment when I would be rewarded for my effort, *when I would know at last,* but rather the moment when *I would no longer know, when my initial anticipation would dissolve into* NOTHING. This is perhaps a mysticism in the sense that my craving not to know one day ceased to be distinguishable from the experience that monks called mystical – but I had neither a presupposition nor a god.[5]

In any case, this way of going in the wrong direction on the paths of knowledge – to get off them, not to derive a result that others anticipate – leads to the principle of the *sovereignty* of being and of thought, which from the standpoint where I am placed at the moment has this meaning: that thought, subordinated to some anticipated result, completely enslaved, ceases to be in being *sovereign*, that only unknowing is *sovereign*.

But the bias that I affirm, and, supreme result, the negation of future results, cannot by themselves give this thought that which engages one's attention. As I said, I will confine myself to the general lines, but at this point I must explain my basic position.

I reflected on unknowing, and I saw that human life was full of moments – which I assign to knowledge – when the ceaseless operation of cognition is dissolved. I referred to those moments in speaking of sobs, of laughter that makes one gasp...saying that in them the train of thought was broken off. I fastened on this aspect, if not of nature, of human life, seeking in the experience a way out of my servitude. The object of tears or of laughter – and of other effects such as ecstasy, eroticism or poetry – seemed to me to correspond to the very point at which the object of thought vanishes. Up to that point, that object might be an object of knowledge, but only up to that point, so that the effect of knowledge would regularly fail. (Every philosopher knows how exhausting is the impossibility of working out the problem of laughter, but poetry, ecstasy, eroticism...doubtless pose problems that are no less exhausting.) It was bound to fail insofar as unknowing, that is, insofar as NOTHING, taken as the supreme object of thought, which takes leave of itself, which quits itself and becomes the dissolution of every object,[6] was not involved in the solution of the problem.

So it is easy to see, if I have been understood, how the "paradox of tears," which would hinder me did I not have this position, could appear to me, quite on the contrary, at the apex of a thought whose *end* jumps the rails on which it is traveling. What appeared to me was not the paradoxical aspect of the equivalences: in my eyes the fact that a happy event might have the same effect as death, usually thought of as the most unhappy event, was not a revelation. I had long been aware of the *banal* character of these relationships, but it made a light that dazzled me a blinding one. A little phrase of Goethe's on death,[7] "an impossibility that suddenly changes into a reality," had the merit of opening my eyes, unintentionally, to the *miraculous* character of the most dreaded event. But what was most striking was the sameness of *uncalculated* reactions which, from a definite point of view, did away with the difference between the positive and the negative, extreme happiness and extreme unhappiness, situating both, indiscriminately *at the point of resolution of our processes.*

The clearest thing was that essentially *an unreasoned impulse gave a sovereign value to the miraculous,* even if the miracle were an unhappy one. What mattered, what the tears maintained, convulsively, in front of us and for us, was the awful yet, in spite of ourselves, marvelous moment when "the impossibility suddenly changed into a reality." While determining our unhappiness, no doubt, this moment nevertheless had the sense of a miracle, the power to dissolve in us that which up to then had been necessarily subjugated, bound up. Moreover, there is no reason at all for thinking that tears of happiness signify gratified expectations, because the object of these tears is itself unanticipated; like death, it is only, all of a sudden, the impossible coming true, becoming *that which is*. In this case the object of anticipation is not that of desire: we anticipate, perhaps in anguish, what it is reasonable to anticipate, the duration of a tiresome state of things, but we don't anticipate, we dare not, cannot anticipate the outcome that desire suggests. Or, if we anticipate it, this is without believing in it, and more truly, we don't anticipate it if we anticipate it *against all reason*. Thus, desire gives rise to unjustified hope, to hope that reason condemns, which is different from the anticipation of the desired object or of its duration. What I call anticipation, which dissolves into NOTHING, is always the unavoidable calculation of reason.

I insist on the fact that, from a point of view that is doubtless limited, but which we can adopt, it is only of secondary importance whether, in the anticipation that NOTHING follows, the surprise is sad or joyful. What matters most from this point of view is that an unanticipated, unhoped-for aspect, considered impossible, reveals itself. This is the place to recall a remarkable fact: in certain islands of Oceania, the death of the king would provoke an outburst of passion on the part of a whole people, where the rules ordinarily determining what was possible were overthrown, where all of a sudden the youngest men would try to outdo one another in killing and violating. When it struck the king, death would strike the whole population at its sore point and then the latent pressure would be directed toward a reckless dissipation, an enormous festival whose presiding theme was sorrow. Whenever it dissolves into NOTHING, disappointed anticipation suggests a sudden reversal of the course of life. Sometimes a fit of laughter or of tears exhausts the possibility of effervescence that opens up at this moment. But often the incipient transgression develops into an unbounded transgression: the disappointed anticipation heralds the reign of the moment, clearing the way for sexual disorder and violence, for revelry and frantic squander. In this way, sovereignty celebrates its marriage with death. A king is the creature par excellence of the miracle; in his person he concentrates the virtues of a miraculous presence. In keeping with a dynamic equilibrium, these virtues may help to maintain order and preserve the possible, but this is to the extent that the integrity of his power, so sacred that no one would dare imagine anything that might affect it, ensures the return of transgression and violence. The "miracle" of death is understandable in terms of this sovereign exigency, which calls for the *impossible coming true,* in the *reign of the moment.*

That which counts is there each time that *anticipation,* that which binds one in activity, the meaning of which is manifested in the reasonable *anticipation* of the result, dissolves, in a staggering, unanticipated way, into NOTHING.

Two

The Schema of Sovereignty

1. The Sacred, the Profane, the Natural
Given and Death

I must now go back over everything I've said concerning death and the link connecting it, in a fundamental way, to man's sovereign being.

I must take it up again from the beginnings, when the *object* became detached from an initial inner experience, which at first did not differ from the experience that animals apparently have.

The tool, the "crude flint tool" used by primitive man was undoubtedly the first positing of the object as such. The objective world is given in the practice introduced by the tool. But in this practice man, who makes use of the tool, becomes a tool himself, he becomes himself an object just as the tool is an object. The world of practice is a world where man is himself a thing, which animals are not for themselves (which, moreover, in the beginning, animals were not for man). But man is not really a thing. A thing is identical in time, but man dies and decomposes and this man who is dead and decomposes is not the same thing as that man who lived. Death is not the only contradiction that enters into the edifice formed by man's activity, but it has a kind of preeminence.

Now, what appeared in the light of contradiction, in the world of practice, appeared by that very fact as something sacred, or in other terms, as something forbidden. Within the world of practice the sacred is essentially that which, although impossible, is nonetheless there,[8] which is at the same time removed from the world of practice (insofar as it might destroy it) and valorized as something that frees itself from the subordination characterizing the world. Its value is not, as it seems, essentially negative. The action that produces things is what negates that which is (the natural given), and the thing is the negation. The world of things or of practice is the world in which man is subjugated, or simply in which he serves some purpose, whether or not he is the servant of another. Man is alienated therein, he is himself a thing, at least temporarily, to the extent that he serves: if his condition is that of a slave, he is entirely alienated; otherwise a relatively substantial part of himself is alienated, compared with the freedom of the wild animal. This relative alienation, and not slavery, defines from the first the sovereign man who, insofar as his sovereignty is genuine, alone enjoys a nonalienated condition. He alone has a condition comparable to that of the wild animal, and he is sacred, being above things, which he possesses and makes use of. But what is within him has, relative to things, a destructive violence, for example the violence of death.

It was the great preoccupation, if not of the first men, at least of archaic mankind, to define alongside the world of practice, that is, the profane world, a sacred world; alongside the man more or less constrained to serve, a sovereign man; alongside *profane* time, a *sacred* time. The divisions were always laid down with a morbid anxiety, but they were far from being sharply delineated. To say nothing of a degree of arbitrariness that inevitably enters into the constitution of the sacred domain, what was felt as a contradiction with respect to the world of things formed a bloodless

214

domain, impossible by definition. What is sacred, not being based on a logical accord with itself, is not only contradictory with respect to things but, in an undefined way, is in contradiction with itself. This contradiction is not negative: inside the sacred domain there is, as in dreams, an endless contradiction that multiplies without destroying anything. What is not a thing (or, formed in the image of a thing, an object of science) is real but at the same time is not real, is impossible and yet is there. It is for example myself, or something that, presenting itself from the outside, partakes of me, something that, being me, is nevertheless not me (it is not me in the sense in which I take myself for an individual, a thing): it may be a god or a dead person, because, where it is concerned, *to be or not to be* is a question that can never be seriously (logically) raised. For that matter, it is not even impossible for me to represent it to myself as a thing. If it were a thing in the coherence of my thought, as is, in a fundamental way, the individual I take myself for, if I took this element for a thing at the moment when my thought organizes itself according to the laws of the world of practice, the negation peculiar to things would reduce this element to a thing, and that is all. But it is a thing that at the same time is not a thing. It is this paradox: a sacred thing, a basically defective and also, from a sovereign viewpoint, very badly made thing: for in spite of everything, the sacred thing ends up having a utility.

From the foregoing, it is evident that the sacred differs profoundly from the natural given, which the action that created things at first denied. The sacred *is*, in a sense, the natural given. But it is an aspect of the natural given that reveals itself after the fact, in the world of practice — where it is denied — through effects that have escaped the negating action of work, or that actively destroy the coherence established in work. Furthermore, it is an aspect perceived by minds that the order of *things* has shaped to meet the exacting demands of this world's coherence: even a person who rejects all those demands is well aware of them; only animals are oblivious of them.

Thus, death in the midst of things that are well ordered in their coherence is an effect that disturbs that order, and which by a kind of miracle escapes that coherence. Death destroys, it reduces to NOTHING the individual who took himself, and whom others took, for a thing identical to itself. Not only was this individual integrated into the order of things but the order of things had entered into him and, within him, had arranged everything according to its principles. Like other things he had a past, a present *and a future* – and an identity through that past, present and future. Death destroys what was to be, what has become a present in ceasing to be. The obliteration of what was supposed to continue being leads to the error that consists in believing that what no longer exists nonetheless *is*, in some other form (that of a ghost, a double, a soul...). No one believes in the pure and simple disappearance of the one who was there. But this error does not carry the conviction that prevails in the world of consistent things. The error is in fact always accompanied by the consciousness of death. It never completely obliterates the consciousness of death.

But what is certain is that the consciousness of death has moved far away from the natural given. Not only do animals not have this consciousness, they can't even recognize the difference between the fellow creature that is dead and the one that is alive. Death, in the disorder which, owing to its irruption, succeeds the idea of an individual regarded as part of the coherence of things, is the appearance that the whole natural given assumes insofar as it cannot be assimilated, cannot be incorporated into the coherent and clear world. Before our eyes, death embodied by a dead person partakes of a whole sticky horror; it is of the

THE SCHEMA OF SOVEREIGNTY

same nature as toads, as filth, as the most dreadful spiders. It is nature, not only the nature that we have not been able to conquer, but also the one we have not even managed to face, and against which we don't even have the chance to struggle. Something awful and bloodless attaches itself to the body that decomposes, in the *absence* of the one who spoke to us and whose silence revolts us.

2. The Fear of Death, the Prohibition of Murder, and the Sovereign Transgression of That Prohibition

This return of the natural given in the guise of the definitive collapse goes against the plenitude of the world of efficacy. This collapse has not ceased to defeat us: it delivers us over to the event from which we remain sick in our inner being. We try to escape from this elementary horror but, in the darkness and the *dead* silence, it maintains the unpredictable and elusive movement of everything we have not been able to reduce to the reassuring order, a movement to which we know we shall later succumb. We tremble, we grow pale when it suddenly appears.... From the very beginning, as a result of an immense confusion in which the consciousness of death takes hold, men have placed the beyond at a safe and distant remove from this undefinable menace, but their effort is futile. What they have perceived in the form of a "ghost" or "double" belongs to this world of trembling, which they cannot control. All the images of paradise, of glorious souls and bodies, or the commonplace representations of the dead reincarnated by metempsychosis, have never kept the true, immutable domain of death from remaining that of a chilling fear. All things considered, death only opposes the happy fecundity of practice with the pullulation of error – beyond a silence that gives us over to the worst. How can one withhold value from efficacious activity, reserving it for that which overwhelms us, for that which makes our powerlessness manifest?

The agreement seems unanimous, but the opposition is perhaps poorly situated.

In efficacious activity man becomes the equivalent of a tool, which produces; he is like the thing the tool is, being itself a product. The implication of these facts is quite clear: the tool's meaning is given by the future, in what the tool will produce, in the future utilization of the product; like the tool, he who serves – who works – has the value of that which will be later, not of that which is. What relates to death may be uniformly detestable, and may be only a pole of repulsion for us, situating all value on the opposite pole. But this cannot be all there is to the experience of death. The basic loss of value resides in the fact that man becomes a thing. Not entirely perhaps, but always. Without death, could we cease being a thing, destroying in us that which destroys us, and reducing that which was reducing us to less than nothing?

The fear of death appears linked from the start to the projection of oneself into a future time, which, being an effect of the positing of oneself as a thing, is at the same time the precondition for conscious individualization. The being that work made consciously individual is the anguished being. Man is always more or less in a state of anguish, because he is always in a state of anticipation, an anticipation that must be called anticipation of oneself. For he must apprehend himself in the future, through the anticipated results of his action. That is why he fully dies; for, in the perspective in which he constantly strives to attain himself, possible death is always there, and death prevents man from attaining himself. Death is what it is for us insofar as it may prevent us from attaining ourselves, insofar as it separates what we were, which is no longer, from the individual being that we cease to be. A being that would exist only in the moment would not be separated in this way from itself in a kind of "traumatism."[9] But subjectively this would not be an individual.

It is insofar as we are subordinate beings, accepting the subordination of the thing, that we die humanly. For to die humanly, in anguish, is to have the representation of death that enables the dividing of oneself into a present and a future: to die humanly is to have of the future being, of the one who matters most in our eyes, the senseless idea that he is not. If we live sovereignly, the representation of death is impossible, for the present is not subject to the demands of the future. That is why, in a fundamental sense, to live sovereignly is to escape, if not death, at least the anguish of death. Not that dying is hateful – but living servilely is hateful. The sovereign man escapes death in this sense: he cannot die *humanly.* He cannot live in an anguish likely to enslave him, to determine the flight from death that is the beginning of servitude. He cannot die fleeing. He cannot let the threat of death deliver him over to the horror of a desperate yet impossible flight. Thus, in a sense, he escapes death, in that he lives in the moment. The sovereign man lives and dies like an animal. But he is a man nevertheless.

Morin agrees with Hegel's conception, according to which the sovereign, the master, sets the risk of death against the horror of death.[10] But Morin thinks that the risk of death, which we take upon ourselves, is the "affirmation of the individual." With the risk of death, on the contrary, the human being in us slips away in the face of individual consciousness. The sovereign being is not an animal, but this is because, *familiar with death,* he resists individual consciousness, whose principle exists within him. To consciousness – and to the seriousness of death, which is its initial content – he opposes a *playful* impulse that proves stronger in him than the considerations that govern *work.* The individual affirmation is ponderous; it is the basis for reflection and the unhappy gravity of human life: it is essentially the negation of play. Sovereign affirmation is based only on the play of unconsidered sentiments, as are the impulses of rivalry, of prestige, the rebelliousness and intolerance toward the prohibition that has death and killing as its object. What the sovereign takes seriously is not the death of the *individual*, it is *others*: to the fact of surviving personally he prefers the prestige that will no longer add to his stature if he dies, and will continue to count only so long as others count.

On the other hand, in a fundamental way the impetus of the sovereign man makes a killer of him. Death is a negation brought into operation in the world of practice: the principle of that world is submerged in death like a city in a tidal wave. It is the world of the thing, of the tool, the world of identity in time and of the operation that disposes of future time. It is the world of limits, of laws and of the *prohibition*. It is basically a general subordination of human beings to works that satisfy the demands of a group. But not only does this world run up against unavoidable contradictions, not only is death its unavoidable stumbling block, but the man who has fully satisfied these demands – no sooner has he satisfied them then he calls *actively* for the negation of a servitude that he accepted, but accepted only insofar as it was imposed on him. The imperatives of the world of practice set many limits on the ravages of death; in addition to customs giving a precise and *limited* form to the moral disorder that results from its coming, civilization responds to it with the interdiction of killing. We find it hard to admit that it's the same with this prohibition as with the others, which are easily transgressed; we need to realize nonetheless that the limits set by civilization can dictate the conditions without which it could not exist. But it is enough for it to dictate them rather often. If the situation appears clear, it is as if the limits were there *to be transgressed.*

220

The limits give passion the contracted movement that it did not have in animality. This properly human movement has forms regulated, relatively, by conventions that are often strange; it has a greater, perhaps less lasting, explosive intensity, but above all it leads to the refinements of pleasure and cruelty that civilization and prohibition alone made possible by contravention. The truth is that although man compels himself – or if he can, compels other men – to become a thing, this cannot go very far. To begin with, that temptation comes up against the fact that, passively, in spite of himself, if only because of death that decomposes him and suddenly makes it all look ghastly, it would be impossible for him to submit unreservedly to necessity (death received passively, and revealing him to be other than he is, by itself proclaims that man is not a thing). But beyond this passive negation, active rebellion is easy and is bound to occur in the end: he whom the world of utility tended to reduce to the state of a thing not subject to death, hence not subject to killing, ultimately demands the violation of the prohibition that he had accepted. Then, by killing, he escapes the subordination that he refuses, and he violently rids himself of the aspect of a tool or a thing, which he had assumed only for a time. At this price, sovereign existence is restored to him, the sovereign moment that *alone* finally justifies a conditional and temporary submission to necessity.

Sovereignty has many forms; it is only rarely condensed into a person and even then it is diffuse. The environment of the sovereign partakes of sovereignty, but sovereignty is essentially the refusal to accept the limits that the fear of death would have us respect in order to ensure, in a general way, the laboriously peaceful life of individuals. Killing is not the only way to regain sovereign life, but sovereignty is always linked to a denial of the sentiments that death controls. Sovereignty requires the strength to violate the prohibition against killing, although it's true this will be under the conditions that customs define. It also calls for the risk of death. Sovereignty always demands the liquidation, through strength of character, of all the failings that are connected with death, and the control of one's deep tremors. If the sovereign, or sacred, world that stands against the world of practice is indeed the domain of death, it is not that of faintheartedness. From the viewpoint of the sovereign man, faintheartedness and the fearful representation of death belong to the world of practice, that is, of subordination. In fact, subordination is always rooted in necessity; subordination is always grounded in the alleged need to avoid death. The sovereign world does have an odor of death, but this is for the subordinate man; for the sovereign man, it is the world of practice that smells bad; if it does not smell of death, it smells of anguish; its crowds sweat from the anguish provoked by shadows; death exists in it in a contained state, but fills it up.

3. The Passage from the Negative Miracle of Death to the Positive Miracle of the Divine

The sovereign world is the world in which the limit of death is done away with. Death is present in it, its presence defines that world of violence, but while death is present it is always there only to be negated, never for anything but that. The sovereign is he who *is*, as if death were not. Indeed, he is the one who doesn't die, for he dies only to be reborn. He is not a man in the individual sense of the word, but rather a *god*; he is essentially the embodiment of the one he is but is not. He is the same as the one he replaces; the one who replaces him is the same as he. He has no more regard for the limits of identity than he does for limits of death, or rather these limits are the same; he is the transgression of all such limits. In the midst of all the others, he is not work that is performed but rather play. He is the perfect image of adult play, whereas we ordinarily only have an image of juvenile play (suited to children). As personified in the sovereign, play is what it would be as personified in God, if we had not imagined His Omnipotence within the limits of the subordinate world. The killing of the king is the greatest affirmation of sovereignty: the king cannot die, death is nothing to him, it is that which his presence denies, that which his presence annihilates even in death, that which his death itself annihilates. The pyramids were only a game giving its most costly form to the imperishable identity of man, but they were the "works" of subordinate beings, *which a limitless sovereignty did not cease to make into a "game."*

In the eyes of the Egyptians, the pyramid was an image of solar radiation. In the person of the dead king, death was changed into a radiance, changed into an indefinite being. The pyramid is not only the most lasting monument, it is also the equivalency of the monument and the absence of a monument, of passage and obliterated traces, of being and the *absence* of being. There death is no longer anything but death's inability to maintain an icy little horror, which is the projected shadow of individual anguish. Horror is the limit of the individual. What it proclaims is man's reduction to thinghood. It announces the world of practice. The intent of the world of practice is always to banish, once and for all, the horror that cannot be separated from it by any means. But at the foot of the pyramid, the world of practice has disappeared; its limit is no longer perceptible.

THREE

The Historical Development of the
Knowledge of Sovereignty

1. The Misunderstanding of Sovereignty and the
Incomplete Character of the World That Results from It

Without question, the indifference to happiness and unhappiness, to absolute power and ultimate powerlessness, which is connected with sovereignty, has something archaic about it. But, above all, this qualification bespeaks the fundamental change in the importance sovereignty has in the mind of man. There exists a recent privilege accorded to rational behavior. The primacy of the miraculous, of that which, even at the price of terror, filled one with wonder, of that which stopped and reversed the course of things, seems to belong to the past. But this is doubtless insofar as *consciousness* deceives us, leaving our most deeply rooted desires in the penumbra of the *unconscious*. Confining ourselves to knowledge structured and guaranteed by the practice of reason, we might believe in the possibility of an ordering of all things, which would exclude risk and caprice and would ground authenticity on nothing more than prudence and the pursuit of usefulness. But what if knowledge, at least the first impulse of knowledge, were servile? What if the servility (the *immediate* servility) of knowledge had resulted in our current inability to see beyond the useful, to envisage, as – in spite of everything – we might expect, the

225

sovereign: beyond the means, an end that would not be subordinate to any other, a *sovereign* end? Then this would have to come to pass, which is simple really, which is rationally conceivable:

The remarkable results of scientific knowledge have not affected archaic humanity, nor even, if you will, that more recent humanity which in part survives in our midst, and which could be called archaistic. But in general modern man has given first importance to a domain that the advancement of learning extended, organized and made ever more coherent, this being the domain of consciousness – clear and distinct, of course. Archaic man was mainly taken up with what is sovereign, marvelous, with what goes beyond the useful, but that is precisely what a consciousness enlightened by the advancement of learning relegated to a dubious and condemnable semidarkness, which psychoanalysis named the *unconscious*. Modern man disregards or undervalues, he tends to disparage or deny, that which archaic man regarded as sovereign. Archaic man endlessly posed the question of sovereignty; for him it was the primary question, *the one that counted as sovereign in his eyes*. It was not posed in his mind in a rational form; he did not conceive of solving it as one solves a problem of mechanics. For, in a way, he *knew* that sovereignty cannot be the anticipated result of a calculated effort. What is sovereign can only come from the arbitrary, from chance. There ought not exist any *means* by which man might *become* sovereign: it is better for him to *be* sovereign, in which case sovereignty cannot be taken away from him, but if he does not possess it, he cannot acquire it. How could anything have been more important, *for everyone,* than the certainty, at one point, of attaining a useless splendor, of surpassing at that point the poverty of utility? Nothing sovereign must ever submit to the useful. Works, all works, had as their final and inaccessible end that miraculous element that illuminates being, transfigures it and grants it, beyond the poverty of the thing, that royal authenticity which never lets itself be reduced to the measure of humiliating labor. Indeed, it appeared, in this reign of the miracle, that the results of labor depended on a virtue without which labor would be fruitless.

The concern for the happy or unhappy outcome remained present in this archaic way of thinking; in fact, it was always a serious concern, but it never *nominally occupied the first place*. The fruitlessness of works itself required the preeminence of the sovereign element, be it felicitous or infelicitous, auspicious or baneful. The circumstances varied and the king could just as easily be put to death as adulated. Were it not for the testimony of history, or that of ethnography, we could not easily make out that initial inversion of what seems so evident to us. We should calmly ask ourselves, however, if the world we have conceived in accordance with reason is itself a viable and complete world. It is a world of the operation subordinated to the anticipated result, a world of sequential duration; it is not a world of the moment. In it, the moment is expressly nullified; the moment is nothing more than a kind of zero with which we no longer see that it is possible *to count*. It is the point, and the core, where the movement of knowledge, which always has elements distinguishable in duration as its object, runs aground and breaks apart.

We have to realize finally that irrespective of any particular form (in any case, needless to say, far beyond its archaic form[11]), the problem of the sovereign moment (this moment whose meaning in no way depends on its consequences) is posed for us, not as a secondary form, but as a need to fill the void of the world of useful works.

2. Crudeness of the Traditional Forms of Sovereignty That Subsist

What apparently justifies a basic disdain for the world of sovereignty, now a thing of the past, is the crudeness of its foundations. In times past, sovereignty asserted itself in the sphere of knowledge, since from the beginning man intended to know. But the exigency given in knowledge from the beginning demanded the observance of those rules that archaic man himself observed in order to put up the roof of his house: to know is, as it's been said, *to know how;* we don't truly know, we don't know anything as well as that object we know how to produce, as that phenomenon we know how to reproduce and whose repetition we can plan. It was impossible to abide by those rules if one posited some sovereign *thing.* But this *thing* had to be situated nonetheless in the domain of things known. Consequently, childish arbitrariness was the custom.

Today we can tell ourselves that without anything sovereign a world of useful works doesn't differ, or rather *wouldn't differ,* any less from full and complete existence than a brick differs from the universe (I say *wouldn't differ* because while we tend not to *recognize* anything sovereign, many sovereign elements survive in our midst, as we shall see, in the most diverse forms). Be this as it may, the foundations of that religious, or military, sovereignty on which the past lived appear definitively childish to us. The truth is that we may suffer from what we don't have, but even though we paradoxically long for it, it would be an aberration for us to regret the religious and royal edifice of the past. The effort to which that edifice corresponded was only an enormous failure, and while it's true that the essential is missing in the world where it has collapsed, we can only go further, without imagining for a moment the possibility of a going back.

In particular in the sphere of knowledge where, to begin, we

228

can't help placing ourselves, we must not even examine, unless it's for their historical interest, the beliefs on which classical sovereignty was based.

If we wish in turn to have an acquaintance with sovereignty, we must have other methods.

In the first chapter of this part, I have already shown their general lines.

I would like now to explain the meaning of these new methods, the significance they have in the historical perspective. I must begin by defining the modern understanding of sovereignty relative to the forms of sovereignty that subsist, or more exactly, that subsist and whose foundations are not worm-eaten, as is true of the monarchic forms.

Today this set of forms composes a diffuse domain, which I will have to describe, briefly, as a whole.

3. Comprehensive View of the Experiences at the Intersection of Which Traditional Sovereignty Was Situated

As I said, to begin with a morphology of the domain in question would mean an endless task, and the exposition would make sense only given a view of the ensemble with which one must in fact begin.

In the absence of a true morphology showing the relations between the different behaviors – thus, the point at which laughter stops and erotic agitation silently takes its place, the specific character of each reaction and the particular conditions of possibility of one reaction or another, the limit on the generality determined by personal inclination, the difference between the ritual forms and the others, the question of the ensembles that unite dance, music and poetry – here I will merely give a rather complete list of those *effusions* in which a keen sensitivity to the pres-

229

ent moment appears at the expense of the subordination of every being to some subsequent possibility. If questions raised by the relations I speak of are treated in this book, it will be haphazardly, without trying to present the overall coherence. But, following the obligatory enumeration, I will indicate what is necessary in this general view: the connections that the sovereign moments generally present, given separately in the effusions, with the existence of a sovereign domain recognized by all, distinct from the poetic or erotic domains, and generally from all the particular domains that correspond to each particular effusion. Obviously, I cannot avoid establishing this relationship, since the understanding of sovereignty, which for archaic man could be given – but never rigorously – in a global way beyond the particular domains that subsist, would not be given to us today did we not attempt to reconstitute it on the basis of diffuse, isolated forms whose unity is never clear.

Laughter, tears, poetry, tragedy and comedy – and more generally, every art form involving tragic, comic or poetic aspects – play, anger, intoxication, ecstasy, dance, music, combat, the funereal horror, the magic of childhood, the sacred – of which sacrifice is the most intense aspect – the divine and the diabolical, eroticism (individual or not, spiritual or sensual, corrupt, cerebral or violent, or delicate), beauty (most often linked to all the forms previously enumerated and whose opposite possesses an equally intense power), crime, cruelty, fear, disgust, together represent the forms of effusion which classical sovereignty, recognized sovereignty, undoubtedly does not conjoin in a complete unity, but which virtual sovereignty would, if we were to secretly attain it.[12] I have not exhausted, I know, those sudden openings beyond the world of useful works, which – even if the *supreme* value of these openings is denied, as it is in our time, when the political game takes the place of sovereign displays – continue

230

to be given to us. Whatever the term, moreover, it would refer to an ensemble so vast that one hesitates to choose one: yet the word *festival*, in a sense, names the modality that comes closest to sovereignty (but perhaps in fact the festival exists, like *traditional* sovereignty, only insofar as it is generally recognized, and so it has lost some of its power). Other terms, finally, would have little meaning in the absence of extensive commentary: terms such as joy, sorrow, pain, hunger and the consumption of food, extreme destitution and extreme wealth (more exactly the sudden abundance of wealth), the gift....[13]

In the world of the primacy of useful values, the overall meaning of these different forms never appears. But it was, on the contrary, the constant concern of archaic man to make that meaning clear, salient, and to give it a material aspect that would dominate. All the miraculous sensations, happy or unhappy, that are connected with the effusions I have spoken of were destined at a single point to flow freely, abundantly. Of course, this unity remained precarious; on the one hand, it constantly tended toward bipartition – essentially opposing the military and the religious, the temporal and the spiritual – on the other hand, toward feudal dispersion. But the first impulse concentrated in the hands of the one designated by a sign of election the virtues of combat and play, of sensuality and wealth, of sacred horror, of intoxication, of ecstasy and of all the arts. At times it became difficult to reconcile the irreconcilable, and substitute kings needed to take upon themselves what was precluded by royal dignity, as it was then understood: the carnival kings had, no doubt successively, the double privilege of drawing upon themselves death or the most joyful ridicule.

The greatest confusion in this area resulted from the belatedly affirmed idea of a fundamental difference between military sovereignty and religion. I will come back to an aberration full of significance perhaps, but based on an obvious error. For the moment, I will merely emphasize the religious character of all royalty and the sovereign character of all religious forms. As a matter of fact, given the failure to perceive this basic unity, the meaning of sovereignty slipped away. More precisely, what slipped away was the meaning of a millennial effort by man to find a place where all the miraculous chances of this world converge.

Becoming flagrant – so much so that, with respect to language and consciousness, nothing is more foreign to us than the meaning of that fundamental quest – the failure at least has the merit of having left an image of ancient humanity that is essentially enigmatic. All in all, man has become a riddle for himself. The elements of this riddle are scattered in history, and in the present only those sovereign moments in a diffuse state, whose constant reality and deep significance we cannot deny, contribute to a possible solution. The contribution comes from within ourselves, but its objective existence is firmly established. We cannot grant the data of history a meaning similar to that which the men of former times granted them. While we require rigor, while we rule out the facile ways of mystical thinking, which relies on inspiration and bases itself on the action of personal choice, while in our pursuit of knowledge we follow rules analogous to those that ensured the exactness, or at least the de facto solidity, of science, we must start from the sovereign moments, which I believe we know from within, but which we also know from without, in order to recover their unity, the experience of which we have only in the past (when it was given from without, but the subjective knowledge of which we no longer genuinely have). That unity exists, in some manner, in the present time, but no tangible datum has made its existence recognizable for us. What is in question for us is to recover that comprehensive view, while meeting our thought's requirements of cohesion, by means of the particular views we may form of isolated sovereign moments (such as poetry, ecstasy, laughter...).

4. The Unity of Sovereign Moments and Deep Subjectivity

Not only will this comprehensive view differ generally from that which archaic man projected in his royal and religious institutions, but its knowledge will itself necessarily have a different form. The sovereign institutions of the past existed *objectively*. On the whole, they were the objective affirmation of the unity of sovereign moments, which, in a diffuse way, occurred throughout human society. Insofar as possible (that is, at least finally, with considerable blanks), the king surrounded by his priests, who annointed him, was a reflection of the global sovereignty implied in the impulses of the throng. The consciousness of these inner aspects was diffuse; these aspects eluded those who could only perceive their external image, their crude embodiment. Only the king crowned under a cathedral's majestic and sacred vaults, resounding with the millennial and tragic tones of the liturgy, satisfied the desire to gaze upon the miraculous image of an unlimited existence. It seemed out of the question to look for this miracle within. (But we can no longer find it on the outside....[14])

Knowledge of the unity of sovereign moments is now given to us on the basis of subjective experience, which may be, if we choose, distinctly conscious. We effect this reversal. Formerly, sovereign moments could only appear from within; we didn't have any objective knowledge of them. But now it is possible to go from a subjective knowledge to an objective knowledge of those moments. We speak of laughter, of tears, of love, beyond the experience we have of them, as objectively conditioned impulses (I am thinking not so much of their physiological aspect, whose meaning escapes us, as of the objective data considered by psychology, the *object* of laughter, for example). If we go instead from an isolated consideration of those moments to the notion of their unity, we are referred back, provided we attain it, to deep subjectivity. The meaning of royalty, in which, after a fashion, the unity of sovereign aspects was objectively manifested *for others*, was not given with a view to the needs of the king himself: it was a matter of responding to the yearnings of a people indifferent to the *personal* problems that the king might set himself. But as we depart in this way from both the domain of positive and practical knowledge of objects and that of subjective and gratuitous beliefs, we meet with the subjective experience of an objectlessness: what we experience henceforth is NOTHING. This disappearance corresponds to the objects of those effusions that acquaint us with sovereign moments: they are always objects that dissolve into NOTHING, that provoke the moment of effusion when the anticipation that posited them as objects is disappointed. The moment when anticipation dissolves into NOTHING is given in the subjective experience that we have of it, but the object itself appears, in the field of positive and practical knowledge, at least as a possible object – but as a possibility that escapes us, and is snatched away from us. Of course the NOTHING does not itself appear, the NOTHING is only the object that disappears, but knowledge can contemplate it as such. Thus, to conclude, this NOTHING is encountered at the very point where knowledge and unknowing are both actual, knowledge being implied in the objectivity of experience, unknowing being given subjectively. But the objectivity in question vanishes to the extent that it is thus posited.

By this means, a clear and distinct notion first takes the place of the childish tales of archaic times, then utterly dissolves into unknowing. This notion is not immediately connected to the *unity* of the sovereign domain, to sovereignty properly speaking, given beyond isolated moments. It is necessary, before one perceives their deep unity in the NOTHING where their different objects dissolve, to view these objects, and their disintegration, separately. However, beyond this unavoidable detour the unity can be perceived immediately.

It can be perceived in a global experience whose composite object is made of the fusion, into a single object, of the different objects of the different effusions at the moment of their dissolution. I can perceive the erotic, laughable, terrifying, repugnant or tragic value of a single object at the same time – that is, of an objectively conditioned aspect. Such an object can be given only in the imagination. But the imagination can make this object, which is precisely what the will of a people could not achieve. To imagine, as Nietzsche said, a tragic situation and be able to laugh as it presupposes an endless mediation; such a thing can rarely be given in immediate experience, in real experience. All the more true, if in some way the mechanisms of desire and the disorder of the passions enter in. These great tides of miraculous possibility, where moreover the transparency, the richness and the soothing splendor of death and the universe are to be regained, presuppose the imagination joining together that which is never given except in parts. The past came close to this experience, beyond the institutional forms, insofar as it granted that a solitary experience, given over to the freedom of the imagination, assumed a role that the one God played in objective sovereignty. And, indeed, it is true that mystical theology understood that through the positive givens it ultimately became the experience of NOTHING. But insofar as it *was only* an extension of objective sovereignty, it had first of all to strengthen the objective and mythological foundations of that archaic form of sovereignty.

The Identity of the "Sovereign" and the "Subject," and Consequently of the Understanding of Sovereignty and Self-understanding

1. The Useful Object and the Sovereign Object

If I have spoken of objective sovereignty, I have never lost sight of the fact that sovereignty is never truly objective, that it refers rather to deep subjectivity. In any case, the real sovereign is a product, no doubt an objective product, of conventions based on subjective reactions. Sovereignty is objective only in response to our clumsiness, which cannot arrive at the subject except by positing some object which we then negate, which we negate or destroy.

The world of things is given to us as a series of appearances depending on one another. The effect depends on the cause and, generally, each object depends on all the others, being the effect, finally, of which all the others are the cause. I don't intend to go further than a summary view of these relations, but the interdependence of things seems to me in any case to be so complete that I can never introduce a relation of subordination beween one thing and another. We perceive relations of forces and doubtless the isolated element undergoes the influence of the aggregate, but the aggregate cannot *subordinate* it. Subordination presupposes another relation, that of object to subject.[15] The subject is the being *as he appears to himself from within;* the subject can also appear to us from the outside: thus, the *other* appears to us, at

237

the outset, as external to us, but at the same time he is given to us, by a complex representation, in the same way that he appears to himself, within, and it is as such that we love him, as such that we make an effort to reach him. We ourselves, in the second instance, see ourselves from the outside, as being like the *other*, who is an object for us. We live in a world of *subjects* whose *exterior, objective* aspect is always inseparable from the *interior*. But within ourselves what is given us of ourselves, objectively, as the body, appears subordinate to us. My body is obedient to my will, which within myself I identify with the presence, perceptible from the outside, of the being that I am. Thus, generally, the object, or the objectively given being, appears to me to be subordinate to subjects, whose property it is. In a world where in our eyes all things would be limited to what they are within themselves, in a world where nothing at all could appear to us in the light of subjectivity, the relations of objects among themselves would no longer be anything but relations of forces. Nothing would ever have preeminence; preeminence is the attribute of the subject for whom another is the object.

I cannot in fact regard myself as a thing within a world of things. I forget that the existence within men continually obliges me to treat as a thing that which I eat, that which serves me, and myself or my fellow beings, as a subject, who eats, who serves himself. What is in the world is no longer, in the knowledge I have of it, anything but a series of appearances depending on one another. Theoretically, no subordination is possible in the series. But actually I overlook the subject, that I am, who considers and mechanically treats as a subordinate that which he eats, that which serves him. Mechanically, I put on the same plane those things that generally appear to me in the dependence where they have no preeminence over one another and those things that I eat, that serve me, that are, with respect to the subject that I am, *servile* objects. Thus, mechanically, the aggregate of things and, more generally, the aggregate of beings, appear to me on the plane of *servile* objects.

When value is sovereignly affirmed, referred to the subject, things are subordinated to him unequivocally. But nothing changes when, once manifest sovereignty is abolished, diminished forms, bogus forms, succeed it.

Traditional sovereignty is conspicuous. It is a sovereignty of exception (a single subject among others has the prerogatives of all subjects as a whole). On the other hand, the ordinary subject who upholds sovereign value against the object's subordination, shares that value with all men. It is man in general, whose existence partakes necessarily of the subject, who sets himself in general against things, and for example against animals, which he kills and eats. Affirming himself, in spite of everything, as a subject, he is sovereign with respect to the thing an animal is, but man in general labors. If he labors he is, relative to sovereign life, that which the object he uses or eats generally is, relative to the subject he has not ceased being. In this way a slippage occurs, which tends to reserve sovereignty for the exception. I can labor for myself; I can even, in a community where each receives an equal share of the obligations and advantages, labor for another without losing my sovereignty for a time any longer than that of the labor. But if the share is not equal, this sovereignty is given up for the profit of the one who doesn't labor but profits from my labor. In traditional sovereignty, one man in principle has the benefit of the subject, but this doesn't just mean that the masses labor while he consumes a large share of the products of their labor: it also presupposes that the masses see the sovereign as the subject of whom they are the object.

2. Different from the Others, the Sovereign Differs from Them As the Subject Differs from the Objective Action of Labor

This unavoidable play on words is awkward. I mean to say that the individual of the multitude who, during part of his time, labors for the benefit of the sovereign, *recognizes* him; I mean to say that he *recognizes himself* in the sovereign. The individual of the multitude no longer sees in the sovereign the object that he must first of all be in his eyes, but rather the *subject*. To be sure, the same is generally true of his fellows, especially those from the same community. But in a privileged way, for him the sovereign is the inner experience – the profound truth – to which a share of his effort is allotted, that share which he allots to others than himself. In a sense, the sovereign is the intermediary between one individual and the others. But from the others, from his fellows, he expected a labor equal to his. As soon as the others had a spokesman, by whom they were represented, the spokesman of the others was such to the extent that he represented their inner selves, not the members who labor, who are analogous to inert things, to subordinate instruments. It must be inevitable, humanly, that a man will give his fellows the feeling of being there for the others, in whose place he can speak, in whose place he can reply. This is not always connected with language, since what matters for the privileged man is to never be placed, with respect to others, in the situation of the object with respect to the subject who is its end and whom it serves. The individual of a multitude cannot in fact see one of their number as the one who represents the others if he is, even for a moment, subordinate to one of them, if he is not, on the contrary, for the others as a whole what the subject is for the object. Thus, the sovereign doesn't labor, but consumes rather the product of the others' labor. The share of this product that is not necessary to the subsistence of the *object* that the man who produces is for the time being, is the share of the *subject* that the sovereign is. The sovereign restores to the primacy of the present the surplus share of production, acquired to the extent that men submitted to the primacy of the future. The sovereign, epitomizing the *subject*, is the one by whom and for whom the moment, the miraculous *moment*, is the ocean into which the streams of labor disappear. The sovereign spends festively for himself and for others alike that which the labor of all has accumulated.

3. What the Sovereign Is for the One Who "Recognizes" Him

What I am saying is perhaps poorly supported, far removed from a reality that is neither simple nor pure. But the *inner* experience that guides me obliges me to maintain the autonomy of this representation with regard to the precise historical data that ethnography, for example, studies. If there is an element that we grasp from within, it has to be sovereignty, even if it is a question, not of the sovereignty toward which we personally tend, but of which we bestow on royal personages, in a way that often seems indefensible.[16] Such an experience doubtless has no meaning apart from the objective givens with which it is connected, but we need to understand those givens themselves in light of that experience, without which they would not even have been *given*. Such conditions of experience appear to us objectively: as production, the surplus share and the share necessary for subsistence – but when the *present time* is operative, even if I speak of *objects*, of the consumed products on which it bears, those objects are *destroyed*, consumed, and the preference granted to the *moment* corresponds to contempt for the objective world. I can still approach the moment from other angles, but it never refers back to anything other than the world of the *subject*. I admit that in that respect I have spoken of it *vaguely*; from what I put forward there doesn't remain anything I can grasp, but this is precisely the point that I wanted to reach. My thought loses its point of support if objects cease to obsess me, if my interest in destroying them at once prevails over the consideration I had for them, over the anxiousness I had to acquire them, over the seriousness they possess by themselves. At that moment, I still consider objects, but in the light of that inner truth where they are no longer anything but the occasion of a subjective play. My thought then passes from one world to the other, from the objective one where it constructs itself to the subjective one where it is undone, but in the time it takes to come undone, before it is completely *undone*, I can still externalize its content. Thus, I could write: "The sovereign restores to the primacy of the present the surplus share of production, acquired to the extent that men submitted to the primacy of the future...." If I could do so, it is because in myself I had distinguished the moment when, the primacy of the future no longer being operative, I behaved as I feel that, in his way, the sovereign behaves. These behaviors, these states of mind are communicable, and sovereignty is an institution, because it is not foreign to the masses, because the state of mind of the sovereign, of the *subject*, is *subjectively communicated* to those for whom he is the sovereign. *Subjectivity* is never the object of discursive knowledge, except obliquely, but it is *communicated* from *subject* to *subject* through a sensible, emotional contact: it is communicated in this way in laughter, in tears, in the commotion of the festival.... In laughter there is not one object that independently determines the same effects in the different laughters. The objective working of the mechanism can perhaps be grasped, but what is missing from it is the subjectivity of the laughter, which is not expressible discursively, but in which the laughers sense an unforeseen, astonishing transparency from one to the other, as if the same laugh gave rise to a single inner torrent. The

emotion designated by the word sovereignty is glimpsed as a contagious subjectivity (like an intimate tidal wave sweeping through
the crowd) less commonly than laughter is. But, on the one hand,
I experience this emotion separately when I have a strong sensation of my subjectivity, which appears to me in a *miraculous*
way, at the end of thought sequences that ordinarily rivet me to
objects; and on the other hand, in the thrill of a crowd on the
miraculous appearance of a king I recognize the same sensation,
less intense in each one of those who form the crowd, at the same
time more intense because of the immensity of the crowd that
reverberates it: what must be exclaimed each time is "Impossible, yet there it is!" What appears each time is in fact the *subject*, always unexpected, relieved of the heaviness that the world
of utility imposes on us, of the tasks in which the world of objects
mires us down.

I cannot at the outset specify the relations and differences
between the various qualities of emotion I have spoken of (emotions connected with laughter, tears, the festival, the feeling of
sovereignty...). Moreover, within the limits of this "theoretical
introduction" I can merely suggest a representation that was made
possible, ultimately, by a recurrence of the emotions described
and the connections that associate them with the particular realities that are brought into play each time. But I needed first to
speak of what made the institution of sovereignty possible and
even easily borne.

That man who assumes in the eyes of each participant of a
community the value of the *others* can do so, as I said, insofar as
he signifies the *subjectivity* of the others. That presupposes the
communication from *subject* to *subject* of which I speak, in which
objects are the intermediaries, but only if they are, in the operation, reduced to insignificance, *if they are destroyed as objects*. This
is the case with the sovereign, who at first is the distinct object

of the one who sees him not just as the man he is but as the sovereign. If I see a passerby in the street, I can regard him as a distinct object, to which I am completely indifferent but I can, if I wish, regard him as a *fellow human being:* this is true if I deny in him, at least in part, the objective character of an ordinary passerby, which is what I do if, suddenly, I think of him as a brother, no longer seeing anything in him but the *subject,* with whom I *can,* with whom I *must* communicate, no longer considering as foreign anything that concerns him subjectively. In a sense, *brother* denotes a distinct object, but in fact this object bears within it the negation of that which defines it as an object. It is an object for me, it is not me, it is not the *subject* that I am, but if I say that he is my brother, this is in order to be assured that he is *like* that *subject* that I am. Consequently, I negate the relation of *subject* to *object* that appeared to me at first, and my negation defines, between my brother and me, the relation of *subject* to *subject,* which doesn't cancel but transcends the first relation. Sometimes the word *brother* denotes a blood tie (objectively definable, conveying the negation of that which distinguishes, the affirmation of likeness), sometimes a tie between beings of the same nature, hence between *every* man and myself. I single out this last meaning, because I intend to contrast it with that of the word *sovereign,* which would refer, if I personally had a *sovereign,* not to the object I would be for the *sovereign,* but rather to the *subject* the sovereign would be for me. As I said, the *subject* in the first instance is myself, and in the first instance the *sovereign* is an *object* for me. But to the extent that I labor in the service of others, whom the *sovereign* represents, I am not a *subject* but an *object* of the one or the ones for whom I labor. I am still a subject, but only when the labor is finished. Moreover, I treat myself as an object, laboring in my own service. I am a *subject* again if, for the sake of the present moment, I deny in myself the primacy of the moment to come, but just as sometimes I regard as an *object* the one I was when I labored — bound to serve the *subject* I am then — the sovereign regards me as an object insofar as I produce what is at his disposal. He knows that I have not really stopped being a *subject*, but I am no longer entirely a *subject* because I labor, and not only for myself but for others and thereby for the sovereign who represents them. I am a subject only in a sense. I can't easily rediscover the unforeseen appearance which is that of integral subjectivity, which nothing bends and which the servitude of effort does not mire down. That capricious, deeply *sacred*, appearance would no longer be available to me in principle had my labor not at least protected the *sovereign* from that misery. In principle, as a result of my labor, the sovereign, if he desires, can live in the moment: what matters, moreover, is not that he desires this, but that he is capable of it and that, being capable, he *manifests* that capability. From the first, the sovereign is this locus of contradiction: embodying the subject, he is its external aspect. But this is not entirely true: essentially, sovereignty is revealed internally; only an interior communication really manifests its presence. (I would prefer that this scheme did not depend closely on particular realities, but I can't fail to point out that often the king's person is so deeply sacred that it is dangerous to touch what he himself touches:[17] what is sacred, what is dangerous is crudely held to be internal, having basically no meaning but inwardness.) But the sovereign is nonetheless objectively determined by the exercise of sovereignty: his subjectivity is never expressed except in crude terms, and even though it alone has a meaning, the means used to reach that meaning are crude as well: they are *external* means. But, in a sense, this is only apparently true. Apparently it is the annointing, the regalia of royalty, the royal prohibitions and the royal splendor that not only distinguish the king as such, but make him what he is: the Jewish king is the Lord's Annointed. But what the king is has nothing to do with the connections of causes and effects. If the king is the Lord's Annointed, it is the Lord and not men, insofar as they have those connections at their disposal, who has determined this. The Lord: He who in the mind of those who name Him is located outside the created world, who does not depend on anything, who, above the king who represents him, is the only true sovereign. Similarly, the Eucharist is not the *spiritual blessing* the Church says it is, owing to the fact that the prescribed words have been murmured; the subjective will of Christ, which nothing objectively determines, is what gives the words of an ordained priest the power to change the objective reality of the bread into the subjective presence of God. Moreover, the need not to leave the royal truth open to an outside determination was felt so strongly that selection of the sovereign usually depended on a factor that fate provided in advance, and for which the utilization of means could not be substituted, such as blood lineage. The subterfuge was crude because, at the beginning of the dynasties, it seems that only an external means could have established the difference between the first sovereign and other men. But the utilization of means may not have had the meaning that objective thought suggests. The qualities that the first sovereign had to display did not in principle resemble those of today's statesman or military leader, who always intervene from the outside in order to change the determinations of the objective world for the benefit of their supporters. He was obliged to evince qualities of a subjective kind: he needed to place himself, with respect to others, in the relation of *subject* to *object*, of the human being relative to the rest of the world, to animals, to things. Doubtless, this was not so simple as it seems to us, and moreover, the equivalence of subject/object and man/animal was not so easily established. But what he had to manifest on the outside was an inner truth. He was in the position of the prophets or saints proving their divine character by *miracles* through which the external efficaciousness of *subjective sanctity* appears.

4. Recognition of the Sovereignty of Others, Personal Rank in the Hierarchy, and Function — Or the Fundamental Difference between Religion and Royalty

The possibility that any man has of perceiving his inner truth in others, and the difficulty he has in perceiving it in himself account for the disarming aspect of sovereignty.

In the first place, it is not so easy to abdicate in favor of others. If the multitudes freely did so, if they repeated the experience endlessly, this was never without a personal reservation: each one strove to be *more like the sovereign than anyone else was,* more like the one who embodied the possibilities of being's infinite wealth. The sovereign surrounded himself with a court where the light that emanated from him shone directly on those who came nearest him. A man might be placed by birth on the verge of that supreme dignity which only one person could assume. From degree to degree, the claim was less and less justified, but it had a good chance of being more legitimate than that of someone else. What wasn't given by birth might be provided by the resourcefulness of ambition, by intrigue or by merit. By being spent, money itself ensured the possibility of one's resembling the sovereign: through the possession of wealth a man escapes the insufficiency of means, which, placing one in the power of necessity, gives one a subordinate look in this world. Insofar as we cannot claim in this world to no longer depend on anyone, we try in some way to receive at least a reflection of that absolute magnificence that properly belongs only to the man whose sovereignty depends on himself alone. Within the bounds of Christianity, there was a violation of this principle: the sovereign was at least answerable to God.... But around the king it was a mat-

247

ter of who would outdo his friends, so as to appear in the light that royalty radiated.

Ordinarily, the royal splendor does not radiate in solitude. The multitude's *recognition*,[18] without which the king is nothing, implies a *recognition* of the greatest men, of those who might aspire on their own account to the *recognition* of others. But the king, who would not have absolute magnificence if he was not *recognized* by the greatest men, must *recognize* the latter as such. Sovereign magnificence always has the appearance of an orderly arrangement that it assumes in the "courts." Whether priestly or royal, the dignities always compose a hierarchy in which the various *functions* form *ranks* that, ascending from one to the other, in some way support that supreme dignity which, surpassing them all, alone possesses the fullness of being. But we have to say, on the other hand, that in this way being is always manifested to us in the degradation of *ranks*, usually tied to *functions*. Inevitably, the function is degrading. Anyone who takes it on labors, and is therefore servile. The theme of the stupendous comedy with which we have entertained ourselves since the beginning of history appears in this formula. In that comedy of splendor, mankind strove miserably to escape from misery. Indeed, the splendor has this very purpose: it reveals the miserable character of work, but claims while revealing it to rise above it, to escape its laws. The difficulty begins with the degradation of ranks, which substitutes a division of labor, be it the least servile division of labor, for the sovereign moment's violent negation. Ultimately, the division does not spare the king himself and the kingship, once a priesthood, is itself no longer anything more than a function, the least degrading one no doubt, but a function nonetheless.

It would be incorrect to say that royalty did not attain the splendor to which it aspired, and that it was never anything but the miring down of splendor. Royalty was, in one and the same movement, splendor and a miring down. A considerable emphasis was placed on magnificence, but it was never able to lift itself out of the mud.

We need to ascertain what being became for its own sake in these meanders.

The mediocrity of the royal forms is undeniable. It stands out when one compares them to the religious forms. The fact is that religion opened up what real power closed off. It is difficult to be clear about this because the principles merge together: royalty is religious and religion is royal, but royalty took on the *function* that religion did not. To the extent that the sovereignty that every man possesses – unless he renounces it for the benefit of another – became, once the multitude had in fact renounced it, the prerogative of one man, this latter accepted it almost inevitably as a political responsibility. Apparently, at first it was officials who assumed it. But the king and his officials[19] formed an interdependent ensemble: the king radiated the splendor without which the officials would not have had the power inherent in their office; the officials derived from their effective activity that share of sovereignty that emanated from them finally, so that if the king had been, as he often was, a victim destined for sacrifice, sovereignty would still have been mired in the functions that it made possible, and which already gave a secondary luster, but a luster nonetheless, to those who carried them out.

Difficulties of the same kind are encountered in the relations of religion and magic: religion, which was not radically different from effective magic (except insofar as it considered the entire community and not the interest of individuals), itself became mired in the world of things. But the religious forms that remained separate from the royal institution were not, like the latter, heavily encumbered by the burden of power. Royalty operated the division of the sacred and the profane essentially *in space*: the

249

royal dignity cut itself off from the multitude, into which rank (which depended on a greater or lesser proximity) introduced a spatial hierarchy where delusion, mendacity and obsequiousness prevailed. Religion in the restricted sense also deployed the separations that it effected in space: it defined enclosures and it ordained sacred persons. But the differences it commanded in this way did not depend as much as in the royal order on the part played by the things themselves (functions, intrigue, force); moreover, the religious distribution was carried out essentially *in time*. The religious principle, insofar as religion contrasts with the royal forms, derives from the need of ordinary humanity to give profane activity a substantial share of its *time*. Even though religion consecrates persons, it does not necessarily have all their time at its disposal. And if someone religiously gives the whole share to the sacred, in principle this is because he has chosen to do so, at the age when choice is possible: for, *choice* is given only in time, but *rank* is in space. Rank depends on birth, which is a spatial difference; on merit, which is established by action on things, whose outcome is ordered in space; on force, which, insofar as it statically bestows rank, is itself a content of space. Thus, religion involves that which is never given statically, that which *gets decided*. The royal order is itself sovereign, it is manifested in the *moment* preferred to the speculation of labor, but the royal moment would, if it were possible, be frozen in regular forms. The caprice on which it is based changes itself into majesty. Religion itself is contained, the capricious impulses that carry it are kept in check; it also derives from the temptation to seize the moment, acceding to it in the way we accede to things, but it is not necessarily bound by that external reality of the thing, which sovereign power has at its disposal. The king no longer can lose himself of his own accord; he has become responsible for the life and welfare of the others. The king and his officials stand in the midst of a sacred world like a dazzling façade that shelters diverse competing interests, some of which are unavowed, others unavowable. Gazing at this façade, we can experience the miraculous fulguration of the moment, but the squalid reality of the order of things is what the light prevents one from seeing.

The inner experience of these complex forms is given to us in two ways: first, a part of our inner experience corresponds to that ground from which the external forms emerge in community life; second, the action of our personal being is made up of the same movement of vainglory and dissimulation, of the confusion of the moment and the thing, as the action of beings in general.

5. Revolution

It is hardly worth saying that so contestable a system is especially contestable for the one who doesn't benefit from the advantages of the sovereign nor from those of rank. The sovereign and the dignitaries cease to provide him the benefits of the subject. He could, if he submitted, receive his subjective truth from them, seeing in the king and his entourage an image of the splendor to which in his heart of hearts he has not ceased to aspire. But he tells himself: "This splendor is false!" (he is not wrong by much), and "What it conceals is the exploitation of poor wretches like me!" (this time he is completely right): he refuses to continue the traditional slide that enables one to mistake for *the others* a magnificent personage surrounded by privileged individuals whom he has wrapped in his magnificence. The most easily perceived deception is that of the privileged attendants who do not dazzle like the king and whose exactions are obvious. But the only true rebellion begins at the moment when the king's person is at issue, when the man of the multitude decides no longer to transfer to another, whoever this may be, the share of sovereignty that is his due. It is only at this moment that he assumes in himself, in himself alone, the full truth of the subject.

Thus, Albert Camus is justified in setting out, as a statement of principle, the formula, "I rebel, therefore I am": the truth of the I-itself is in question when we cease to subordinate ourselves, but the rebellion does not begin when *we* rebel. When the sovereign himself refused to fully accept the prohibitions on which society is based, when he took it upon himself to transgress them in some way, on behalf of his followers, the rebellion had begun and the sovereign could say on behalf of the others: "I have refused to submit, therefore I am." This reservation is more serious than it appears. The rebel is defined by the categorical no he opposes to the world of sovereignty as a whole. But what if, in this burst of negation, the rebellion – the *subject* itself, that inner truth that suddenly dawns at *sovereign* moments – were itself negated?

6. *The Marquis de Sade, or the Sovereign Rebellion*

I cannot omit at this point to introduce the views that are connected with the position of a singular man, the Marquis de Sade, who by birth received a share of the sovereign magnificence, but who nonetheless pushed rebellion to its extreme consequences.

In speaking of this figure, about whom I can say what Voltaire said about God, that if he had not existed he would have had to be invented, it is difficult to avoid misunderstandings. Moreover, it was because of misunderstandings that his outbursts of temper were associated with the revolutionary convulsion of his time. This *grand seigneur* told himself with good reason that we should have command of ourselves and free access to the world: otherwise we are dupes or we are servile. His mistake was doubtless in imagining we can choose to consider *the others* as being external to us, so that they can never count for us except absurdly, or because of the fear we have of them or the advantage we hope to

gain from them. Thus, we might kill or torture those others, who
are nothing to us, whenever a pleasure would result. It is a gross
mistake in this sense: we can choose to regard another, a few or
even many others, in this way, but my being is never *myself alone;*
it is always myself and *my fellow beings.* Even if *my fellow beings*
change, if I exclude from their number this one whom I regarded
as such, if to him I add that one whom I regarded as external, I
speak and so I am – the being within myself is – outside myself
as I am within myself. Consequently, to have ourselves and the
world at our disposal has at least this limitation: that if not the
world a part of the beings it contains is not entirely separate from
us. The world is not, as Sade tended to represent it, made up of
myself and things. But the idea he formed of rebellion is nevertheless at the limit of the possible. If it involves contradictions,
these do not deprive it of its meaning.

Sade called the abolition of the monarchic order a crime. Consequently, the throng of revolutionaries were partners in crime;
each revolutionary was the other's accomplice, and because each
one had taken part in crime he was bound to continue in crime.
The society of criminals must devote itself to crime; each citizen could attain the supreme pleasure by killing and by torturing.
We know that Sade coupled the abolition of the death penalty
to this freedom of crime. He maintained that the coldness of the
law cannot justify a killing, which would be justified only by the
passion of the criminal, which at least has transported him outside himself. I can put this singular way of thinking in different
terms. Killing is a transgression of the prohibition of murder. In
its essence, transgression is a sacred act. Legal killing is profane
and as such inadmissible.

I will now use this terminology (which is personal to me,
in a sense) to convey Sade's thought as a whole. The man who
stopped seeing his own subjective truth in the king, who meant

253

to find it in himself, found it, as essentially the king had found it, only in crime. If he has found it, this is through the killing of the king, but if he abandons crime he submits in advance, if not to the king, whom he has killed, then to that power which, in the name of the king, limited the freedom of anyone who did not have the sovereign prerogative and which, the king being dead, limits the freedom of all men.

This fundamental truth is schematic; the king's sovereign freedom has little to do with the unlimited crimes of the monsters spawned by the imagination of the author of *Juliette*. Just think of those moments of lustful butchery when the crimes that their joy wrung from them mingled with their vomitings. The principle is the same, however, sovereignty being the negation of prohibition. Actually, the cruel monstrosities of Sade have only one meaning: their excessiveness brings out this principle. The only thing that matters in my view is to show how the rebellion stumbled. The rebel refused to transfer to another the sovereignty that was his, but as Sade felt it and paradoxically expressed it, he was not able to keep to the path he went down. He liquidated that royal subjectivity that imposed itself on him and deprived him of his own subjectivity, but he was not able to regain for his own part that of which the king's glory had deprived him. As far as monarchic society is concerned, he was only an object, but nothing was changed in republican society, except that in front of him there was no longer a *subject* whose sovereign character seemed to be the sole cause of his limitation. In a society that has done away with institutional sovereignty, personal sovereignty is not given, for all that. Even the man who fought to abolish that which oppressed him, which reduced him to the level of things, must still by some stroke or other recapture that of which oppression had deprived him. What is more, he has lost what the monarchic society at least had, a rather complete representation of the human being, such that this being could not allow himself to be confused with things, reduced to objectivity.

7. Sovereignty with No Hold on ANYTHING, or Poetry

The foregoing is doubtless a gross simplification. The world is always richer than language, especially if we extract a momentarily recognizable perspective from an immense disorder. Language then impoverishes reality, and it must do so; otherwise we could not glimpse what is not visible to begin with. But I endeavor in this way to describe a common and communicable inner experience, which reaches precisely that sovereign subject which feudal society so clearly failed to reach and that rebellion all too often missed by following the paths that I have traced out. The miraculous openings, through which we are suddenly inundated by light, are always close to these emergent perspectives. At least we can, in the deep darkness (in the darkness of the intelligible), arrange appearances in such a way that they cease to close the wall of objectivity around our vapidity.

It was not chance that opened in front of us, in that wall, the breach that Sade's *imagination* saw there. Indeed, the breaches in that wall are imaginary; only the stones that raise it up are *real*. They are things, but the *reality* of things is not deep: it is basically superficial, and above all it is important to show that the wall it confronts us with, while it is impassable, faces in every which way. What once seemed to close the wall was due to the ponderousness that tended to make sovereignty into a thing. At all events, the wall became closed in the eyes of the one who was not deceived by the magnificence that the king and the priests commanded. He was right to proclaim their mendacity and to combat them. But the past did not lie in the way he believed: *in truth,* it lied only insofar as, in its *ponderousness*, it represented as a thing that which in principle could not be one. (It did this in

255

two ways: in the ponderousness of a thought that was powerless to free itself, and in the ponderousness of the material profits derived by those who used, like a screen, the splendors whose meaning lay in not being used.)

I would now like to end this quick overview (my introduction) focused not on the *object of study* (which is taken up, rightly, by the history of religions), but on a *problem* (which is nothing less, for the mind, than a tearing [*déchirement*]). I think I have adequately accounted for the impossibility of grasping sovereignty as an object.... I spoke a moment ago of mendacity; in a sense, I am pursuing the rationalist critique, speaking of the lies of the past. But in those lies I have placed the only truth that counts, in my view (and in that of all men who have not been alienated by the service of things). In those lies? But not in those alone. Also in the lies of all those who sought or *who will seek* what I seek. Sovereignty is NOTHING, and I have tried to say how clumsy (but inevitable) it was to make a *thing* of it. I refer now to the opening of art, which always lies but without deceiving those whom it seduces.

Once again, it was not chance that, in his Bastille room,[20] reduced Sade to the imaginary. In the world of fallen sovereignty, only the imagination has sovereign moments available to it. The domain of eroticism, limited by the relative solitude of rooms, is itself profoundly imaginary. Eroticism seems at first to delude the mind less than the imagination of art, and so what it opposed to the tradition of sovereign individuals was less insubstantial: is there anything more dreadful than those figures raised by Sade's imagination against that of a divine majesty that the kings embodied? It was precisely by rising to the level of this "dreadfulness," by recognizing in the work of Sade the extravagant standard of poetry, that the "modern movement" was able to bring art out of the subordination in which it almost always had been left by artists *in the service of* the kings and the priests. But nowadays the "modern movement" is relatively sluggish and its first burst of energy was mixed with a tiresome braggadocio. The antecedents it appeals to have more meaning than it does. It often seems to me that art gained by serving a system that was organized by the greater or lesser miring down of bygone sovereignty: in this way, it avoided the trap of individual vanity, which substitutes a ludicrous, more degrading, miring-down for the heavy solemnity of times past. But I will never forget the "dreadful" moment when modern art denounced servitude, the least servitude, and claimed the "dreadful" legacy of the fallen sovereigns. Those who spoke in its name were perhaps only fleetingly aware of an "impossible" to which they dedicated their words. They deluded themselves in turn, asserting rights, privileges, without realizing that the least protest addressed to those who represented things placed them in the line of the privileged ones of the past. Whoever speaks on behalf of a sovereign art places himself outside a real domain on which he has no hold, against which he is without any rights. The artist is NOTHING in the world of things, and if he demands a place there, even if this only consisted in the right to speak or in the more modest right to eat, he follows in the wake of those who believed that sovereignty could, without being surrendered, have a hold on the world of things. His business is to seduce: everything is risked if he cannot seduce the spokesmen of that world. It only remains for him to be silent, and he must never regret the time when sovereignty subordinated itself to things by attempting to subordinate them: it is not his business to know whether the spokesmen are qualified.[21]

PART TWO

Sovereignty, Feudal Society
and Communism

ONE

What Is the Meaning of Communism?

1. Sovereignty in the Perspectives Generated by the Communist Upheaval

I intend to consider the problems of sovereignty in the present world. In former times these problems were posed in the general consciousness, directly. But present-day humanity fancies that it is detached from those old concerns, which it preserves perhaps, but without ever thinking about them. Present-day humanity has the communist horizon before it. And we may say that, on the whole, what once seemed sovereign has become inadmissible, unworthy of other considerations, depending on the case, than the archaeologist's curiosity or the uncomprehending struggle aimed at complete destruction. If we consider things in general, we have to say of the universe where the life of man in all places aspired, naively, to sovereign forms, that it made "a clean sweep of the past." Today, sovereignty is no longer alive except in the perspectives of communism. It is only insofar as the convulsions of communism lends life to it that sovereignty takes on a vital meaning in our eyes. Hence I will not seek the meaning of sovereignty directly, but rather that of communism, which is its most active contradiction. To begin with, communism is the countermovement, it is the repercussion that drew its strength

261

from sovereignty only to overthrow it – and that owed its effectiveness to the opposition that sovereignty gave rise to. Communism is also that vast world where what is sovereign must come back to life, in new forms perhaps, but perhaps in the most ordinary form. At all events, it would be hard to justify looking elsewhere than in these cloudy perspectives for aspects of sovereignty that vitally affect men limited by the present time.

2. Difficulty and Timeliness of Knowing What Communism Ultimately Means

In today's world nothing is more familiar than communism.[1] Everywhere in the world, communism has commanded attention as a fact or as a possibility of first importance: there are few human beings left who don't have some idea of it, sometimes associated with hatred, sometimes with devotion, more rarely with indifference. Everyone agrees on one point: it involves a contestation of private property, especially with respect to the means of production, the industrial enterprises above all. No one disputes this. But if it's a matter of the role of this extraordinary movement, of its place in the *history* of humanity, the disagreement doesn't confine itself to the usual opposition of adherents and opponents. At the behest of their leaders, not only do the adherents stick to the principle of practical truth, of effective truth, which is tied at the same time to the propaganda value and to the result, but they suppress the part of the truth that detracts from the propaganda; they affirm in the course of purge trials whatever they have deemed necessary for the condemnation of those political friends of theirs who are no longer in agreement with them. These practices are not new, they have always been inherent in political action, but since this action in their case is justified by an ideology, that is, by a rigorous positing of truths, a great malaise emerges from the attitude of the communist leaders.

This malaise, by definition, does not have a paralyzing influence in the domain of efficacy; but it slowly withdraws the reality of communism from the free play of human thought, which becomes inconceivable if it is no longer accessible to all and sundry.

Inevitably, these considerations are regarded by adherents as being inopportune and hostile. But if the communist action succeeds, that is, if the revolution that has begun absorbs the world and finishes its tasks, they will be found in the end in much the same form as I have given. In fact, let us take as an example the differences between the history of the revolutionary events that was written when Lenin was alive and the one that the Stalinist apparatus dictated fifteen years later: we have the choice of two things: either we will pass, as Marx expressed the hope that we would, from the world of necessity to that of freedom, in which case it would be easy to explain these changes by the need, later no longer the case, that forced Stalin to modify the historical role of those opposed to him; or finished communism will still be a world of necessity, something that an orthodox supporter cannot grant any more than, in his conscience, he can disregard the role of Trotsky in 1917.

Of course, militant intellectuals call these kinds of questions postrevolutionary, but that amounts to saying that the concern to understand communism is itself a postrevolutionary concern. Today, when the fate of the revolution is at stake, "the point is not to understand the world, but to change it." Be that as it may, a communist should not be surprised if some day the desire to understand appears as the consequence of an action in which, in practice, in some degree, the actors are required to consider understanding as secondary, and untimely.

In actual fact, the lack of interest in understanding communism evinced by practically all noncommunists and the involvement of militants in a cohort acting almost without debate – according

263

to directives in which the whole game is not known – have made communism a reality that is foreign, as it were, to the world of reflection. To a large extent, the action is carried forward in darkness: those who know its hidden design had to give up the idea of making their knowledge available to others, and assuming that an intense work left them the time to define the most general aspects of their game, they would not be able to freely communicate them. It is likely that no one today could even attempt to do what Lenin did within the limits of his power. In any case, Lenin knew only the dawn of the endless day in which the revolutionary experience continues, and his successors have not given proof of an intellectual genius equal to his. Even those whom opposition freed from the necessity of cloaking a game in silence, even during the period when they had the benefit of exceptional information, ultimately demonstrated the growing powerlessness of reflection tied to the concern for action (of which the concern for criticizing action is only a variant). After Lenin's death, Trotsky was the most brilliant of the communist theoreticians, but his luminous insights and the accuracy of some of his forecasts don't alter the fact that the events he comments on staggered him.

Even if the value of the theoretician is connected with the final defeat of the leader of the game, this would merely point up the superiority of practitioners over theoreticians; measured against events that never cease to outstrip those who live through them, the inadequacy of Trotsky's theories would be unchanged.

3. Difference between the Original Marxist View and the Current View

I cannot develop here a new interpretation of communism recalling Hegel's reflection on the recent revolutionary events, such as *The Phenomenology of Mind* set forth in 1806. I will merely submit some preliminary thoughts. They are connected with Stalin's death and are a response to that death's invitation to look back on the life of a man who loomed large.[2]

From the outset it must be said of Stalin that he gave communism its unexpected form.

If one wishes to judge communism, it is necessary to begin by noting the differences between the development that Marx forecast and the facts subsequent to that development. (Actually, it is accepted practice to emphasize these differences for the purpose of denigration; that seems rather simpleminded to me.)

Today history's main divergence from Marx is evident. For Marxism, the socialist revolution would respond to the situation that obtained in countries having achieved the highest industrial development. The standard of living of the proletarians of these countries could not be seriously improved so long as the revolution had not smashed the framework of capitalist society. The industrially underdeveloped countries, which have kept the forms of feudal society, were ripe for bourgeois revolution, not for socialist revolution. But in the most advanced countries, wage-earners' standard of living improved significantly: consequently, revolutionary activity in those countries was ineffective or nil. Socialist revolutions, carried out by the militants who quoted Marx as their authority, succeeded in countries with an agrarian or feudal social structure, and peasants had a decisive part in them. The events in China have given definition to this unforeseen and paradoxical turn.

4. Stalin's Views Prior to 1917

This aspect of modern revolutions is well known, but it is curious to see the influence that the belief in the impossibility of such developments once had. Isaac Deutscher's work has the great merit of giving, in connection with Stalin's politics, the details of a revolutionary activity whose actual results were different from what they were represented as being by those who achieved them. Deutscher says it with a remarkable clarity: there was not one of them who had not at first seen a measure of absurdity in the political direction that the political revolution was eventually to take. The subject matter of *Stalin* is the life of a political man who finally opted for "socialism in one country," who made the Russian Communist Party the agent of industrial investment. To appreciate the paradoxical character of this position adopted by Stalin, one must go back to the political climate of the first years of the century. In that period the young Georgian militant followed Lenin faithfully. It was taken for granted, says Deutscher, that "the armed insurrection... would result in the setting up of a Provisional Revolutionary Government."[3] But

> Russia was not ripe for socialism; and, therefore, the Provisional Revolutionary Government would not be a "proletarian dictatorship." Nor would it be a parliamentary government, since this was not possible in the middle of a revolution. Lenin's label for the Provisional Government was "a democratic dictatorship of the proletariat and the peasantry." That cumbrous and self-contradictory formula was never clearly explained either by its author or his disciples although it was the basis of all Bolshevik propaganda from 1905 till 1917....[4]

According to Stalin, in 1905,

> These were the tasks of the Provisional Revolutionary Government...: it would disarm the 'dark forces' of the counter-revolution; it would lead in the civil war; it would then convene a Constituent Assembly, issuing from a general election. Between the emergence of the Revolutionary Government, deriving its power from no constitutional source, and the convocation of the Constituent Assembly, the Government would decree a series of radical reforms, none

266

of which would go beyond the limits of bourgeois democracy. The reforms would include: the proclamation of the freedom of the Press and of assembly, the abolition of indirect taxes, the imposition of a progressive tax on profit and of progressive death duties, the setting up of revolutionary peasant committees to take charge of land reform, the separation of Church and State, the eight hours working day, the introduction of social services and labour exchanges, and so on. Altogether the programme was much more moderate than that that was to be adopted . . . later by the moderate Labour government in Britain. For Russia, it spelt a thorough-going upheaval.[5]

Stalin, adds Deutscher,

> argued that the programme just outlined could be put into operation only by an alliance of the Socialist working class with the individualistic peasantry, because the urban Liberal middle class would not support the revolution. He realized that in the long run the working class and the peasantry were pursuing different aims, and that eventually their interests and policies were likely to clash. But the clash would arise only if and when the Socialists attempted to overthrow capitalism "and this was not the task of the revolution in Russia." Thus, the "democratic dictatorship of the proletariat and peasantry" was to be purely democratic because in its programme there was "not an ounce" of socialism proper.[6]

Oddly, Trotsky, although he had thrown in with the Mensheviks (but for reasons of party organization), was at the time the only socialist who believed that a victorious revolution in Russia was bound to lead to proletarian dictatorship and to socialism.

We know that from February to April 1917 Stalin, who was part of the Bolshevik Central Committee since 1912, had control of Bolshevik policy in Saint Petersburg. During this period he adhered to that program with which Lenin was formerly in full agreement. But Lenin, in April, was able to go to the capital, where he immediately assumed the leadership of the movement. When he delivered the speech that would define the new Bolshevik policy, asserting that the revolution was entering a socialist phase, that the banks should be combined into a single national bank, that industry could not be socialized immediately, but that production and distribution should be placed under the control of the workers, those who heard him were taken aback.

> A non-Bolshevik writer, who by chance was present at the conference, described later the impact of Lenin's words: "I shall never forget that thunderlike speech, startling and amazing not only to me, a heretic accidentally present there, but also to the faithful, all of them. I assert that nobody there had expected anything of the kind. It seemed as if all the elements and the spirit of universal destruction had risen from their lairs, knowing neither barriers nor doubts, nor personal difficulties nor personal considerations, to hover through the banquet chambers of Kshesinskaya, above the heads of the bewitched disciples."[7]

This shows how firmly established was the Marxist principle of socialist revolution resulting from the accentuated development of capitalist industry, and how far the Marxists of 1917, whether hard or soft, were from admitting this disarming possibility: a socialist revolution that would begin with Russia and continue in China!

As a matter of fact, Lenin himself, coming around to the thesis that Trotsky has defended as early as 1905 (so that the earliest disciples exclaimed, "That's Trotskyism, not Leninism!"), did not believe any more than Trotsky did in the possibility of a socialist revolution limited to a society emerging from the feudal stage.

Lenin and Trotsky believed revolution was near in all of Western Europe, and they didn't think that the construction of socialism in Russia would go very far without the help of the victorious proletariat of the advanced countries. Only cooperation on a global scale would enable the working-class organization of production to experience a complete development. Lenin till 1921 and Trotsky till the failure of the German revolution in 1923 lived with their eyes fastened on the Western horizon, waiting for the conflagration that would herald salvation: the extension of proletarian dictatorship to its chosen domain. But the industrial world remained unshaken: the proletarian movement, if we exclude the revolutions from above of the European East, was not to win a significant victory up to the present time, save in China.

5. Stalin after 1917 and the Stalinist Perspective

After 1917, Stalin, as he was wont to do, realigned himself with Lenin. However, among the communist leaders he represented an anti-Western tendency, which revealed itself long before he decided in favor of "socialism in one country." He expressed himself as early as July in terms that show his clear awareness of the situation of the advanced industrial countries as well as a basic orientation: "You cannot rule out the possibility," he said to an opponent,

> that precisely Russia will be the country that paves the way to Socialism.... The base of the revolution is broader in Russia than in western Europe, where the proletariat stands alone against the *bourgeoisie*. With us the working class is supported by the poor peasantry.... In Germany the apparatus of state power works with incomparably greater efficiency.... We ought to discard the obsolete idea that only Europe can show us the way. There exists a dogmatic Marxism and a creative one. I am opting for the latter.[8]

269

At this time,

> Stalin did not yet expound the idea of Socialism in one country, the
> view that Russia by herself, in isolation from the rest of the world,
> could build to the end the edifice of socialism. Only seven or eight
> years later would he formulate that view jointly with Bukharin and
> against Trotsky. But already now there was a stronger emphasis in his
> words on Russia's peculiar Socialist mission than either in Trotsky's
> or in Lenin's.[9]

Perhaps there was also a keener awareness of the seemingly
insurmountable obstacle that a proletarian movement meets in
countries where the feudal chains are broken, in countries where
the peasantry possesses most of the cultivated land: an isolation
of interests that, at the decisive moments, the cleverest propaganda can't disguise. As Deutscher makes clear, the difference
between Stalin and the others was barely perceptible. Stalin did
not commit himself to "socialism in one country" until later. And
even then he was careful to affirm the fictitious belief in the coming general revolution, despite its unlikelihood. All one can say
is that, in addition to his aversion to Europe, his practitioner's
realism and his distrust of dogmatic positions made him the right
man to lead a revolution whose course must necessarily turn aside
from the paths that theory had laid out for it.

In 1924 Stalin was alone, abandoned to the misery of an immense backward country in which the peasants no longer had
to send to the cities the money from the income of the big landowners, without it being possible yet for the cities to pay with
manufactured objects for all the necessary agricultural products; he reflected on the impossibility of defending the Russian
soil without substantially increasing the industrial resources.
But he was still so imbued with the traditional Marxist doc-

WHAT IS THE MEANING OF COMMUNISM?

trine that he wrote at the beginning of the year that

> the overthrow of the power of the bourgeoisie and establishment of
> the power of the proletariat in one country does not yet mean that
> the complete victory of socialism has been ensured. The principal
> task of socialism – the organization of socialist production – has still
> to be fulfilled. Can this task be fulfilled without the joint efforts of
> the proletarians in several advanced countries? To overthrow the
> bourgeoisie the efforts of one country are sufficient; this is proved
> by the history of our revolution. For the final victory of socialism,
> for the organization of socialist production, the efforts of one coun-
> try, particularly of a peasant country like Russia, are insufficient;
> for that, the efforts of the proletarians of several advanced countries
> are required.[10]

Finally, in the autumn, he "first formulated his ideas on socialism in one country...."[11] Soon, "belief in socialism in one country was to...become the supreme test of loyalty to party and
state."[12] But to begin with, it was a secondary point, "put forward by Stalin almost casually.... For many months, until the
summer of the next year, none of Stalin's rivals, neither the other
triumvirs nor Trotsky, thought the point worth arguing...."

Moreover, in itself the formula didn't have the value we might
be tempted to attribute to it. It didn't entail an industrial policy
different from the one advocated by Trotsky. "Trotsky...had,
since the end of the Civil War, urged the Politbureau to begin
gearing up the administration for planned economy; and in those
early days he first sketched out the ideas that were later to be
embodied in the five-year plans."[13] The formula merely had a great
practical value. No one could have asked the working world to
furnish the necessary effort and then add, "but, needless to say,
the efforts of a single country are insufficient." At least the pop-

ular imagination demanded prospects contrary to those which Marx's teaching had defined.

6.

The doctrine of "socialism in one country" has long been official. In our day, it is a basic truth whose value has been proved by practice. But, in this case, while the theory and the experiment met with success, there were few consequences: Stalin himself did not draw the lesson from it.

Deutscher says of him that "he reached his formula gropingly, discovering, as it were, a new continent, while he believed himself sailing for quite a different place."[14] That is true as far as it goes, but one must also understand that Stalin and his crew conferred the name of the Indies on America. If the lesson of Russia had taken effect, it would have become easy to see in China a revolutionary situation of the first order. In the case of Stalin it was the contrary that occurred. Stalin backed Chiang Kai-shek because he didn't believe in the possibilities of the Chinese communists. He advocated a compromise formula analogous to the one he had recommended, up to 1917, for an agrarian country like Russia. The business had regrettable consequences. Chiang turned against those who had supported him and crushed them. Yet Stalin was later to oppose an agreement between the communists and the social democrats of Germany, which was the only thing that might have countered the rise of National Socialism. The working world still seemed to have the only potential for overthrow: a movement of reaction did not cause alarm. The strange theory of Social Fascism, lumping socialists together with Nazis in the same vituperation, made sense only in connection with a communist upsurge, natural in a highly industrialized nation. On the revolutionary chessboard, China appeared all the more insignificant because the communist party of the cities, led in 1925 by Li Li-san, had

272

gradually transformed itself, at the prompting of Mao Tse-tung, into a communist party of the fields, into a vast agrarian guerrilla movement. Nothing could be more paradoxical, and, above all, nothing could be less important from the point of view of that Marxism which Mao took as his basis nonetheless. No doubt this explains the fact that after the war Stalin, decidedly closed to the prospects of a communist movement whose privileged domain would be agrarian and feudal society, and not the industrially advanced countries, negotiated in August 1945 with this same Chiang Kai-shek who in 1927 had massacred his communist friends, and who was then preparing to destroy the armies of Mao Tse-tung. Citing James Byrnes,[15] Deutscher tells us moreover that at Potsdam, a little earlier, he had gone "so far as to disavow the Chinese Communists opposed to Chiang Kai-shek and to say that the Kuomintang was the only political force capable of ruling China."

7. Communism Limited to the Destruction of Feudal Forms

I don't intend to dwell on errors. Undoubtedly, the German policy at the time of Hitler's coming to power and the Chinese policy up to the eve of Mao Tse-tung's success represent the weak parts of Stalin's policies. Stalin nonetheless holds, in Deutscher's words, "the foremost place among all those rulers who, through the ages, were engaged in building up Russia's power."[16] To which it must be added that his action tended to mix the interests of Russia with those of communism.

My object is situated opposite to these individual controversies. I wish to emphasize here that Stalin's action gave communism an unexpected form, that of a movement whose chosen terrain is found in agrarian, industrially backward countries with a juridical structure that is more or less feudal. Stalin did not draw the lesson from this in a clear way, but on the day of his death he left a world in which, because of his calculations or in spite of them, he had helped communism to take on this meaning.

But in itself this first proposition has only a superficial value. The only thing that matters is that communism, for the poor countries, is the only means of bringing about that "industrial revolution" which the rich countries accomplished long ago.

As Deutscher points out, the essential work of Stalin inevitably calls to mind that period of intense "primitive" accumulation in England whose excesses and cruelties Karl Marx described in the last chapter of volume one of *Capital*. "The analogies," says Deutscher, "are as numerous as they are striking."[17] He goes on to say that Marx gave an account of

> the first violent processes by which one social class accumulated in its hands the means of production, while other classes were being deprived of their land and means of livelihood and reduced to the status of wage-earners. The process which, in the thirties, took place in Russia might be called the "primitive accumulation" of socialism in one country. Marx described the "enclosures" and "clearings" by which the landlords and manufacturers of England expropriated the yeomanry, the "class of independent peasants." A parallel to these enclosures is found in a Soviet law, on which Stalin reported to the Sixteenth Congress, a law which allowed the collective farms to "enclose" or "round off" their land so that it should comprise a continuous area. In this way the individual farmers were either compelled to join the collective farms or were virtually expropriated. Marx recalls the "bloody discipline" by which the free peasants of England were made into wage-labourers, "the disgraceful action of the State which employed the police to accelerate the accumulation of capital by increasing the degree of exploitation of labour."[18]

I don't intend to pass judgment on a revolution that was the doing of Stalin himself: I believe that it was just as much the result of the development of events as the English industrial revolution. Deutscher deserves credit for having made this development visible. It is certain that the revolution demanded cruel measures, but without cruelty would the same measures have been effective? It is apparent from the foregoing that all accumulation is cruel; all renunciation of the present for the sake of the future is cruel. The Russian bourgeoisie not having accumulated, the Russian proletariat had to do it. And the Chinese proletariat will have to do likewise. We shall see that the accumulation of resources with a view to industry falls upon the proletariat whenever the bourgeoisie is not able to do anything, and that the new role of the proletariat calls for changes that Marx couldn't have foreseen, changes that seem destined not to be easy ones, but whose extraordinary consequences ought to again determine the relations of force.

TWO

The Collapse of Feudal Societies and

the Great Revolutions

1. The Limit of Lucidity Derived from Action

The communists, who thrive on the tension and contained violence of action, are – avowedly – obliged to make little allowance for the capricious and oblique course of history, which reaches the goal via bypaths. Not that they cannot themselves take it down such paths (thus, in 1939 they engaged in a fight to the death against Hitlerism over Poland). But in this case they can't speak.... And when they act while passionately giving their reasons, they aren't apt to recall the difference between the language of the revolutionaries of 1893, for example, and the change in the relations of production that occurred in the background, discreetly, far from the angry voices of the popular tribune. It is true that they think, along with Marx, that they have taken account of the real changes that are in play. I'm not saying they are mistaken, but history sometimes goes astray, and those who precede it with a confident commentary don't always keep in mind the successions of errors by which the most judicious men went astray. Even if, in the end, history were to justify thought, it would not do so without having given silent and painful lessons to those who presumed to define its raison d'être and its end. So that the man of action – who meant to command history – if he were attentive would see that another, who doesn't act, who waits, may in a sense be ridiculous, but takes the consequences of the event more seriously: the one who waits without acting disregards those immediate ends that never have all the importance, nor the exact importance, which action bestows on them.

It may be, in short, that today it is once again possible – and even appropriate – to see what action prevents one from seeing. Others say: What if no one acted!... As if it were inadmissible that a man might avoid the deafening crowd and try to see better and farther than those who bark and bay. What is coming is never easily recognized by those who see mainly what they wish to see. Would what is coming be commensurate with readymade ideas, with ideas formed at a time when no one would have imagined what sort of monstrous, dreadful, and at the same time the craven, flat thing we were going to become? I don't know if it is reasonable to propose a "radiant future" to tomorrow's humanity, but we would do well not to close our eyes to a truth that in part the fight "for a radiant future" keeps one from seeing. We will be able to distinguish the present shape of this truth, whose effects cannot yet be known, only if we are not obliged to get ourselves approved by the masses.

2. Revolution Considered As the Subversion of Sovereign Power

This way of thinking implies, needless to say, value judgments different from those of Marxism. Moreover, it calls for a critique of those judgments. Now this critique, it seems to me, might be derived first of all from the unexpected forms that present-day communism assumed.

We have seen what was paradoxical about the development of communism beginning with Russia and China. These countries, with an analogous social structure, both had at the outset a mainly agrarian economy; their undeveloped industry was based in large part on foreign capital. According to the perspectives of Marxism, both of these countries, which, given their immensity and their isolation, formed a veritable world apart, appeared open only to the developments of a bourgeois revolution. They were not ripe, so it seemed, for a proletarian revolution. Indeed Stalin, who before 1933 had not allowed even a temporary alliance of the German Communist Party with social democracy, despite the disastrous experience of 1927 in China, still gave his support in 1945 to the Kuomintang, alone capable of transforming an essentially agrarian country. Stalin was not prepared to recognize, and he died without recognizing, the affinity of the communist revolution with countries with a feudal structure. The possibility of a communist revolution in Germany seemed to him, in 1933, to outweigh the risk of Hitlerism, but the unseasonableness of such a revolution in China, in 1945, led him to support Chiang Kai-shek.

I cannot help but insist on these aspects: I wish to stress, against both classical and present-day Marxism, the connection of *all* the great modern revolutions, from the English and the French onward, with a feudal order that is breaking down. There have never been any great revolutions that have struck down an established bourgeois domination. All those that overthrew a regime started with a revolt motivated by the sovereignty that is implied in feudal society.

We have a poor understanding today of the initial role of sovereignty in the decisive political crises. Generally, we consider the institutions of the past, from the materialist point of view, if not as alluring curiosities then as realities alien to what we are. We don't take them seriously, for themselves, except when it is a matter of the most remote times or of archaic societies, with which our relations are the most distant. But I want to make an effort, on the contrary, taking these institutions seriously, to show what the transition from societies based on the requirements that sovereignty satisfied to societies of the modern type signifies *for us*. Thus, I will try to show the meaning of what we have suppressed without being sufficiently aware of what we were doing.

As the exposition of Volume I suggests, in the feudal world there was a preference for a *sovereign* use, for an unproductive use, of wealth. The preference of the bourgeois world was reserved, quite on the contrary, for *accumulation*. The sense of value that predominated in the bourgeoisie caused the richest men to devote their resources to the installation of workshops, factories or mines. The feudal world erected churches, castles, palaces, whose purpose was *to evoke wonder*. The bourgeois works satisfied the desire to multiply the means of production. An immense project, the construction of Versailles, is perhaps the most notable form, although in human terms it may not be the richest, that was given to the principle of a noble existence dedicated to the scorn of useful activity. Just imagine, in this day and age, an effort as spectacular as that of Donzère-Mondragon, for example, whose sole result, whose sole profit, would be that yearly maintenance budget which was doubtless to finally make the revolution inevitable.

I don't mean to suggest that the revolution was wrong in its opposition to Versailles. But neither do I see any reason to regard Versailles as an aberration and not to seek its meaning. An exigency remains within us of which the bourgeois attitude is the denial. Versailles is doubtless a distorted, even detestable, expression of that exigency, but it nonetheless affords the opportunity to clearly distinguish the focus of attraction around which the world has revolved up to our time. Versailles is far from being the only example of such a focus, but for anyone who would refuse to see what its splendor signified, humanity would never take on that limpid and irrefutable solar appearance which is that of sovereignty. Versailles is the symbol of the order that the bourgeois and proletarian revolutions meant to abolish. The great revolutions of both types had as their purpose the abolition of the feudal order, of which sovereignty is the meaning, and of which Versailles gave the universal form. I would like to speak of this less vaguely, but I wanted to use a familiar symbol of the sovereign order without delay.

Of course, sovereignty – in a practical sense, the use of resources for nonproductive ends – cannot be given as the goal of history. I even maintain the contrary: that if history has some goal, sovereignty cannot be that goal, and further, that sovereignty could not have anything to do with that goal, except insofar as it would differ therefrom. That goal is perhaps, on the contrary, classless society; classless society is at least the direction that history has taken in our time. Obscurely still, the vast majority of men are ceasing to consent to the existence of privileged classes. Apparently, the point toward which we are converging, drawn by a gravity analogous to that of flowing water, is undifferentiated humanity. In his last piece of writing, Stalin, who evokes the struggle of his party "for the peoples' radiant future," speaks earnestly of "the abolition of the antithesis between town and country, and between mental and physical labor, and elimination of the distinctions between them."[19] How better to formulate the fluvial movement that must slowly, inevitably, mingle all our waters at the same level? But not only would it be useless to go against the current, it is desirable, without any doubt, that the differences be obliterated; it is desirable that a true equality be established, a true nondifferentiation. And, as Stalin shows in the same publication,[20] this demands the utilization of new means. But while it is possible that, in the future, men will concern themselves less and less with their difference from others, that doesn't mean they will cease to concern themselves with what is sovereign. What is sovereign stands in opposition to what is bourgeois, or servile, just as the enjoyment of production is in opposition to accumulation (that is, to the production of the means of production).

Indeed, perhaps it is finally possible to show that sovereignty, being generally the condition of each human, is neither anachronistic nor insignificant. And that having played the leading role in the history of revolutions, it still raises a discreet but crucial question at the end of a debate burdened with this double excessiveness: the rampant acceleration of technical progress and the militarized organization of revolutionary tension....

3. Feudality (1): Property and Sovereignty

Revolutions, I asserted, have occurred in societies of the feudal type, in which the use of wealth was not yet reserved for the accumulation of productive forces. Marxists have acquired the habit of designating by the name of feudality rather diverse social states which at times it would seem logical to name differently. Conventional historians have preferred in many cases the terms royalty, monarchy, empire: they have reserved the term feudal for society of the occidental Middle Ages, or for societies that seem close to this model, like ancient China, or like Japan prior to the recent industrialization.

Here I will only add one reason to those that led Marx and Engels to give the name *feudal* to all juridical structures previous to societies of bourgeois predominance (to structures characterized by an economic life based on the agricultural domain, a social life based on the eminence of landowners). Personally, the feudal world does not seem to me to designate only landed property, which may still today be held by bourgeois proprietors investing part of their fortune in land. It seems to refer essentially to a regime implying at least a certain degree of sovereignty on the part of the owner. I cannot overlook the fact that for a good many minds schooled in pedestrian ideas of economy, the word sovereign, insofar as it denotes a form akin to the *sacred*, is scarcely intelligible: it refers to an archaic state of things whose arbitrariness seems fundamental to them; in their eyes, this state of things had no meaning apart from the naked self-interest of those who profited from it. This conception is justified by the existence of a source of income that is not based on labor. But might there not be a share of income which, in principle, would not come from labor?

If the income from a piece of landed property were the product of the owner's labor – of the labor connected with stock-breeding and, a fortiori, of field labor – there would be no sovereignty on the part of the owner. The point is that labor is the exact opposite of the sovereign attitude. For Hegel, in an aspect of this doctrine that was at the origin of Marx's, labor is the action of the man who, rather than *die* free, chose to *live* in servitude.[21] That doesn't mean that a definitive downfall is connected with labor: on the contrary, Hegel clearly saw that only labor will produce the consummate man, and that, of necessity, the consummate man labors. But irrespective of Hegel's thought, I insist on one point: our sovereign moments, when nothing matters except *what is there,* what is sensible and captivating *in the present,* are antithetical to the attention to the future and to the calculations without which there would be no labor. Thus, landed property, feudal property, imply sovereignty of the owner only insofar as it frees him from labor.[22]

Feudality (2): The Use of the Surplus

Except for hunting, which was never considered to be work, and even to a certain extent stock-breeding, less closely tied to the pursuit of profit than farming,[23] the sovereign enjoyment of the ground presupposes laborers in the service of the owner. But in spite of the oppression usually connected with ownership of the ground for the purpose of enjoyment, it is impossible to overlook the fact that sovereignty is man's primordial condition, his basic condition: if voluntary labor seems to limit this condition, and if violently imposed labor changes it into its opposite, into slavery, sovereignty is nonetheless inviolable. The sovereignty of a human being, of any human being, subsists even from the most servile point of view. Moreover, labor, which is its negation, can never annihilate sovereignty, because in time and over a large enough territory labor always produces more than is necessary for those provisions without which it could not continue, and the accumulation can never be total. There is always something left over and, when all is said and done, it is the surplus that falls to the landed proprietor; oppression deprives the slave of his share of the surplus, but it is still because there exists a surplus that the owner benefits from a share of the sovereignty which is possible in the world. Economically, the sovereign attitude is exemplified by the use of the surplus for nonproductive ends. The ground is the sign and equivalent of the seasonal surplus: of what man receives, not without labor, but beyond his labor, beyond, more exactly, the provisions necessary to the worker for the production of his labor. The fact that an organized authority allots the surplus share to someone other than the cultivator can be viewed as one wishes, but the connection of sovereignty with the possession of the ground has a precise meaning. We can picture, in a backward country, a group of lands that are exploited to capacity: starting from there, the possible accumulation is nil or negligible. The same is not true of the industrial plants of an advanced country: their ownership does not oblige but induces one to accumulate. Hence, landed property and sovereignty are historically linked.

Ordinarily, it is true, this link seems itself to be directly tied to the manpower that is exploited by the owners. But sovereignty, which did not depend on the ownership of the ground (but which often entailed it), is even less the result of slavery; the slavery that accompanies it as a general rule enriched the forms of sovereignty, but slavery was not its precondition. Sovereignty comes first.

5. Feudality (3): Concentration in a Single Individual of the Right To Use the Surplus

The sovereignty of the one who compels a defenseless fellow human being to labor is obviously different from that initial sovereignty that must have been, in the equality of the clan members, that of the hunter or shepherd of ancient times. But this difference is less important than it seems. It is only after the event, once the thing is experienced, that a man is troubled by the results of the sovereign temper. Such a difference is perceptible to one who is concerned not to destroy, on account of his sovereign attitude, the possibility of others. But without the final failure of immediate sovereignty, which nothing limits, this unhappy sovereignty would not be conceivable. The initial sovereignty is naive and differs from that of slaveowners and kings only by a lack of opportunities. Moreover, in the fact of asserting a limitless sovereignty, we must see a force that casts a spell, that does not just prevent the sovereign from taking heed of the suffering of those he subordinates. This action prevents even those who let themselves be subordinated from gauging their downfall. It draws them into an agreeable resignation, so long as there is a slight possibility of participating in that glory whose appearance fascinates. Is anything more common than the differentiated life of one man, a life magnified by the veneration of which he has become the object on the part of an entire people? The agreement of all gives the incomparable dignity of one its profound truth. The desire to see, at one point, sovereignty produced, without limitation, in the anticipation, the silence and the trembling of the subjects, sometimes becomes so great that the latter no longer know that they themselves confer on the king the quality which they should have claimed, which they should not have given up. Sometimes the important thing is no longer to be sovereign oneself, but that man's sovereignty exists and fills the world where, at that point, it no longer matters that those servile labors are organized and perpetuated that make hateful a humanity degraded by an excess of hate. But while another's sovereignty may be pleasant to one who is not really the sovereign's property and slave, it is nonetheless unsatisfying in the long run. The subject may not have any resentment, but he cannot arrange it so that a mute demand does not remain within him. He expects for himself a limited share of the grace he bestows on the one whose preeminence he recognizes. What is solicited by the one who serves the sovereign is not just the granting of lands, it is also, in keeping with an alternating movement of condensation and diffusion, the granting of a share of that sacred existence which emanates from him.

6. Feudality (4): Dispersal of the Right of Use

It is logical that, virtue being condensed in one person, all the sovereign resources of the people, including property which is its principle and its source, would issue from the prince. Landed property, ownership of all the ground, is in fact the consequence of the supreme dignity. It was from the pharaoh that the priests or the administrators who served him were to receive the just reward for their services, mainly in the form of lands. But the essential aspect of this reward was the shift by which the grantee strove to establish between the land and himself ties similar to those that initially connected that land and the pharaoh. It was a matter of making a *benefit*, in the meaning the word received in medieval law, of what was at first one of the attributes of a function, of an *office*. The passage from *office* to *benefit*, the principle of all feudality, is in fact the passage from subordination, which is the service of the sovereign, to the sovereignty of the feudatory. It is not a complete sovereignty, which moreover is in fact never achieved since it is never a pure benefit (an enjoyment), but is always, even on the part of the suzerain, in the last instance an *office*, and even a service.[24] But once the grant is hereditary, the *office* has truly become a *benefit*, there is truly a feudality, and hence a sovereignty, at least a relative sovereignty, of the domain owners. "Nobility" is at the very least the indelible mark of the sovereign grace, retained even by the descendants of those who were blessed with it.

The delegation of diffuse sovereignty to a single person is always followed by a more or less broad dispersal. The dispersal is itself followed by a new condensation. Things arranged themselves in this way at least as early as the Egyptian monarchy, when, after a period of revolution, and above all of anarchic revolt, the twelfth dynasty relegated the great feudatories to the background. In societies where the concern for sovereign works prevails, this movement of systole and diastole is inevitable: the power that directs the prodigality is constantly divided, organized, and decomposed. But politically, the main thing is the economic domination of a caste of landed proprietors connected with sovereignty, either through service of the sovereign or through hereditary prerogatives; the main thing is the absence of accumulation,

SOVEREIGNTY, FEUDAL SOCIETY AND COMMUNISM

the continual consumption of the available resources for non-productive purposes.

7. The Equivalent Position of the Bourgeoisie and the Proletariat with Respect to Feudality

All the great revolutions of the modern world, which are linked to the struggle against feudality, have tended to oppose these sumptuary expenditures, regarded as aberrant. They were the doing of masses united by their incomprehension of the preoccupation with and habits of prodigality, which the landed proprietors as a whole represented. When the bourgeoisie established quite different systems, based on the accumulation of a large part of the resources with a view to industrialization, the popular masses never joined together to overthrow the established order. These masses have never united except in a radical hostility to the principle of sovereignty. The bourgeoisie may disappoint them, but it never appropriates a large enough share of resources for nonproductive purposes to bring about a general upheaval: such an upheaval never occurred except in countries dominated by a feudal caste.

If the bourgeoisie is sufficiently strong, as with the English or French bourgeoisie, it can exercise power. But if the bourgeois class is weak compared with the class of landed proprietors, if by itself it does not have the strength to impose its principles on the survivors of the feudal world, the power passes over to that social class which possesses nothing. These propositions would soon gain acceptance were it not for the prestige of traditional Marxism, which the Marxists of our day cannot relinquish. In any case, it is not necessary to push the analysis very far in order to see that nothing contradicting these propositions has taken place. That doesn't mean that other factors will not supervene, factors that will change things. But it accounts for the disappointment that followed the anticipation of events consistent with the schemas of Marx; but it replies to the assertions of Stalin quoted above:

> You cannot rule out the possibility that precisely Russia will be the country that paves the way to Socialism.... The base of the revolution is broader in Russia than in western Europe, where the proletariat stands alone against the *bourgeoisie*. With us the working class is supported by the poor peasantry.... In Germany the apparatus of state power works with incomparably greater efficiency....

Indeed, in Germany the apparatus of power did eventually pass into the hands of the bourgeoisie; from then on, the bourgeoisie had an immense force and standing, and the popular masses could not muster against it a force strong enough to overthrow it. Since the bourgeoisie became the ruling class of Western Europe it has never given rise to an opposing revolutionary dynamism comparable to that of Russia and revolutionary China.[25] The days of June, the Commune and Spartakus are the only violent convulsions of the working masses struggling against the bourgeoisie, but these movements occurred with the help of a misunderstanding. The workers were misled by the lack of obstacles encountered a little earlier when the bourgeoisie, in concert with them, rose up against men born of that feudality which irritated everybody. The bourgeois apparatus of repression had no trouble crushing those insurrections that confronted forces more suited than they for the exercise of power. As to the Russian bourgeoisie, it was defeated before having fought. Subsequently, only the feudal lords engaged substantial forces against the communists. For its part, the Kuomintang had time to show its unfitness for governing without the support of the class of landed proprietors: if it united superior forces against it, this was because it embodied the feudal order.

289

THREE

The World of Denied Sovereignty

1. The Primacy of the Means of Production and the Soviet System

In the end, the revolutions of the twentieth century are not very different from those of the seventeenth and eighteenth centuries (nor from that antifeudal bourgeois subversion which sixteenth-century Protestantism was, in part). Essentially, what all these revolutions prepared the way for was the change of economic structure known by the name of "industrial revolution." Begun in the eighteenth century, this fundamental overthrow shook the most advanced countries; it spread in our day to Russia; tomorrow it may spread to China. It is the result of a subversion of the principles that preside over economic life. We are passing from the primacy of sovereign works, tied to agricultural predominance and the feudal order, to the primacy of accumulation. The basic determination, in the superstructure of a society, involves the use of the excess resources for the production of the means of production. It is not so much a question of whether these means of production are, individually, the property of the bourgeois or, collectively, that of the workers: what matters primarily is the *growth* of the means of production, the increase of the total amount of a country's productive forces. In terms of economic structure, this

291

is the crux of the difference between feudal society and developed industrial society.

Ownership of the means of production is also very important, but only in a secondary way. At bottom, incomes and wages depend on the mode of ownership, but the distribution of manufactured products is carried out, once the resources of each individual are given, according to the law of value. On the whole, the difference is essential only in one particular: with the collective accumulation of the State, the law of value does not limit the production of the means of production. This is what Stalin, in the last writing he published himself, meant to make clear. Stalin points out that if the value of the manufactured products is determinant in a market economy pure and simple, the various branches of production must be developed according to the profitability of each enterprise. But, he says,

> it is totally incorrect to assert that under our present economic system...the law of value regulates the "proportions" of labor distributed among the various branches of production. − If this were true, it would be incomprehensible why our light industries, which are the most profitable, are not being developed to the utmost, and why preference is given to our heavy industries, which are often less profitable, and sometimes altogether unprofitable. −...If this were true, it would be incomprehensible why workers are not transferred from plants that are less profitable, but very necessary to our national economy, to plants which are more profitable, in accordance with the law of value....

If such were the case, he adds

we should have to cease giving primacy to the production of the means of production in favor of the production of articles of consumption. And what would be the effect of ceasing to give primacy to the production of the means of production? The effect would be to destroy the possibility of the continuous expansion of our national economy, because the national economy cannot be continuously expanded without giving primacy to the production of the means of production.[26]

Thus, collective ownership of the means of production, which, needless to say, cannot by itself ensure growth of the economy, is the only thing that can ensure its steady growth. Individual ownership of those means, which makes it necessary to consider the limits of profitability of an isolated enterprise (whereas collective ownership is only bound by the overall profitability of a nation's enterprises), can inhibit accumulation. Periodically, this kind of control through profitability can result in crises of overproduction. Wishing to differentiate the "basic economic law" of socialism from that of capitalism, Stalin makes the essential distinction when he contrasts the continuous force of the one with the alternating form of the other. With socialism, he says, "instead of development of production with breaks in continuity from boom to crisis and from crisis to boom – unbroken expansion of production."[27]

2. Difference between Individual Accumulation and Collective Accumulation

The bourgeois, whose attitude toward feudal squander is similar to that of the workers, still cannot be as rigorous in pursuing the consequences of the primacy of accumulation. Their individualism stands in the way, tying them to the pursuit of the greatest profit.

The bourgeois world, without any doubt, is closer to the feudal

world than the working world. Bourgeois individualism "drives...
capitalism to such risky undertakings as the enslavement and systematic plunder of colonies and other backward countries, the
conversion of a number of independent countries into dependent countries, the organization of new wars – which to the mag-
nates is the best 'business'....".[28] Such an individualism, devoted
on all sides to ruthless profit-seeking, prevents the bourgeois
industrialists from ensuring economic growth with a rational regularity. Generally speaking, the bourgeois opposition to the feudal order, which could, at the time of the French revolution, be
violent, was content not with half-measures but at least with
incomplete measures. Let us say nothing of the fact that justice
never really interested the bourgeois unless they themselves were
injured: the only thing that mattered to them was developing the
productive forces and putting an end to the political power of the
nobles. The bourgeoisie became what it was by making it impossible for the nobility to remain the value and the limit of the
world: the primacy of sovereign works was not admissible for it,
either materially or morally; sovereign works paralyzed and denied
it. But it was not eager to confront the world of sovereignty with
that negation which the latter had not spared it. With regard to
the sovereign magic, the bourgeois, if they were no longer its
victims, were inconsistent, obtuse and tolerant; little by little
they pushed inconsistency to the point of displaying rather often
a kind of regret.[29]

Only the workers pursue the consequences of a condemnation
of everything that, in the course of time, endeavored to appear
sovereign. But they don't speak a language very different from that
to which the bourgeois world has accustomed us. If they touch
the essential, the workers speak plainly: what they speak of is "the
extension of production, the promotion of education and public
health, the organization of national defense...." The communists,

if they state the reasons for human activity, use the vocabulary that is familiar to us: the lack of allurement and the matter-of-fact quality of this language are connected in both cases with a hatred of the costly splendors of the feudal world. This limited vocabulary, implying a reprobation of the concern with ostentation that is the prerogative of sovereignty, is shared by the politicians of the bourgeoisie and those of the proletariat. It is merely firmer, it takes on a narrower meaning if it is employed in the Soviet world. Stalin considers the workers' labor: in capitalist society this labor is divided, according to Marx, into two parts: with the first, the only necessary labor, the worker ensures his livelihood and that of his family; the second, which is *surplus labor*, ensures the profit of the owner. But – Stalin stresses this point – in Soviet society it would be "strange to speak of 'necessary' and 'surplus' labor." Indeed, under the conditions created by the dictatorship of the proletariat, "the labor contributed by the workers to society for the extension of production, the promotion of education and public health, the organization of defense, etc.," is just as "necessary to the working class, now in power, as the labor expended to supply the personal needs of the worker and his family." Marx defines as surplus labor what the owner basically regards as an excess available to use as he pleases, either for nonproductive personal expenditures or for accumulation. But this free disposal disappears in the socialist world. There, the product of labor furnished beyond the personal needs of the worker is no longer a surplus. The need it meets is collective and its necessary character is held to be indisputable. The military and medical functions and education are radically different from the corresponding feudal activities, whose dominant aspect was glory, nonproductive culture, ostentation or voluntary charity. In the capitalist world, development goes in the same direction as in socialist society, but nothing is blocked. It is only in the precise language of Stalin that things appear blocked. Take accumulation in particular: it is not by chance that accumulation is cited in the first instance. On the part of the bourgeois, accumulation was the result of a choice; the bourgeois were, and they remain, *free* to invest their resources in productive enterprises; they were *free* to indulge rather in extravagant spending. The workers, if they accumulate, emphasize the *necessity* that accumulation satisfies; by this very fact, they dismiss – at least temporarily – the possibility of giving the present moment precedence over the future.

This is doubtless what must be done if it is foolish to live enjoying one's resources, not caring about increasing them. In this case, the individual's freedom in the bourgeois world is the freedom not to be reasonable. But in socialism only the collectivity is concerned, and by definition the great number is consistent with reason; in principle, socialist rigor alone is consistent with reason.

3. The Dialectic of Ends and Means in the Denial of Sovereignty

Communism, or, if we prefer, Stalinism, has proved to be the most effective means of increasing a country's productive forces. In this sense it replaces chance with necessity, and for that it sacrifices free initiative. But the need to accumulate is variable, and it isn't always necessary to go fast. We may ask ourselves whether the proletarian revolution, bringing about a change of the same order, but faster and deeper, as that of the bourgeois revolutions, may be suited to situations different from those that led to bourgeois regimes.

The communist method is in fact appropriate in countries that have very limited actual resources, assuming there is the possibility of increasing them. In relatively wealthier countries (to say nothing of those having little in the way of raw materials and little means of obtaining more), it is not necessarily so foolish to be less concerned about the primacy of production of the means of production. It is not always so foolish to prefer *the present moment to the future,* or rather, it is only a matter of knowing *when* the present moment is preferable to the future. But without speaking of a total overthrow, the situation may not be so bad. It may require that one settle for incomplete measures. The lack of rigor in the distribution of products and defective justice and equality doubtless do not have all the importance that is commonly attributed to them: in any case, this lack of rigor goes hand in hand with a slower accumulation — that is, with an easier life in spite of everything, and not just for the privileged class but for the people as a whole.

The general question of the opportune moment and of the value of methods is obviously not susceptible of a simple answer. It would be convenient to define economically the situations that accord with private accumulation and those that call for collective accumulation. But it seems better to me to judge *after the event,* on the basis of results. The future brings into play too many factors that will only appear later; moreover, numerous reasons support my decided intention to adhere, in the present circumstances, to the principle of uncommitted reflection.

However, I do think it is possible to speak of the advantage that collective accumulation represented for those who made that choice, of what they expect from it in exchange for the privations they have borne.

I drew attention to the fact that in a communist system the basic ends of the effort do not seem at first sight to go beyond the ruling necessity. It is a matter of satisfying not superfluous requirements of *luxury* but those requirements that it is *necessary* to meet.

Indeed, it is with good reason that Stalin defines as a necessity the requirement to expand production, health services, national defense or education. But is it possible to think that the *end* of the effort comes down to the satisfaction of these needs? How can one fail to see that such ends are actually means? Education, for example, understood in the spirit of communism, is only a means, as in the phrase "the production of the means of production." Education is itself a means of production, and production cannot be understood as anything but a means. We might be tempted to imagine that the Soviet conception of life resembles that of all men whose resources are small but whose character is firm, that it actually resembles the conception of proletarians of capitalist countries to whom the bosses granted only the possibility of surviving in exchange for their labor: ownership of the newly produced means of production would not necessarily change this conception. But in the bourgeois world, all the surplus labor is not reserved for the accumulation of the capitalists; only part of the profit goes into investment; another part is the basis of luxury.... The proletarian frame of mind might in fact exclude luxury, but does this mean that it tolerates nothing that goes beyond necessity?

The truth is that it would be crude to imagine a world in which this sequence would close everything. It might be easy to say that this is the case, but the essential point would be missed. In Stalin's view, socialist production has an *end* that he is anxious to distinguish from the *means* that it is: "Men produce," he says,[30] "not for production's sake, but in order to satisfy their needs." Thus, he vigorously criticizes a rather confused Soviet economist, L. Yaroshenko, for whom "production is converted from a means into an end," and who refuses to recognize that "the aim of socialist production" is "to secure the maximum satisfaction of the constantly rising material and cultural requirements of the whole

of society," who refuses to see that this aim is man and consequently his needs.[31]

An unavoidable difficulty begins at this point. In part, these
requirements consist in the necessity of ensuring useful functions
such as food supply, technical education, medical services and so
on. And when Stalin evokes the "satisfaction of material and cultural requirements" it is difficult not to place such functions in
the foreground. Would this man and the satisfaction of his needs,
to which Stalin refers, be themselves anything else but "means
of production"? Even if Stalin tells us that these needs are constantly growing, it is difficult not to think that this growth might
be the result of the constant growth of productive forces.... That
is doubtless true in part, but the important thing is that it is not
entirely true.

4. Only Complete Nondifferentiation Has the Power To Deny Differentiated Sovereignty and Thereby To Frame a Preliminary Affirmation of Undifferentiated Society

In his *Economic Problems of Socialism*, Stalin attempted to define
"the basic conditions required to pave the way for the transition
to communism."[32] In Stalin's view, this transition presupposes
"substantial changes in the status of labor. For this it is necessary,
first of all, to shorten the working day at least to six, and subsequently to five hours." But it is not a question, we should say, of
obtaining this free time for workers in order to give them an
enjoyment of the present moment. Indeed, for Stalin this reduction of labor time is "needed in order that the members of society might have the necessary free time to receive an all-round
education." With this it seems that we are brought back to the
obstacle of those needs that are nothing more, finally, than useful functions of production. Moreover, Stalin specifies the aims
of this supplementary instruction: he foresees a "universal com-

pulsory education, which is required *in order that the members of society might be able to choose their occupations and not be tied to some one occupation all their lives.*"³³

As to these last words that I have underlined, I suppose they will seem insignificant at first. Yet, they and they alone introduce into this sequence of subordinate activities, into this series of requirements that are functions, an element that is not reducible to a means. Doubtless, Stalin has taken into account the need to use technicians with multiple capacities to meet the changing requirements of production. But it is not at all important from my point of view to consider the practical value of these ideas. They may be utopian, or judicious. I don't imagine the possibility of knowing this is within my reach, and in a sense it doesn't matter. But we would be mistaken, seriously mistaken, if we thought this resolve to negate social difference with a view to annihilating it was insignificant.

Social difference is at the basis of sovereignty, and it is by positing sovereignty that the men of distant times gave differentiation its full scope: it was the developed forms of sovereignty that created the greatest possible difference between persons at its inception. This radical will, this central will to suppression represents a modest contribution on the part of Stalin, if one must account for a formulation that goes to the heart of the matter. The will to abolish differences is not attributable to Stalin's initiative. It was a theme of Marxism from the beginning, but Stalin gave it a precise form: the unexpected, anodyne and pedestrian form that I have spoken of. This proposal issuing from a statesman holding absolute power is surprising for its lack of solemnity, peculiar in such a case. We might even imagine, but wrongly it seems to me, a certain thoughtlessness on the part of its author. No doubt, it is more simply a matter of not wanting to dwell on a point perceived in the long view. It is not characteristic of men

THE WORLD OF DENIED SOVEREIGNTY

of action to think too insistently about the end they have in view; for them the interest of the action, in some sense placed in the light of the end, is substituted each day for the interest of that end, *in the present time*. The unremitting and inexpiable hatred of sovereign forms, of everything that expresses and arbitrarily ensures the personal sovereignty of a master, does seem to have been the basis of Stalin's revolutionary rigor (as it definitely was of all that was irresistible, contagious and ultimately overwhelming in the workers' movement).

Stalin's father was born a serf, "a chattel slave to some Georgian landlord,"[34] His mother was the daughter of a serf. For him, the condition of a man under the feudal master's thumb was the most familiar thing. His father had attempted to extricate himself, trying, but in vain, to become a petit bourgeois. Moreover, Stalin hated his father, who drank, his mother and himself being the victims.[35] He was first in his class, he was gifted and his ascendancy asserted itself early on. But, because of these very gifts, the only place accessible to him in this world was the one that revolutionary activity allowed him to carve out for himself. The authority he came up against was violent, it was that of the feudal world; he could not submit to it, and against it he undertook not the parliamentary struggle of Western politicians but a struggle for life or death.

For such a man, then, the suppression of differences, and of the sovereignty that is their major consequence, clearly denotes that return to sovereignty which is represented by all the forms of the sovereignty of others. But the absence of differentiation as a goal does not just have the negative meaning of an abolition of sovereign values. It cannot help but have a corresponding positive meaning. If every man is destined for complete nondifferentiation, he abolishes all alienation in himself. He stops being a thing. Or rather, he attains thinghood so fully that he is no longer

301

a thing. In becoming, by means of an *all*-around qualification, a fulfillment of the thing, a perfection of utility, hence of servility, he stops being reducible to a *particular* element, as things are. A thing is *alienated*, it always exists *in relation* to something else, but if it is connected with *all* that is possible, it is no longer determinate, nor alienated; it is not any more a thing than would be what I imagine in front of me, which I could not name, and which, being neither a table nor a stream, could be a stream, a table – or whatever one wanted....

If the all-around education that Stalin wanted to give to communism's consummate man were relatively worthy of the name, this man, at a time when the works of material civilization cannot be abandoned, would draw as close as possible to that kind of sovereignty which, linked to the voluntary respect of the sovereignty of others, would go back to that initial sovereignty that we must ascribe to the shepherds and hunters of ancient humanity. But the latter, if they respected the sovereignty of others, respected it only, it must be said, as a matter of fact.

5. *Stalin and the Meanders of History*
The perspective of nondifferentiation can obviously be given as the *end* of history. But in the first place, here sovereignty is not itself an *end* (quite on the contrary): in a fundamental way, nondifferentiation is even, in the first place, the negation of sovereignty. Insofar as we speak of an *end*, what is wanted is to arrive at nondifferentiation through *all*-around education. But sovereignty cannot be understood as a form that history would realize. If it appears in the perspective of history, this is because it was already given; history merely rids men of that which kept them from finding it. Still, it goes without saying that the perspective revealed through Stalin's vision is given only through a thick fog. It is necessary to look first, toward that distant and scarcely visi-

302

ble point, at the meanders of historical turmoil, whose complexity is definitely greater than Stalin thought (or said).

I am not talking about those difficulties inherent in human changes that, aiming at a perfect state, are produced in the imperfect milieu we know. Apart from a general hindrance, which is gravity, the meanders I speak of have disconcerting aspects.

Stalin could have seen for himself what the detours of history have about them that is ultimately not just disconcerting but terrifying. Nothing prevented him from observing the paradoxical character of the paths taken by the liberation of the worker-slave, which Marx propounded, when those paths lead to nondifferentiation and all-around abilities. How could he have kept from being troubled by that perfect disposition of human possibilities that presupposes the elimination of the choice that man can personally make? In spite of being well accustomed, it is surprising to read this proposition: after the exhausting labor of Soviet industrialization, to envisage the reduction of the working day to five or six hours, in order to devote one's free time thus obtained to *compulsory* all-around education!

I would like to say it without repugnance, and without undue admiration: in Stalin's destiny there is an element of excessiveness that fills one with awe; this destiny is not comparable to any other. This party leader near death, defining man liberated from the sovereignty of others and from difference (a future, but still distant result of the effort in which he had involved an immense people), had given himself the prerogatives of a sovereign![36] One could not imagine a longer detour on the paths by which history ensures (is supposed to ensure) the development of human possibilities. We cannot doubt his sincerity, but the effects of his action, which are prodigious by any standard, at least demanded of him a strength of nerves without parallel.[37] This is true to such a degree that if we reflect on that life, and on the moral consequences that follow from it, we ourselves need to have an exceptional tranquillity. Reflection, which gravitates toward simplification, must constantly be brought back to complex perspectives, which are often imposing and nearly always unclear. No one, in any case, was able to bring into sharper focus an ambiguous and sticky element that made historicist thought an uncontrolled mechanism, insofar as it engaged in its battles.

6. Digression on Stalin's Governing Thought

In any case, Stalin's own thought, far from being able to solve the problems that the enormous scope of his action presented to him, could not clearly discern that which, in Marx's ideas on the revolution of advanced peoples, departed from the actual course of history. He was not able to see that such a revolution was to be the prelude to a final antagonism between the poor countries and the rich, opposing, once the feudal world was destroyed, poor proletarians and rich bourgeois.

Indeed, it is time to point out that, in a notable instance, his faithfulness to the Marxist schema involved him in a real oddity. This time it is a question of faithfulness to one of Lenin's theses (but this thesis makes sense only if nothing disturbs the Marxist doctrine concerning the revolutions of industrial countries). Moreover, the relevant passage from *Economic Problems of Socialism* is the only one that has attracted general notice. Section six of the first part is titled "Inevitability of Wars between Capitalist Countries." Paradoxically, Stalin asserts in this section that "Lenin's thesis that imperialism inevitably generates war" is in no way obsolete. Even after World War II, the antagonism between the different capitalist countries would be, according to him, stronger than the antagonism between capitalists and communists. Everybody thinks that, in the present world, the only important wars to anticipate would set bourgeois against proletarians. But Stalin doesn't agree.

> When Hitler Germany declared war on the Soviet Union, the Anglo-French-American bloc, far from joining with Hitler Germany, was compelled to enter into a coalition with the U.S.S.R. against Hitler Germany. Consequently, the struggle of the capitalist countries for markets and their desire to crush their competitors proved in practice to be stronger than the contradictions between the capitalist camp and the socialist camp.

For Stalin nothing has changed!

This way of looking at things, which made sense at a time when the group of capitalist countries was much stronger than the communist power, undoubtedly expresses a logic of the situation that Stalin must have found compelling. He set himself to the task of averting a new world war by means of the "peace movement." There is no reason to question his intentions. But "the aim of this movement," he says, "is not to overthrow capitalism and establish socialism – it confines itself to the democratic aim of preserving peace."[38] "It is possible," he adds, "that...the fight for peace will develop here or there into a fight for socialism...." But above all, the peace movement, which may prevent a "*particular* war," "will not be enough to eliminate the inevitability of wars between capitalist countries generally."[39]

This is what, in my opinion, can be concluded from Stalin's statements. Stalin envisioned the recurrence of a war between imperialists, analogous to the Hitler war, in which the *USSR* would intervene in the last instance. This accords with a principle that Stalin had adopted as early as 1925 with a view to the war that was in the works, which would become inevitable: he said, "not tomorrow, nor the day after tomorrow, but in a few years." Today we know Stalin's basic scheme from the secret speech he made to the Party Central Committee in 1925, and published in 1947. This is the crucial passage:

> Our banner is still the banner of *peace*. But if war breaks out we shall not be able to sit with folded arms. We shall have to take action, but we shall be the last to do so. And we shall do so in order to throw the decisive weight in the scales....[40]

It's true that this principle does not exactly correspond with Stalin's attitude during World War II, but only because Hitler brought him into action earlier than he had anticipated. Further, we can know precisely what Stalin thought concerning World War III. Taking Stalin's place at the Twentieth Congress of the Communist Party of the USSR, on October 5, 1952, Malenkov read a report, partly inspired by the *Economic Problems of Socialism*, in which he returns to the theme of "the inevitability of wars between capitalist countries." "As a result of the First World War," says Malenkov, "Russia dropped out of the system of capitalism, while as a result of the Second World War a whole series of countries in Europe and Asia dropped out of the system of capitalism. There is every reason to assume that a third world war would bring about the collapse of the world capitalist system."[41] This outlook is what one could expect, but it is of some interest that this final corollary of Stalin's thought was furnished by the current head of government of the USSR.

This thinking, in which blindness so often followed visual acuity, persisted after a half-century's experience as if nothing had changed. Stalin died without having perceived the world's division into two homologous halves, much closer to one another than he thought, and than most people think today. He overlooked the

fact that the economic mechanisms of these two halves were similar and he didn't see that their opposition essentially concerned
relative poverty and wealth.

This way of thinking, which is elucidated – and nicely completed – by the Malenkov quote, yields an easy inference. Stalin
evidently thought what Marx and Moltke both expounded: that war
was the motor of history, and that without wars the world would
stagnate. But he expressly thought that nothing was changed. We
are only half-surprised at this. Who could forget the clear voice
of Lenin: "Do you think that we might lay hold of a world that
has not bled to the bitter end?" We can no longer ignore the
meaning this *to the bitter end* now has, of that implication which,
if Stalin had not lacked imagination, would have taken his breath
away. But Stalin gave no heed to it. He didn't care to ask himself
how a world that, this time, would have literally *bled to the bitter
end* could still be liberated. He didn't ask himself, in the interro-
gation of the night, whether he might not rather abandon any concern with liberation. But enough said: *What this world will be* we
don't know; we can even say that this world is in no way susceptible of being known – *what it will not be* suffices. It is not reasonable to envision, through *the immensity of its ruins,* the radiant
future that Stalin announced to his supporters. Marx had seen the
proletariat as the heir of the bourgeois industrial plant. But all
indications are that instead of benefiting from the riches that capitalism accumulated, the victorious proletariat would find the
entire world in the situation in which Germany would have been
in 1945 if the damage had been much more extensive and if it
had not been able to expect any aid from the outside. Stalin made
other mistakes, which chance repaired, but would his successors
have any reason to count once again on chance to set things right?
In the present case, it's obviously a matter of resorting to a strat-
agem *that has succeeded:* let the bourgeois nations tear one another

307

to pieces and intervene only at the end, in a decisive manner.... Let us remember, however, that the old dictator seems basically to have realized that the responsibility to start the war – *or to make it inevitable, which might easily result from the development of revolutionary activity* – could hardly be envisaged by a socialist power. He intended at all costs to count on the bourgeoisie to unleash the inevitable conflict. With this in mind, he forgot that the bourgeois, properly speaking, have themselves never started a conflict of global importance, but only the feudal lords – the Germans or the Russians – or the Nazis. But in that way, he expressed the irreconcilability of revolution and war, and of the coming world war and the imperialist political calculations. But there is an awkward contradiction in this: without the error of imperialist war there would be no revolution to win the rest of the world; only "a third world war would bring about the collapse of world capitalism." It is possible to doubt the likelihood of an American preventive war (the American people and the bourgeois democracies of Europe are opposed to it). So it was necessary to imagine that war was *inevitable* between the great capitalist nations.

If I have interpreted the facts correctly, that "governing thought" is not convincing. Stalin's mistakes were numerous and they did not all result from that ruthlessness that Lenin worried about in his testament. In any case, we can't see how the darkness in which the nations are now floundering could be illuminated by a dogmatic assertion. I will come back to the situation of the threat of war and to the consequences that follow from it, for the reason that not only does what I am talking about depend on it, but this situation itself depends on what I am talking about. What I wanted to show, first of all, in Stalin's quite ambiguous and complex position, is the shape that sovereignty necessarily assumes in revolutionary circumstances.

Sovereignty within the Limits

of Soviet Society

1. The Necessity of a Deeper Search for the
Meaning of Communism

Thus far, I have focused only on the most immediately visible aspects. I have spoken of the general opposition of accumulation and nonproductive consumption, without examining its underlying principles. Further, with regard to bourgeois society and Stalinist society, I have merely shown that they opposed feudal society in much the same way. If one got down to fundamentals, the opposition between the West and the USSR would cease to be negligible. But examining the system of values peculiar to the USSR leads to a deeper inquiry, without which the meaning of communism could not be entirely grasped.

I tried first of all to bring out aspects of communism that are obscured in equal measure by the contrary propagandas.

Stalin, like Marxists in general, did not see that communism might finally amount to being a means of development of the poor countries; that, all things considered, the hostility of the USA and the USSR is mainly that of the richest countries to the poorest – and of the poorest to the richest.... This is, no doubt, an altered form of class antagonism: in both nations, from the top to the bottom, all the social strata are in it together. Even in countries where the internal opposition continues (France, Italy), certain factors are lacking, which gave the class struggle its vigor, and which depended on the opposition of the sovereign principle of feudal hierarchy to the utilitarian principle of the productive masses. This opposition disappears, or lessens, if the workers no longer lay the blame on idle lords, but on hardworking bourgeois.

As I have said, Marxists in general nonetheless differ from the bourgeois: they push to its strict consequences the negation of the principles on which human societies as a whole were based prior to our revolutions. Like the Marxists, the bourgeois oppose consumption and affirm the primacy of accumulation. But the bourgeois revolutionaries never had a closed system: they only upheld free choice against the squandering tradition of the past. Free choice, in their eyes, would guarantee a preference for rea-son, which condemned nonproductive spending. They combated tradition, certain of defeating it. They were half-mistaken, but they were mistaken.... The Marxists replaced free choice with a blanket decision, in the face of which, caprice – whether war-ranted by tradition or not – ultimately became criminal. Each individual must, of necessity, put an end to his deviations, each one must make his behavior depend on decisions of a State that assumed a leadership becoming increasingly meticulous. The Communist Party – or rather the machinery of the Party, whether this came down to one person or not – determined for everyone a system of values that could no longer be questioned. However, as I see it, the question is not whether the general decision can be condemned on principle. I think that it can't, but that an inter-pretation by one individual, or a small number of individuals, or the thought of an immense people, bears the stamp of dispropor-tion: the overly constrained decision, be it constrained by an unquestionable need, must be adjusted, in the second instance, to general behaviors that are less deliberate, unsystematic and popular, in the sense of thoughtlessness, of unthinking blindness. Without a general decision overriding individual mood, no society would be possible. But the result of constraint never has any meaning except after the fact, once the constraint has relaxed.

Be that as it may, the question of sovereignty is usually poorly formulated; in particular, it is poorly formulated if we confuse it with the autonomous decision of an individual. If it is not the calling into play of a sovereign principle, going beyond what is useful, an autonomous decision may have no sovereign quality at all; it may even be servile; it may show the subservience of the one who freely made it. Basically, sovereignty never has anything personal about it. Only a personal value is involved in the decision that sets accumulation (the concern with increasing production) against consumption (the immediate pleasure). The individual decision is meaningful only to the extent that it expresses a value supported by a common approbation. As a rule, the individual is inclined to nonproductive consumption[42] – more so than society as represented by the State – but this means only one thing: the individual is more readily, less dangerously, blind and thoughtless. He is (perhaps in the aggregate, but especially in the person of the privileged few) happier in a blind and thoughtless society. But one can be sure that the individual never decides except ostensibly: indeed, it is his fate to submit, to follow: it's true that in our societies he chooses for himself, but the effect of this choice is perceptible only when it is that of the masses. It is the *prevailing values* that decide concerning accumulation and expenditure (and one might even say that the value that gives primacy to accumulation is favorable to individual autonomy: one might, I imagine, more easily say the opposite). No doubt, these prevailing values are themselves determined; they are determined, it appears, by economic factors (thus primarily agricultural production is more favorable to sovereign values, and chiefly industrial production to productive values), but for the moment I don't intend to dwell on that: I wanted to come around to the way the prevailing values function in communism, for the reason that communism means above all the values that it causes to prevail. As in every society, in communism these values are of two kinds. Every society is based on the affirmation of certain useful values, but also on a sovereign value. And the deep meaning of communism is conveyed only by the principles it brings to the fore in these two categories, and by the relations of these principles among themselves.

I arrive then, beyond the simplified forms of the accumulation-expenditure opposition, at a critical analysis of the operations that may be designated by these terms and, at the same time, at an analysis of the value judgments that accompany them.

2. The Utilitarian Justifications of Classic Nonproductive Expenditure, or the Reduction of Sovereign Values

In principle all *useless consumption,* all nonproductive spending, implies recognition of a sovereign value that justifies it, whereas the value involved in accumulation is a function of productivity. But if we engage in nonproductive spending, spending that, in principle, is not justified by any clear utility, this is rarely mere squander: we are always, or very nearly, looking for some result. This spending may be socially useless, it may be, from the standpoint of the overall wealth of a people, a pure and simple loss. Suppose a pretty woman buys an evening gown. The labor used to make this gown could have gone into a more useful product, for example warm clothes for children. But this woman may think of her gown as a means. First of all, she will use it to make herself alluring. Perhaps in making herself alluring she intends to do a useful deed, for example by seeking funds that will make it possible to give warm clothes to poor children. In a sense, this is the most favorable case, but the utility would not be any less, she would only be selfish, if she sought a wealthy lover, or generally speaking, more prestige, hence more power. The same holds true in nearly all cases. Let us take the example of the saint, of the woman who in the search for ecstasy consumes the means of life that society grants her. She might have taken care of sick people, but instead of action she chooses contemplative unproductiveness, a choice sanctioned by the Gospel: to Martha, who attended to the necessary duties, Jesus preferred Mary, who spurned low tasks in order to lift up her soul to God. The Gospel may be essentially on the side of sovereign values. The saint nonetheless feels that she must justify her behavior by asserting its utility. She justifies it to herself by making the contemplative life the price of her salvation. True, Saint Teresa said she would do the same thing if the fires of hell were waiting for her. But religious contemplation is still listed on the balance sheet as one of the divine graces owed to the population that surrounds the convent. We may think what we wish of salvation and of those graces, but no matter: in any case and in every instance, the utilitarian interpretation is given of the most brazenly nonproductive behaviors. A nun intoxicated with God, a coquette intoxicated with clothes come to seek in the same way for the meaning of that which is perhaps at bottom only a senseless passion.

3. The Sovereign Value of Communism Is Man, but It Is the Man Who, in Order To Produce Better, Has Renounced Sovereignty

In reality, sovereign values, which alone justify nonproductive expenditures, are not necessarily conscious, and if they are conscious they are seldom affirmed. Passion, desire and their immediate satisfaction put on reasons that disguise them and give them the appearance of a useful means. Conversely, if the principle of

313

a sovereign value is affirmed beyond the value of utility (the pure means), it remains vague and, lacking definition, is hard to distinguish from that which it aims to contradict. Stalin arguing against Yaroshenko, who paradoxically limits value to productivity, does not cite desire, but "man and his needs," which may be different from productivity, but not very different. For this man, cited by Stalin, is above all a producer and the satisfaction of his needs, far from harming production, serves to increase it.

The first way of reducing the sovereign order to the utilitarian is the rule in the bourgeois world. But precisely this way of transposing the truth cannot withstand the communist critique. If it is a question of utility, most nonproductive expenditures are inadmissible. From the communist point of view, those expenditures that are not selfish are futile. Moreover, communism would reject a justification that would be based on their sovereign value: why would it accept on these grounds that which its enemies defend by alleging useful values it does not deem to be such? For a Marxist, a value beyond the useful is conceivable, and even inevitable, but it is immanent in man or it is not a real value. What transcends man (man living here below of course), or likewise that which goes beyond ordinary humanity (humanity without privilege), is unquestionably inadmissible. The sovereign value is man: production is not the only value, it is but the means to satisfy man's needs; it serves him, and not the reverse.

The Marxist position is obviously the most solid one. The bourgeoisie maintains those values that it no longer dares to call sovereign, which, modestly, it has named "spiritual," but doing so it pays tribute to utility, and thus to productivity, which, barely outdone by Yaroshenko, it makes the measure of things.

We still need to ask whether man, to whom communism refers production, did not take on this sovereign value on one prior condition: to have renounced, for himself, everything that is truly

314

sovereign. He becomes the measure of things, it's true, but perhaps to this end he had to deny himself? He is still a man, no doubt, he brings production into his service; but if he brings it into his service he does not do this without having given in to its demands, that is, without having abdicated. For the irreducible desire that man *passionately, capriciously* is, communism substituted those of our needs that can be reconciled with a life entirely taken up with producing.

We should finally ask ourselves, then, whether this world, communist or bourgeois, which gives primacy to accumulation is not obliged, in some form, to deny and suppress (or at least attempt to) what there is within us that is not reducible to a means, what is sovereign.

4. The Need To Stop, by Means of a Decisive Negation, the Movement by Which Language Always Makes a Sovereign End into a Means to Something Else

The mania of the present world may be pointless. Here or there, a sovereign share is somehow inviolable within us – in each of us perhaps, in a certain number of individuals at the least. To deny or suppress it makes no more sense than the effort of Sisyphus. That effort, it must be said, was under way long before the triumph of accumulation. What has always been peculiar to sovereignty lies in the strange and elusive quality that makes it both inevitable and impossible. In the present age, which ignores it or opposes it, and is excited by little else but possible productivity, the elusive character of that which is properly sovereign ensures its decline (if not its disappearance). But the past itself could never truly affirm it, and could never ensure its preeminence with any certainty. The point is that sovereignty, sovereign value – which language itself requires, since it always goes back a little further in the concatenation of means and ends – is never given unambiguously in that very language which requires it. Indeed, although language tells us that the means postulates an end, it must, no sooner than this end is stated, still answer the question – What is the use of it? – which, in some manner, and like a threat, remains suspended over the final cause, whatever it may be. Language implies the necessity of ends, in relation to which it defines the means, but it cannot isolate an end and say of it, positively, that it is of *no use:* it cannot keep from inserting that end into an endless circle of propositions where there is never any apogee, where nothing ever stops, where nothing is *lost.* The *loss,* at the apogee, is what is extremely disconcerting to the speaker, and it is something that only the movement of "negative theology" has the power to contemplate as an object, if it is true that in that movement the object in question negates itself as an object, that it becomes an absence of an object. It is strange, no doubt, to bring God into these unavoidable reflections – but avoided up to now – on accumulation and expenditure. It is all the more strange as the author is an unbeliever, an atheist even. But this affords me the opportunity to recall that God, initially, *historically,* is the hypostasis of sovereignty. The language difficulty to which I refer was first encountered by the theologians, who were the first to speak of what is sovereign in the world, of what is not subordinate: "positive theology" inserted God in the chain of ends and means, of means that serve ends and of ends that are always the means of some other effect (God, in "positive theology," is the Creator), but the impasse of "positive theology" is emphatically underscored in the reversal that "negative theology" constitutes. Here I must return to something I said elsewhere,[43] which I introduced with this passage from Dionysius the Aereopagite,[44] one of the most famous spokesmen of "negative theology": "Those who by an inward cessation of all intellectual functioning enter into an intimate union with ineffable light...only speak of God by negation."[45] I went on to say:

> This is what one finds when it is experience and not presupposition which reveals (to such an extent that, in the eyes of the latter [Dionysius], light is "a ray of darkness"; he would go so far as to say, in the tradition of Eckhart: "God is Nothingness"). But positive theology – founded on the revelation of the Scriptures – is not in accord with this negative experience. Several pages after having evoked this God whom discourse only apprehends by negating, Dionysius writes,[46] "He possesses absolute dominion over creation..., all things are linked to him as to their center, recognizing him as their cause, their principle, and their end...."

Thus, in this desperate tension – which theology comments on, and which men maintained in order to grasp that which, beyond the useful, is authentically sovereign – nothing short of the vehemence of negation – aggressive, *provocative* – would foil the stubborn effect of reasoning, bound and determined to link every entity to its effects, to reduce it to its actions. Even within "negative theology," the doggedness of language reappears, making, positively, the divine entity into an action creating something other than itself. This other thing is, it's true, subordinated to the entity that is the cause, the principle and the end. But God nevertheless has in his positive representation a sense that must be denied with passion, if he is not to be reduced to the *Good Lord* whom his works manifest, who is conceived, so wretchedly, only in his works.

317

5. *Man as the Sovereign End of Man,*
Heir of the Kings and of God

Insofar as it derives from Feuerbach, the Marxist tradition sees
in man what theology saw in God. In other words, it substitutes
an anthropology for the theology of the Christians. This means,
above all, that a Marxist regards man as the heir, and the sole heir,
of divine sovereignty. Being nothing more in his eyes than a mythical, objectified form, of which, subjectively, man is the underlying and sole reality, God has this still possible meaning: what
His sublime attributes have represented and continue to represent
is an image of *human* sovereignty. Not the sovereignty of a privileged human being, *of royal blood:* this sovereignty that Marxist
thought can and indeed must envision is that of the nonalienated
man, which *every* man potentially is. There is really nothing more
contrary to the extremely troublesome image that ancient humanity, personified by the kings, gave itself.

It is even necessary, in order to define the meaning of sovereign
value in a Marxist world, to point up what was negligible and
profoundly inhuman about the sovereignty of the feudal world.
However, the all but general determination to disregard those sovereign values that are immanent in man, that dominated humanity
up to our time, can be suspected of being finally just a reflection of sensibilities affected either by a still living hatred or by a
somnolent accord. Unquestionably, royal sovereignty became
dull, more so than any other, because of the reduction of the end,
which it aimed to be, to the means that it always was in the hands
of those who were invested with it. But this aspect is secondary,
and the ignorance in which we have persisted as to the precise
meaning that, over millennia, the kings had for their subjects, our
deliberately maintained incomprehension of the demand – so lasting, so insistent – which they satisfied, which indeed, in a number of countries, they still satisfy, only demonstrate one point:

that the present movement of the intellect has dodged and continues to dodge the problem of the sovereign end.

This tendency is even what defines the modern intellect, and it cannot surprise those who, on the other hand, are led to see in thought, as in every superstructural phenomenon, that which the infrastructure conditions. In a world whose forces of production would not exist had capitalist accumulation not made their development possible, the intellectual mainstream readily considers the means and, on the contrary, it turns away from the problems that the ends of activity leave open. These problems are considered in the Marxist world, which must take up again the whole problematic of action. As I said, for Stalin, following Marx, man, man alone and, potentially, every man, is the sovereign end of man's labor. But this response is given in a devil-may-care manner: it is first of all a matter of denying those sovereign ends of the past that God and the kings constituted. But the glorification of man, whose charm has taken the place of God's in particular, is only sketched out in the communist tradition. The meaning of this glorification is not deepened, on the contrary: it is only touched upon, as is the fashion in a world where we are so tightly constrained to act that we always have a sense of what we are *doing* and never of what we *are*.

Yet, the fact of retaining that aspect of God which is the truth manifested in man obliges us, in principle, to take into account the ancient and, on the whole, popular form of man's divine prestige. It is true that a disclosure in man, and by man, of the sovereign end that the divine in essence is, seems fallacious, no doubt even detestable, if it occurs in the person of a king. But it does occur and it is not enough to say, as a Marxist would, that economic privilege is the only reason for, and meaning of, the royal dignity. The opposite comes closer to the truth. It is the appearance of excellence in the first kings that gained them their great material advantages: if force enabled war chiefs to seize the throne, it never *created* thrones. The thrones, which is to say, the custom of seeing in a single individual, objectified and condensed, the splendor that is common to all men insofar as they are not alienated, and which in any case was common to the most ancient men, who were doubtless neither chiefs nor sovereigns.[47]

What made royalty contestable, especially in a time of fever and revolution, of impatience, was that the sovereign end, which royalty was meant to embody in the eyes of the subjects, became, never more scandalously, a means for the very individual it was supposed to transfigure. The king received the royal prerogatives as a possession, which he could use unreservedly for his *personal* ends. Actually, if this had not been the case, he would not have been a sovereign: the royal function considered as the responsibility of a head of government is a conception rooted in the decline of the institution; this function, if the word fits, has always been to satisfy the crowd's expectation of splendor (of splendor, or if not, and much better, of religious charm). The royal dignity was an end, it was in no way a means. The embodiment of this end would have demanded that the king become one with that movement of cessation, of rupture, which the end constitutes, but often he was only a selfish man, sometimes even a miser. And all things considered, it was only in death, which he received from his own subjects (but doubtless, in principle, of his own accord) that the royal person could assume in everyone's eyes that unconditional charm that sets a sovereign end against the servile means. But the ritual of the "slaying of the king," although it was widespread and left many traces, did not have the force to oppose the ordinary wretchedness of royalty with a counterstatement as profound – or as obstinate – as the one that "negative theology" opposed to "positive theology."

Insofar as the memory of them remains in us, the kings none-theless continue to satisfy the impulse to make manifest an aspect of the human being that the necessity of labor has not entirely altered. If we lingered on this aspect, so evidently archaic, so clearly adapted in the past to the trickery and debasement that *interests* impose on it, we would lower ourselves to the rank of lingerers who still yearn for a regime less openly devoted to the primacy of utility. But if we attempt to rediscover an effaced figure visible through the royal forms, as one discovers on a palimpsest an ancient text beneath a medieval scripture, we respond to the concern that might, that should, haunt those who decided to give to man what our recent ancestors still gave to God.

At this point I can still only indicate the direction of an inquiry, but concerning the problem of sovereignty of present-day man, I can say that it is not connected merely with the struggles that this man had to conduct against the sovereign ends of the past (which determined, as I said, the two political forms that oppose us to one another): this problem could not be raised if we did not seek in the structures we have destroyed not the answers that are now antiquated but, beyond them, the primary exigency that these answers evaded. We can now recognize that man is himself and that he *alone* is the sovereign value of man, but this means above all that man was the real content of the sovereign values of the past. There was nothing in God, or in the kings, that was not first in man, and that without the alienation that reduces him I would rediscover in him what was enchanting in God or in the magnificence of the kings. I am mindful of the disappointing and tiresome aspects of those fallen figures, of the ways in which they were inhuman or paltry, but in front of their stiff grandeur, indeed in front of grandeur in general, I have to laugh and my laughter does not cease to confront their solemnity with defiance. I would be their slave without this defiance, I would not be the man who refuses their authority and whom their authority no longer alienates. But neither can I grant that man should remain in the lowly state in which they put him.

6. *The Sovereignty of Soviet Man Linked to the Sovereign Renunciation of Sovereignty*

I am well aware that I have not yet clearly defined the nonalienated man I have spoken of. Moreover, by placing him on an equal footing with God and kings, in particular with that God who, according to Eckhart, "is nothingness," or with the king who willingly allowed himself to be slain by those whose king he was, I may irritate or perplex a reader whom I am doubtless unable to enlighten. In contrast, the "man and his needs" that Stalin speaks of form a figure that is easy to grasp and I myself said that, because of the basic nondifferentiation with which Stalin associates him, this man satisfied the principle of the sovereign end – Stalin speaks discreetly of "value." Identifying value with productivity (as Yaroshenko did) left no meaning or place to the *end* of labor: the absurdity of this position was flagrant, since by itself labor is only a means. Yaroshenko merely brought out the impossibility for man to work without giving work a general justification, beyond obligation. To put it another way, the obligation must itself be justified by a positive, desirable character of the result. It is true that man defined as an end by Stalin does not himself have a sovereign character: his requirements are measured against the need to ensure and increase production. But this time we are dealing with an incontestable principle. I said that, in Stalin's view, man would himself become the sovereign end, but only provided he has renounced his claim to that sovereignty he discovers in himself; he loses it no doubt, but in a sovereign fashion, without losing it for another's benefit.

322

True, this last assertion is questionable: we might say, in the first place, that the subjects of the Soviet State were not free to renounce their potential sovereignty; second, that they apparently renounced it for the benefit of another, Stalin, who actually had rights over the Russian people analogous to those of a sovereign. These are perhaps superficial aspects. It is certain that the principles of life of the USSR, in particular those I am speaking of, even if they have not been the subject of a popular agreement, expressed under the conditions to which the populations of the West are accustomed, are spontaneously those of countless revolutionary militants. Further, it is true that the equivocal forms of Stalin's personal power – the humiliating flattery addressed to him, and even some of his character traits[48] – may have corresponded to the archaic spirit of a part of the Russians, indeed even to the longing for sovereigns that was scattered among the whole people, where the past obscurely survived perhaps. But these superficial aspects did not signify that Stalin was really, and for everyone, the sovereign for the benefit of whom the crowd, in order to make him the exterior object of its contemplation, formerly gave up its share of sovereignty: in actual fact, Stalin himself never accepted the essential attributes of a sovereignty of which he only had the *power* and not the *enjoyment*; Stalin is even the best example of man sovereignly renouncing the sovereignty he has at his disposal. What other men are capable of discovering in themselves is de jure sovereignty, whereas in a sense the sovereignty that Stalin found in himself was de facto sovereignty. This is not entirely true since, if he was in fact sovereign, this was conditional on a prior renunciation: he would never have been able to arrogate to himself the prerogatives of the king; the leisure and the dazzling ostentation were denied him; productivity was his lot. To be exact, war (but modern war in this case, which is labor from the first) is a part of sovereign glory that he might have

323

claimed for himself, but he does not appear to have given him-self up to military splendor. Apparently, he had no taste for it and, in any event, he owed his power to the responsibility he assumed of developing the communist domain, where man is sovereign, but provided he denies in himself the disposal of himself and of the world.

7. Sovereign Renunciation, unlike the Renunciation We May Effect for the Benefit of Another, Is Favorable to Accumulation

Stalin's uncertainty seems to have caused his successors to decide more clearly in favor of undifferentiated man, who abdicates. It seems that they renounce personal glorification, which is to say, that external manifestation of the concentration of power which is one of the signs of sovereignty. It furnishes an example, one that is not only concrete but actual, of the oppositions I speak of – that I sometimes speak of abstractly or by citing the past, which is no better. My decision not to try to clear up the prob-lem of the *ends* of labor without addressing the problem of roy-alty receives in this way the semblance of a justification. In my view, Stalin's life reveals a rather strange dilemma. It appears that not only is the question of the end of activity really raised, but that it is raised in the context of current politics. It is raised as follows: Men must always renounce personal sovereignty, but their renunciation can occur in two ways. If they renounce for the ben-efit of a sovereign, they can identify with him and, transposing their sacrificed sovereignty onto him, by contemplating it in his person they find the religious rapture that is their end; if, on the other hand, they are certain that the alleged sovereignty of the kings belongs to them, is none other than their own, they can renounce in a different, *sovereign* way, without bequeathing to another, a possession that seems inalienable to them but that they renounce, rationally, for their own sake. They place their sovereignty in renunciation.

Moreover, these contrary reactions are extremely significant: they correspond to the two systems of production whose diametrical opposition gives definition to the modern world. The greatest interest is accorded to sovereign *ends* in societies in which the population is monarchized; it is accorded to *means* when individuals renounce in a sovereign manner, but renounce, sovereignty. The pamphlet by Stalin that I remarked on is essentially concerned with productivity. Of course Yaroshenko is mistaken, and even seriously so, to make productivity the end of labor, but Stalin merely offers a quick correction in which man as an end is associated with requirements that are those of a producer. The primacy of nonproductive expenditure goes hand in hand with the popular interest that once constituted the strength of the monarchic institutions, but if, on the whole, the men who have the authority deny themselves, and deny others, any sovereign attitude, accumulation is favored. In a period when development of the productive forces compels accumulation, it is obviously desirable to minimize the attention that is given to the disinterested ends of productive activity.

PART THREE

The Negative Sovereignty of Communism and the Unequal Humanity of Men

ONE

Equivalence and Distinction

1. The Contesting of Values That Don't Concern the Working-class Militants

Whatever its effects, the sovereignty that is won and at the same time renounced could doubtless be offered as the best solution to a problem that, moreover, is of another age. In any case, this solution answers necessity, to the extent (questionable, it is true) that accumulation forces itself upon us.

Further on I will say from what perspective and in what way the present, in spite of everything, in spite of itself, transcends it. But the situation of communism raises, from the point of view of sovereignty, a new problem, as fundamental as the first one.

One of the least apparent results of communism is the rift it brings about, in the consciousness of the most sensitive men, between what they love and what they affirm: on the one hand, what secretly sustains them, on the other, what they openly say that they care about. A kind of timidity, of bad conscience, of shame, takes hold of minds at the idea of the lack of value, the lack of weight – compared with the concerns of communist politics – of what engages them personally. In itself, the individual feeling of a worker does not necessarily appear to them to be preferable, but the general importance of the proletariat give it preference: the only true value is the one that concerns a worker. What captivates only men who are relatively rich and cultivated does not count.

In these circumstances a kind of dispossessed man has formed, a man who no longer grants himself the right to live, except to deny what he deeply is, effacing himself at the least alarm. Often it's a question of persons who are well off, enjoying possessions that make life worth living in their eyes, but which, on the first occasion, they are sincerely prepared to declare of no acccount.[1]

Such an attitude is capable of displaying various aspects, according to the circumstances or values involved, but in any case communism is there, contesting the value of that which moves the most sensitive men.

The problem always comes down to the interest presented by such and such a product of a civilization whose generally human character is overlooked: this civilization's system deprives it of meaning; it has become the symbol of a defect, which is bourgeois life. Sometimes this object is a poem, a painting, a personage endowed with prestige; sometimes it is a strong feeling, a passion, an excessive joy: for men of bad conscience, these goods have a secondary importance, *working-class humanity* counts before *humanity* (before the forms of life that are common to men, but unevenly developed in the different classes).

2. Justification and Flimsiness of the Protests against Working-class Coarseness

Far from this bad conscience, minds given to anxiety – and to avarice – claim that civilization is fragile; that, perhaps even reluctantly, a social revolution would destroy the most precious assets of the civilized world. What is worthy of being loved requires oases in the midst of a society controlled by an awful necessity, refuges protected from what the theoreticians of communism regard as a fundamental reality. For communism, and perhaps with good reason, reality is manifested above all in the set of human relations that is connected, for example, with the activity of a mining center. Those who see civilization as fragile, who worry about it, think on the contrary that the values that don't have their place close to mine shafts deserve to be defended. Dissatisfied with their living conditions, the miners struggle to obtain other conditions, which answer their requirements, not the desires of certain idle profiteers of the "established order." In this way, they reduce civilization to the standard of basic needs. In principle, a pure and simple reduction, in the practice that is inherent in communism, is considered a bad thing by the communists themselves. On the whole, it nonetheless explains – and no doubt justifies – the "directives" concerning Soviet literature and art. I don't really see why a working-class world, exhausted by labor, would concern itself with the possibilities accessible to the minority that doesn't work. Actually, the bourgeois pessimists are right to take account of a radical difference between their value judgments and those of the workers. But the question goes beyond the narrow purview to which they deliberately confine themselves.

Here I will set out the primary terms of that question: *Isn't the generosity of the communistic intellectuals – and bourgeois – preferable to the avarice of the conservatives? Do those goods that make life worth living for both these groups deserve to be defended? When the voice of a throng condemned to the labor of the mines makes itself heard, what importance does the protest of a negligible refinement and a morbid sensitivity have?*

331

3. Classless "Humanity" and the More or Less "Human" Character That Founds the Division into Classes

Under the present conditions, this protest remains in the throats of most people. Even those who accuse communism of an error have received as their share that "bad conscience" which communism imposes on most of those whom it alarms. In our time, the moral effect of communism predominates. Refinement and morbid sensitivity are not openly defended (they are defended only from the angle of comfort).

The attitude of the communists is in fact the major position, to which anticommunism opposes only a line of insignificant positions, of contradictory positions. But this primary character of communism usually goes unrecognized because of a determination not to talk about it. Assuming one were to ask communists to state the *principles underlying* their morals, they would probably refuse. Everything is clear in their eyes; they have no need for discussion. The *consequences* of their moral stance are explicit. I will nevertheless attempt to bring to light the principles that justify it.

With respect to the various principles of living to which men have adhered, communism, by affirming nothing, and indeed "by the fact that it affirms nothing," implies a system of values that it is possible to define *after the event.*

The very silence of the doctrine places this first point beyond doubt: that the value principle is *man*, and man alone, *irrespective of any meaning or specific attribute* that we give him. It is not the attainment of a civilization, represented by those who benefit from it, it is any man, black or white, skilled or unskilled,

332

coarse, brutal or absurd, educated or illiterate.... The apparently sacred value thus implied in man must not be tied to any definition that would establish this sacredness. For communism there is not, and there cannot be, any other definition of man than that of the *natural* sciences, which sees no clear-cut difference between us and the animals: man is that primate, anatomically different from the (vanished) hominids and the apes, who are definitively characterized by the use and fabrication of tools.

If I introduced, beyond this rudimentary definition, any notion of the value that man has and that animals, plants or stones don't have (such as religiosity, consciousness), I would have to envisage a gradation whereby some men, more than others, would have this value as their share. The decision to assign in this way a *particular*, definable if not actually defined, value seems to us to be one of the attributes of the human race. For humanity as a whole – and even, in the end, for the communists – the human quality is not distributed equally among all men. Leaving aside religion properly speaking and consciousness, certain basic behaviors, our way of eating for example, or of evacuating, or sexual activity subject to rules, distinguish man from animals. From this point of view, each man is certainly superior to animals, but *more or less so:* the way in which he satisfies his *animal* needs is *more or less human.* Doubtless, the introduction of these particulars will surprise some people. Be that as it may, these kinds of distinctions are found in everyday life, at all levels of society. There are few men who have not on occasion been disgusted by the relative animality of another: this *more or less* humanity involves primary value judgments – based on repugnance and sympathy – which stand in contrast with the communist principle of equal value and which don't depend on a calculation of interest.

333

In this way, mankind gave rise to social classes that are distinguished not only by privileges, but also by a higher or lower degree of humanity. Often this division into classes overlaps the division of the species into different peoples and races, considered superior or inferior. But at bottom it is differences in the manner of eating or evacuating, or others, less simple, that are ultimately reducible to them, that underlie the judgments of superiority or inferiority of the different "classes."

Later I will try to elucidate the meaning and specify the range of these gradations, which operate in *religion* and in *consciousness*. But the morals implicit in communism are connected from the start with the principle of leaving the value judgments that are tied to these gradations in the background.

4. The Secondary Prohibition against Racial Hostility

External to the different material interests, the immediate judgment that decides about the relative humanity of an individual, a social level, or a people usually adapts itself to those interests. This is what leads Marxists, with apparent good reason, to deny the sense of the judgment.[2] This judgment is brought to bear in fact from the top to the bottom, hitting the oppressed classes or races and also operating at the lowest rung. The bourgeois are not the only ones to regard blacks as an inferior form of humanity, less removed than the whites from animality.[3]

But a secondary prohibition falls on these immediate reactions.[4] There is no question that primary prohibitions concerning the races have the most *inhuman* consequences (on the more or less human scale, nothing is more *animal* than Auschwitz). It is humiliating for the species to find in contempt for the other's animality an opportunity to slide toward a lower – and the least pardonable – brutality. But it is not logical to summarily condemn judgments and behaviors that only a higher prohibition has

334

defined as *inhuman*. From the bottom to the top of the scale, the impulses are of the same nature; it is never a question of anything else but putting a check on animality everywhere it appears. The lowest racism cannot hide the fact that in these aversions with regard to races or civilizations held to be inferior the primary problem is posed: it is a matter, for humanity, of what gives a meaning, a worth, a *sacred character* to the difference between man and the animals. It is a matter of judgments that establish the *human* quality.

5. Rationalism and the Prohibition against the Exploitation of Man by Man

It is always possible, however, to attribute to man a value without content, with only the most general, the vaguest, meaning. Such a thing is not so easy to maintain.

A judgment of this sort is not based on ordinary behaviors, given in experience. It derives from questionable intellectual operations. Reason sees in man in general a definite biological reality, but not the distinct and incomparable *value*, not the *sacred* entity. The sacred is given only in experience, as a fact, not as the result of a judgment, of a rational operation. No doubt, it is always possible to link irrational behaviors to a judgment of reason, behaviors such as those ordinarily connected with a flag, a fatherland, a leader. But this last operation is always illegitimate. It cannot truly satisfy reason. Nor does it have — at least it cannot have straight off — the "unquestionable" value of an irrational judgment based on the identical affectivity of a large number of people.

It would be crass to give too much importance to these kinds of ill-wrought representations. In the world where we *really* move, most intellectual operations are faked. The irrational is *explained* and the police limit the possible discussion (otherwise, how could the deserters be judged?).

335

It is easier to give an unjustified explanation of the irrational than to affirm its de facto existence, owing itself to chance, to the fortuitous agreement of the masses. There is *man* having over animals the privilege of the strength that a manufactured weaponry brings to him. We agree to give ourselves, as men, a dignity that animals don't have. We assert that reason justifies it, without seeing that this function bestowed it on us only after giving us weapons. If reason gains us a privilege, this is rationally; it is the cause of which privilege is the effect. Reason, not being the gift of the irrational, is not in a position to claim over the profane animals the irrational privilege of a sacred creature. But this incorrectness with respect to reason is sufficiently justified by its reasonable consequences.

Thus, communism does not have to consider the arbitrariness, in terms of reason, of the value that man traditionally attributes to himself.

Similarly, it does not have to pay too much attention to the difficulty implied in the condemnation of "the exploitation of man by man." This condemnation is based on the equivalence of men, just as exploitation is justified (insofar as the exploiter needs to justify it) by the inequality of their value. In one respect, moreover, communism has limited the principle of equivalence. For it, the word *human*, implying human dignity, is equally applicable to all men, but not to those among them who exploit their fellows. The exploiter is himself a man, but he has excluded himself from that quality which communism grants to all men alike. Communism returns in this roundabout way to the selection that by its nature it must deny. It appraises in its turn individuals, governments or classes according to the respect given to the prohibition, formulated by it, against exploitation.

It is by no means possible, on this basis, to claim that communism is poorly grounded. What is involved in this principle is

336

shifting, and the only reservation rests on the resistance of those unstable realities that action denies but does not abolish except by winning out.

However, I feel that a certain number of remarks are called for:

– *If "man in general" is worthy of respect, the impulse that establishes this respect is the same one that, from the very beginning, made unworthy of respect those men who did not behave in a "human" way.*

In other words:

– *If man is respectable, this respect is tied to the shame of the original animality, to man's repudiation of nature.*

·Or better:

– *If the universal man of communism has a value so great that it is criminal to exploit him, he gets it from the ancient "curse of man by man." The man of "classless society" owes the value in the name of which he destroyed the classes to the very impulse that divided humanity into classes.*

No one can deny it: The respect due to man is meaningful only insofar as I remain associated with the impulse that led men of all times to contest the humanity of all the others. Often this contestation is crude, but without it there would not have been any humanity since, at bottom, its initial impulse was the repudiation of animality. But it is this contestation that we find from one end to the other in the apparent ascent of man, as well as in the moments of decadence, of unjustified contempt, of baseness. The principle of equivalence is contrary to the essence of a species constituted in the ceaseless exclusion, in the malediction, of that which it placed lower than the stage it reached. It may be that this impulse is by itself a "curse of man by man." We live under these conditions, hating in ourselves that which we denounce but do not have the strength to distance ourselves from. We make a comedy of our life, a web of lies and pretensions. We are nevertheless doomed to a contempt for others, expressed in violent

337

prejudices against them. The inescapable cause of this is the desire to be *more human*. But it is easy to yield to it by condemning *in the other* that which we judge to be *inhuman*.

Whether it's a matter of communism or, generally, of humanity, the agitation in question, in which sovereignty is involved, is at the same time so strong and so obscure that, experiencing it, we lose what little lucidity, what little wisdom we have. Convulsively, all values get mixed up in it. . . .

Particularly if we consider communism, which has raised objections to those things that men previously held to be sacred.

TWO

1. On the Relationship between Human Dignity and Prohibition in Its Association with Transgression

I must now go back to what I was arguing. I spoke of *animal* needs and of the more or less *human* ways that men have of satisfying them.

I needed to do this before I related my thought to *everyday* experience (that is, the inner experience — often painful — that we have of the objective behavior of others). In my view, it is essential, at the outset, to disregard the precise data that we derive from established knowledge. But we must come around to that nonetheless. We have to tell ourselves finally that the transition from animal to man resulted from prohibitions that changed the way the animal satisfied its animal needs. It was the observance of prohibitions, not the use of reason, that gave men the feeling that they were not animals. This problem is difficult: it is certain that archaic humanity is not always sure of being different from animality. At least the hunters often liken the animals they hunt to men; they do not regard them as things but as subjective beings, that is, in short, as their *fellow creatures* (it is true that they see them as being dead or remote from themselves). This first difficulty prompts us to be cautious, but it does not go against the principle: man set himself against the animals to the extent that he observed prohibitions. These prohibitions changed the way in which he satisfied his animal needs. A difficulty just as great is connected with transgression. We have seen that men observe prohibitions but they set aside fateful moments when they violate them. They don't feel the need to transgress each prohibition systematically: in general, the moment of transgression becomes irreplaceable in human life, but it does not change the everyday observance of rules that determine the human attitude. Thus, the way in which man satisfies his animal needs, which the prohibitions determined, is not modified by transgressions that do not result from a slackness. A man satisfies his animal needs in an animal way if, as it happens in rural areas, on the death of his wife he obliges his daughter to take her place beside him. The same is not true if some magical operation requires, among an archaic people, a similar incestuous union. The prohibition guards the possibility of the transgression and, likewise, an *extraordinary* transgression guards the rigor of the prohibition. Transgression, on the one hand, and on the other, the blending of man and animal (which correspond to the same guarded submission with respect to the prohibition), cannot prevent us from seeing the connection of human dignity with the general and rigorous observance of the prohibition. But here is the most serious difficulty: of human dignity no doubt, but not of *sovereign* dignity.

It's true that up to now I have neglected a basic aspect of sovereignty, which is owing to the particular prohibitions of the personages who embody it.[5] Kings and priests observe rules stricter than the others, but these rules derive from their nature; they are rules that derive from a fundamental transgression of the rule. "Every precaution must be taken to prevent the dispersion of their sacredness." This is because they carry within themselves that transgressive impulse which at one point throws off the established rule, and from which might spring the disorder in which animality and violence would reign. Webster points up a strange aspect of these precautions: these "sacred persons (are) treated in much the same fashion as polluted persons."[6] Often, for fear of the worst (on pain of death), everyone must avoid touching them, but in return they must observe restrictions that do not apply to other men. At times they must eat alone, in secret. At times they cannot touch the ground with their feet; at times they cannot look toward the sea. Some are not allowed to leave their enclosures. Webster writes: "The almighty divine king is hedged about with so many taboos that he loses all freedom of action."[7] The taboos that the king himself is constrained to observe are complementary to, they do not go against, the sovereign principle embodying the world of transgression. Indeed, it's a question of *associating* the transgression with the prohibition: the sovereign does not cease to be an integral part of the society of which he is both the mortal danger and the supreme good. But if human dignity depends on the observance of prohibitions, would this dignity be contradictory, finally, with that of the *sacred*, of the transgression and the violence, which the sovereign personifies?

The problem framed in this way, returning to the dialectic of Volume II, obliges us to engage in this continual composition.

2. Human Existence Forever in the Breach, or the Basic Unity of Human Dignity and Sovereign Dignity in the Negation of the Given

In its complexity, what I have just said reveals what I believe is the main weakness of my exposition: the real world never offers simple moments, it never corresponds to any situation that I might describe, but rather to the imbroglio of relations that arise from the continual opposition of the most diverse possibilities. It's true that, if I spoke of a particular aspect, I was never unmindful of the ensemble into which it might enter. To begin with, I never lost sight of the complementary aspect of the possibility directly opposed to the one that my exposition described – thus the transgression if I considered the prohibition, the prohibition if I considered the transgression. That goes without saying, but I wish now to emphasize the composite aspect of the forms to which we are accustomed, the ones that we may observe, and of which, up to this point, I have not spoken in a systematic way. I said concerning sovereignty that it got mired down but, in the first part of Volume III, I stressed the regrettable character of this miring-down. I have come to focus instead on the sense of composite forms, which we must envision as such, no longer being concerned with their impurity, in order to link the *human quality* to their composition.

As soon as I contrast humanity with animality I must take into consideration *at the same time* the primordial opposition and the hybrid effects that ultimately result from it. Not only does the return to animality that we perceive in sovereignty – and in eroticism – differ radically from the animal starting point (transgression is not the absence of limits), but it goes into the composition of the world to which it is opposed. The human world is finally but a hybrid of transgression and prohibition, so that the word *human* always denotes a *system* of contradictory impulses, some depending on those that they neutralize but never entirely eliminate, and others delivering a volence mixed with the certainty of peacefulness that will follow. Hence the word *human* never denotes, as simpleminded people imagine, a stabilized position, but rather an apparently precarious equilibrium that distinguishes the human quality.[8] The word man is always connected with an *impossible* combination of movements that destroy one another. I am not speaking so much of utilitarian man, who avoids these torments as best he can (efficacious activity and reason presup-

pose at least a provisional resolution of the inner being). But insofar as sovereignty is in question, it has always been, willingly, and
it will remain, *in the storm*. The storm is the lot of a conditioned
being who bears within him not only the conditions of being, of
the particular being he is, but the general aspirations of beings
to be free of their conditions, to negate them. Utilitarian man is
he who concerns himself above all with his conditions, of which,
ultimately, sovereign man is the negation. Both are contestable
in principle. We cannot reduce ourselves to utility and neither
can we negate our conditions. That is why we find the *human
quality* not in some definite state but in the necessarily undecided
battle of the one who refuses *the given* – whatever this may be,
provided it is *the given*. For man, the given was originally what
the prohibition refused: the animality that no rule limited. The
prohibition itself in turn became the given that man refused. But
the refusal would restrict itself to the refusal to be, to suicide, if
it exceeded *the limit of possibility*. The composite and contradictory forms of human life are tied to this position *in the breach*,
where it was never a question of retreating, nor of going too far.

Hence the apparent opposition between that dignity which
is the property of all men, and the supreme dignity. It's true,
prohibition and transgression are opposed to one another in the
formal definition that we give of them. Ordinarily, from the standpoint of a commonplace affirmation of our human quality, prohibition, contravening the animal satisfaction of animal needs, is
given precedence. But it is bound up with transgression, with the
sovereign dignity, which has remained the basis of that *sacredness*
with which the most wretched man is invested. Something sublime is the principle of our being, which maintains the millennial contest in which men have always tried to be more worthy
of admiration than their fellows. Ways of eating or of evacuating
only concern those elementary behaviors where men perceive a

343

relative independence with respect to conditions. Further, ways of giving and sacrificing, which do not share in the same movement, establish commonly felt principles of *distinction*. Bravery in war is of the same order, still partly determining in our day those judgments that we bring to bear on each other to decide the degree that one has reached in the human dignity. Finally, art accords with those movements of negation of the conditions that do not just partake of the horror of animal behaviors and of the prohibition. Only the refinement of technical civilization brings us back to the lower level of distinctions based on the manner of satisfying animal needs, whose forms derive from the material organization of society.

3. The Bourgeois World, or Dignity Dependent on Things
I must emphasize, at this point, the most important aspect of the distinction that men make among themselves, according to the place that falls to them on the scale of dignity.

On this scale, the sovereign occupies the highest degree, but the sovereign is always surrounded by those who exercise sovereignty as a burden, those who are burdened with the task resulting from the effective power of the sovereign. Sometimes these men who approach the sovereign actually work, but sometimes they leave the work to others, who are their inferiors, not being adjuncts of the sovereign by birth as they are. The thing to note is that, from this perspective, it is a matter of coming as close as possible to that sovereign dignity which is the prerogative of a single individual, but which we approach by degrees. To be more or less truly a man depends on the degree of sovereign dignity that we attain.

In the order of traditional sovereignty, whose principle is not to belong to the world of things, which nonetheless tries to act on this world, to dominate it (the *object* being *for* the *subject*),

344

this dignity comes to issue from the degree of domination that a man has over things. The king himself, insofar as chance alone gave him the kingship, remained outside this deep subordination: in society as a whole, rank gradually came to depend on the possession of wealth, and not wealth on rank.

Feudal society was itself altered by this inevitable tendency, but deep degradation begins with bourgeois society. In bourgeois society, "difference," the greater or smaller dignity of each man, appears in the most painful light. Because of accumulation, bourgeois society is, like communist society, the society of things; it is not, in the image of feudal society, a society of the *subject*. The *object*, which lasts, matters more than the subject, which as long as it is under the domination of the object does not yet exist for itself and rediscovers itself only in the dazzle of the moment. In bourgeois society, the concern for dignity does not cease, but it ultimately merges with the desire for the thing. *Apparently,* dignity did not derive from things in the feudal order, it depended on them *more and more,* but without ever going so far as to neglect appearances. Today the search for a human dignity, as close as possible to being sovereign, is a caricature in our eyes, and rarely corresponds to the reality of the movements that I have described. Our breathless efforts are devoid of meaning insofar as they cannot envisage the NOTHING of sovereignty, but rather the inverse that is the thing, and the ponderousness of those who believe it to be sovereign. In the place where we had reason to anticipate the dazzling appearance of the *subject*, in the dazzle of the moment, the reign of money remains. For all that, the prestige of sovereign moments or of the freedom for which nothing matters any more has nonetheless continued to be enormous: it continues in fact to arrange that caricature, in the archaic framework associated with the behaviors I have described. The manner of eating, of evacuating, the respect of sexual rules, the manner of giving, of dressing

345

and of decorating one's house, the use of the most recent technical processes, constitute an immutable framework within which we place ourselves more or less high on the rungs of a ladder.

It is not the pursuit that is implied in this enumeration that is ludicrous, but the fact that it stops short and that it nonetheless pretends to make the one who takes it on the measure of man. The manner of eating or of evacuating isn't, and hasn't been for a long time, much more than an opportunity for looking down on those who don't have the means to do such things with an equal refinement. But the manner of dressing and of decorating one's house, which comes down to the desire to outdo one's rivals who don't have the profound sense of dignity that is proper to man, is an opportunity to reveal, not the lack of dignity but the comedy of dignity, or the comic dignity of anyone who *uses* art without knowing what magnificence it calls into play. War is, it is true, the crude detour by which, if such is possible, modern man is brought back to what is at stake, which he avoided seeing and which only emerges from the suddenness of the moment. In principle, the rest is caricature.

4. The Gift in Bourgeois Society and the World of Material Reality

I must now reconsider the problems that are raised by the gift. The manner of giving is the most important of the behaviors that entered into the pursuit of rank.

The manner of giving deserves, it seems to me, a somewhat fuller treatment. Where accumulation is concerned, the one who gives loses what he has given, but in the traditional world his dignity grew in proportion to his material loss. In principle, the bourgeois manner of giving has only one distinctive aspect: it is the most limited. Great lords and poor folk have other manners. Yet the comic character of the bourgeoisie is never far off: thus it emerges at the restaurant where it's a question of who will avoid paying, while protesting loudly at seeing the other person pay. But just as hypocrisy is vice's homage to virtue, the repeated affirmation of the pain the other person causes us by disappointing the desire we had to pay for him still testifies to the universal aspiration to the sovereign dignity of the gift-giver.

I spoke in the first volume of the aggressive nature of the gift. There enters into some archaic forms of giving a desire on the part of the giver to humiliate, to overwhelm the receiver by showering him with presents so valuable that sometimes he cannot reciprocate. This meaning is linked to the greater dignity of the one who gives and the loss of prestige of the one who receives, who benefits from a gift whose purpose is to harm. The gift places the giver under the sovereign sign of the moment and the receiver accepting the gift cannot contest a selfish impulse before reciprocating.

We cannot give precedence to the principle of rivalry over the sovereign generosity that is at the origin of gift-giving; to do so would be to reverse the terms of the discussion. Calculation would be on the side of the giver.... The game would end if this were the case. Even if the giver feigns it, at bottom it is still generosity that overwhelms. And doubtless it was a rule, in these archaic forms, that the giver should feign, but his generosity would still not have taken effect without *excessiveness*. Ultimately, it was the one that overdid it who prevailed and whose sovereign character compelled respect.[9]

The meaning that bourgeois *moderation* gives to the game is quite different. The gift has remained at the basis of rank, and the pursuit of rank has kept for bourgeois society the value it had as a sovereign end for the nobility. But the bourgeois cannot *violate the sense of proportion*. Feudal society had itself limited ostentation by rules: everyone must *keep to his rank;* it was unseemly to have a lifestyle that a predetermined social position would not

347

have justified. But Versailles exhausted the royal resources, and was Versailles anything else but the endless, and in a way *miraculous*, gift of the royal house to the nobility? Within the limits of the bourgeoisie, the essential thing is rather to *calculate in terms of one's means* that portion of the gift that constitutes the way of life. On certain occasions, presents are still displayed, but it is important not to ruin oneself by making them. They can still be sumptuous but they are not entirely so unless one can say: "There you have just an inkling of his fortune. . . ." If some dangerous generosity, if some excessiveness, in a word, was manifested in the gift, it could not contribute to the rank of the giver, and the suspicion would arise that he were about to meet his downfall.

In reality, rank in archaic society was owing to the sacred presence of a subject, whose sovereignty did not depend on things, but swept things along in its movement. In the bourgeoisie, it is owing only to the possession of these things, which nothing sovereign or sacred provided. The worst thing about it is that in the bourgeois pursuit of rank, while sovereignty properly speaking is not involved, the subjective end always is. But since the subjective end does not differ in any way, as I have said, from the dignity of man, from his sovereign dignity to be exact, bourgeois man is only a means, he has no end but the semblance or the illusion of dignity, and that rudimentary humanity connected with the body proper and its instincts, with society and family. In him the pursuit of sovereign dignity is no longer anything but the pursuit of material goods that pertain to that dignity, and beyond the possession of these goods there only remains a vacuous urge, where the sovereign truth is reduced to its objective form, to its material form. In the bourgeois world, the gift no longer has the directly aggressive value it often had in archaic society: it is not expressly the receiver whom the bourgeois giver is intent on diminishing. It is still a gift of rivalry, but in one sense only. Rank continues

348

to depend on behaviors that were originally sovereign, and ostentation is still directed against rivals. In this way, the enormous sum of efforts, the substantial expenditures involved in the human classification have ceased to be referred to the sovereign image that would illuminate its meaning: there remains, for the purpose of being *formally* more human, the inexpiable combat of every one against all the others.

Consider those piles of commodities meant to distinguish their buyers from one another, those clothes, those pieces of furniture, those foods and those utensils.... Consider the houses, the apartments or the public places, the more or less expensive automobiles, or the coaches divided into classes! There is nothing, almost nothing, that does not help to perch us on a rung, the highest one possible, of that ladder of democratic dignity where the meaning that justified the climbing of it is no longer given.

5. Communism, or the Sovereign (Subjective) Dignity Negated

This is where communism comes in. In the division into classes, communism only sees the armed oppression of the propertyless by the proprietors, so it negates the "distinction" that opposes the inferior classes or races to the propertied class or peoples. But the communist negation has a special form: it does not negate with full knowledge of what is at stake. It puts forward the dictatorship, that is, the violence, of the proletariat. This dictatorship would suffice to create a society in which nothing would subsist of what once controlled the division of men among themselves, making them more or less human depending on how close they came to the sovereign quality. I said this earlier (I said it in several ways): "Social difference is at the basis of sovereignty, and it is by positing sovereignty that the men of distant times gave differentiation its full scope...."[10] There is no doubt that communists are sharply opposed to every form of divine or human sovereignty, and the coherence of their action is not in question. Without qualification, the communist movement is essentially a machine for eliminating the difference between men: everything called "distinction" must disappear forever, overwhelmed, crushed in the cogs of this machine. Stalin's last writing would show, if need be, that this basic application of communism has never ceased being its deep meaning. It is a matter of abolishing sovereignty and extirpating it, root and branch, from a humanity undifferentiated at last. No doubt, as I have shown, the original sovereignty belonging to all men alike is spared in this crushing, but this is conditional on the renunciation of it which the revolutionary has made in advance.

The communist intention is not in question; but Stalin himself had to appeal to a differentiated salary scale. Since rising on this scale is conditioned by acceptance of the whole system, and since the material advantage gained in this way depends on some revocable function, even though the difference involved might be as great as in bourgeois society (which is not even likely), we are not simply dealing with a return to the human relations of which I spoke, wherein the pursuit of rank and the rivalry of men among themselves, of all men, took precedence. Indeed, no one can climb a rung of this ladder without having proved that the ladder did not have the least meaning in his eyes. In any case, the deep meaning (or the ultimate meaning) of the gradation is still explicitly denied: it is not in any sense a matter of approaching the sovereign magnificence that formerly dominated the social structure. The material advantages gained are the signs of a culminating effectiveness on the part of the power holders, but this effectiveness is collective: for each one it is a matter of participating as best he can in the general effectiveness and, situated within an immense activity, of coming as close as possible to those who control it. Taking things as a whole, it would be foolish to see an affectation in this attitude. In the Soviet world, there is a competition that is not a comedy: on the contrary, nothing is more *serious*. Because sovereignty – sovereign subjectivity – is no longer at issue, the element by turns comical or sublime is finally lacking. Sovereignty is renounced: the objectivity of power takes its place.

6. *The Objectivity of Power*

We must now consider the relation of the *objectivity* of power and *sovereignty*. So long as power is an individual end, it is really only a *means* of which sovereignty is the individual end. Within the limits of traditional sovereignty, or those of the world in which sovereignty is simply abolished – so long as sovereignty is not at the same time individually regained and individually renounced as it is in Soviet society – power, whether it is due to political or administrative position or to wealth, cannot in principle have an *objective* meaning, or at least not fully: the subject individual cannot identify himself with the power of the thing. So long as he is a subject, he tries to attain subjective sovereignty, either by drawing near to the sovereign, or, when he is no longer a subject, inasmuch as he can, by straining ludicrously, in a bourgeois manner, toward a sovereignty that is inaccessible to him because to that end which no one can reach through effort, he has made use of a means. Doubtless, in the case of bourgeois power, the honesty of the thing comes into play (in this sense the Soviet world helps us understand the bourgeois world), but the collective impersonality, which requires the *equivalence* of *all* human beings, can never prevail over *distinction*. The bourgeois in power is never completely ridiculous: he fastens on to the remnants of the past, to those exalted forms of military society[11] that are a kind of extension of a sovereign institution. His honesty is formed,

351

on the one hand, by utility and by what he derives, on the other hand, from the reflections of vanished sovereignty that come to him from the past. It is only to the extent that he denies the meaning of the ladder, even though he climbed its rungs one after another, that Soviet man accedes to the complete objectivity of power. This objectivity alone effects the radical negation of sovereign subjectivity. Everything about it that is sovereign stems from the initial possession of sovereignty, from the fact that the revolutionary overthrew the sovereign power, but objectivity would not be possible if the sovereignty acquired in the overthrow had been the object of a self-interest, if renunciation had not been linked to it, with the strength that things give to the one who identifies himself with their exigency. This involves a deep change, a change in the very structure of man and of the things with which man is associated. In the sovereign world, things were what the sovereign and his family had the enjoyment of. But this enjoyment was in opposition to the exigency of the things themselves, that is, to the accumulation of the means of production. Things, insofar as they are in the possession of those who serve them, if they escape from those who subordinate them to consumption, if nothing opposes their movement, develop. Then those who serve them no longer have the enjoyment of them, but rather the increased power that results from their development. Power is to sovereignty what "potential" energy is to the possible radiation of light. But since it is *human*, power is the *refusal* of sovereignty: in the same way, a man who decides not to light his lamp refuses the light. He who possesses and serves things by developing them enjoys a greater and greater power, but he doesn't make use of it. He is not subordinated to anyone else, in the sense that no one else possesses it, in the service of whom he would be placed. He has sovereignty in principle, but he replaces it with the objectivity of power.[12]

352

Yet this decision was not made in isolation; it is the decision of all men and not that of one individual. The individual cannot go back on it, and the sovereignty that belongs to him is potential only in a certain way: in no case could he light the lamp, in no case could he exercise the power that belongs to him.

7. Might Soviet Power Be the Reality of Which Sovereign Dignity Is the Shadow?

Such appears to be the shape of the Soviet world. At any rate, this is how it differs from ours, from this comical bourgeois world. But there is little need to say that such differences are never fully operative. Indeed, I imagine that the individual becomes, in Russia, all the more important as he seemed no longer to matter, as he identified himself with things. The impersonal individuals that hold power occupy a considerable place nonetheless. A place so great even that it became necessary to reduce it. But a short time ago this place was still the object of a life-and-death struggle.

The life-and-death struggle for sovereign dignity was once implied in the essence of the sovereign. The sovereign by definition was he who, in extreme cases, had put magnificence before life. But magnificence cannot really exist without power. We do not generally speak of a struggle for sovereign dignity, but simply of a struggle for power. At this point, we must even wonder whether power is not the real object of which sovereign dignity is the shadow. In point of fact, the Soviet leaders do not have the advantage of any dignity recalling the fallen sovereignty. The name Father of the Peoples, often given to Stalin, cannot be assimilated to the formal titles of the sovereigns. The half-ritual praises to which Stalin lent himself introduced an ambiguity. But in its origin and its substance the power he commanded was nonetheless naked power, without any of the genuinely religious attributes that founded the fallen sovereignties. The recent change and the repudiation of Stalin have, in any case, made the Stalinist ambiguity a thing of the past. Apparently the life-and-death struggle is itself rejected in turn, but the execution of Berya is close to us. And if the de jure institution of the Soviets is clear, the relations of force that dominate the current political reality still seem to be reducible to de facto situations for which a fight to the death was formerly engaged in. No judicial mechanism seems to have been established that would lead one to underestimate the power – collective in some degree – that the Soviet leaders still have. This power continues to justify the question that we have posed: "whether power is not the real object of which sovereign dignity is the shadow."

8. The Power of Bourgeois Leaders

If I am to proceed with my exposition, I must clear up a difficulty. From a materialist standpoint, if subjective truth is disregarded, the material or tangible advantages are brought to the fore at the expense of the others. Thus, the material advantages of sovereignty constitute its substance, and it is to benefit from them that sovereignty is desired. But if I have been understood, it will be clear that these advantages have no other purpose than the rank they procure, and rank is meaningful only in the subjective order. What is signified by the amount of meat or alcohol, the size of a dwelling, if not the resulting difference between the one who has these things and the poor person who doesn't? A rich man consumes a little more than a poor man and what he consumes is chosen. But considered in quantitative or qualitative terms, objective differences have little meaning. They cannot in any case justify the life-and-death struggle. The capacity the rich man has of influencing the decision of the poor man might give us more to think about, but it concerns subjective life (vainglory) or is reducible,

354

as an indirect consequence, to those objective differences that I just mentioned.

What I have said up to now enables me to lay down as a principle the relationship between surplus resources and rank. The surplus is bound up with the rank of the one who has it at his disposal; it is connected with a position approaching to sovereign dignity, and, more rarely, with that dignity itself. Insofar as things alone determine rank, and not rank the enjoyment of things, the subjective truth that rank signifies is ridiculous. Let us now consider the position of a prime minister, a "mayor of the Palace" for example, vis-à-vis the hereditary sovereign. For his part, the mayor of the Palace has the reality of "power": in his eyes this reality signifies the rank that he acquires, and that will soon allow him to depose the hereditary dynasty. The same is not true of the modern prime minister. In the first place, his position as prime minister is precarious: it depends either on the king's decision or on a vote of the parliament: this decision or this vote replacing the life-and-death struggle, the value that "power" has for him is smaller. The prime minister sometimes appears in the halo of sovereignty: his function in the monarchy places him very high on the scale of dignity. A coefficient of personal *illustriousness* comes into it,[13] and the same light, less bright and even dulled as it were, shines on a republican prime minister. But we're already far, in the sphere of prime ministers, from man's subjective truth. We distance ourselves from it to the extent that "power," not greater or lesser dignity, is involved. The "glory" of the prime minister belongs essentially in the category of false glory, of the untrue reflection; it is always a bit comical, and the prime minister is not serious unless he holds it in contempt, adhering to the objective truth of "power."

For the bourgeois leader, gravity is always the objective truth of power, but he is radically excluded from it by the persistent possibility of a comical subjectivity, to which the possession of things or power contributes. To put it differently, the politician of our democratic world is always situated in ambiguity;[14] he does not attain the impersonal objectivity of power, but even less the subjectivity of being. In him, nothing is more alien than the dissolution of the moment, but pretension to subjectivity, the pursuit of rank to which, beyond the mediocrity of a personal position, he becomes linked by struggling, either for a class or, what is often the same thing, for his country, keeps him in the sphere of that dignity which is the aping of dignity. Only the gravity of the communist leader allows us to see what is, in the bourgeois world, just a constantly thwarted possibility, the power that the development of things requires apart from that pursuit of rank for which men use it in contradictory ways. When a politician had clearly assumed the objectivity of power, he placed himself effortlessly on a level with the sovereignty that he had supremely denied, with weapons in his hands. This also demanded the negation of every difference between men, under the conditions that I have specified.

9. The Equivalence of Sovereignty and Power Implies the Renunciation of Sovereignty

This is remarkable: at no time does any element appear that is worthy of interest, except for sovereignty and power. Sovereignty often entails power, but then it is sovereignty that is power's end. Material advantage is insignificant. Between one pure form and the other, we perceive hybrid forms whose interest is secondary. Once pure power is cleared of compromises, precisely if it escapes from the comedy of sovereignty, it is as though the negation of sovereignty were, in a sense, identical with sovereignty. It seems that its pure objectivity has the virtue of sovereignty itself. *The objectivity of power implies and only implies the abolition of sovereignty:*

356

if there subsisted an element of subjectivity, of striving for rank, sovereignty would continue to exist, but complete objectivity is situated on a par with the sovereignty that it has the strength to abolish. He who exercises supreme power in its objectivity aims in any case to put an end to sovereignty's dominion over things: things must be freed from any particular subordination: henceforth they must be subordinate only to undifferentiated man: in this respect, the man who wields this power but who deliberately deprives himself of the enjoyment of those things that he administers (as if the things administered themselves) is the equal of the sovereign whom his predecessors dethroned.

10. Soviet Power Subsidiarily Tied to an Archaic, Secondary Form of Traditional Sovereignty

But the power that puts an end to the play of fallen sovereignty materializes itself.

It commands accumulation, since it is in its nature to oppose the expenditures that create rank. An incomparable composition of forces results. But for the one who holds it, what does this material power signify? If we generally grant that the power to do *this* or *that* possesses an attraction in itself, is it not the attraction which *this* or *that* presents? Or would it be the possibility of choosing? Or again, is it desirable to command, to play for the others when their destiny is at stake? But that can only increase the interest of a game: the interest of the game is not created by the multiplicity of those who are at stake. The inclination to have subordinates cannot be regarded seriously. One has the choice of two things: it is a question of services or goods that one can expect from their labor (these services or these goods relate to rank), or the one who commands them desires to be for them what the subject is for the object, but this relationship itself is of the order of rank.

357

The objective power of which I speak is itself an end, and this power may be viewed as the end that goes beyond these aspects, which are limited to the remnants of sovereignty. Doubtless we must consider such remnants; nothing humanly happens that has – at least that has for long – a genuine purity. But the composition of forces of which I speak does not actually have the objectivity of power as its sole end. We must not forget the origin and the *military* form of this power. It was not appropriate at the outset to emphasize that, in a sense, Soviet power is a *military* authority and that the Communist Party has the organization of an army. Communist activity is a battle. The class struggle is a war, which truces interrupt, but the truces change the mode of combat, they cannot stop the war. The communists would prefer that their adversaries and even their friends forget this if possible, but the doctrine and the facts combine to remove the doubts.

It was hard to speak of *sovereignty* without speaking at the same time of *military authority*, if only to establish the difference between the two. Indeed, this difference is never clear. If need be, I can even speak of a military kingship and a religious kingship, as if *sovereignty*, generally religious, could also be military. Actually, the affinity of sovereignty and the organized convulsion of armies is so great that the resort to arms has often designated the sovereign. The sovereign, properly speaking, is passive and the military commander, by contrast, gives activity its decisive form. It is true that archaic war was apparently the affair of violence. Ritual violence, subject to few rules, was its most striking aspect. The fact of religious transgression, the violation, in some way a sacred violation, of the prohibition of murder, accentuated the sovereign character of that warrior who involved the others in violence. Calculation distanced *military authority* from the religious qualification of the sovereign, but it could not do away with that qualification. And insofar as the force of circumstances wrongly decides that which, however, only *is* on the condition that it be distinct from it and that it be autonomous, that it be *above* it, calculation sometimes even created that qualification. Yet military authority, which could designate the person of the sovereign, did not create sovereignty: the people's expectations remained tied to some form of sacred origin (the Caesars invented a clever religious drama; Napoleon revived the legacy of Charlemagne; and the latter had joined that of the Germanic kings to the dignity of the Caesars). In connection with communism, I don't intend to take up the "theological"[15] development, which I have decided not to include in my exposition because of its importance. But I believe I can say, concerning communist power, that in this respect it is the analogue of sovereignty. Military organization and combat formed and designated the power holder; they even determined its personal character, but *in the realm of sovereign truth, where it is situated,* Soviet power is essentially given in the inner experience of a sovereignty that is available and abolished.

In the deep sense, the purpose of the power that is generated by the Soviet machine is indeed this "theological" truth. This is true, however, only in the deep sense. That power also has an immediate sense: by the conditions of its origin and the training of its holders, it is necessarily a military power. There is a danger in communism that comes of the impossibility for accumulation to be applied to any other end than war. The pursuit of distinction, and the use of wealth that corresponds to it, *may* find a favorable possibility in war, but the suppression of the difference between men tends to close off the other outlets. The die would be cast if the power holders were not free to open them.

11. The Ultimate Value of Subjectivity
This freedom implies deep changes. A stranger to communism, I do not have, as far as the future is concerned, the ability or the

responsibility to speak of it. And in any case, if I evoke those possible changes, that cannot be the opportunity for me to recall the interest that differences of rank have in bourgeois society! This society enjoys a kind of equilibrium, but a shaky equilibrium cannot be cited as an example in the face of a world that tried to force destiny. No one on this side of the curtain is in a position to give lessons to those whose lot was to put everything at stake.

Wanting to finish with the question of difference, the possibility to which I will allude has no meaning except in the indeterminacy of all things, which is characteristic of a society grown old.

Concerning the suppression of difference, I have spoken thus far as if suppressing it completely seemed possible to me. But I was mainly considering the subjective difference arising out of an objective difference, that is, the proprietor deriving a comedy of sovereignty from the enjoyment of a beautiful house. The feudal lord himself drew part of his glory from the enjoyment of a domain: at least he emphasized the subjective difference, the nobility, to which he owed his rights as a landed proprietor. But the bourgeois was comical if he claimed the subjective difference, nobility. His existence, situated in the world of things, was never anything but one of the things of that world. But for all that, humanity did not cease being a subjective truth: multiple errors didn't change this in the least.

Insofar as the deep difference has subjective truth as its end, it will always have the ultimate human value. It is the bourgeois debasement of sovereign subjectivity that communism destroys. If, in the same movement, communism generally opposes the pursuit of subjectivity, this is in order to confuse it with that traditional confusion to which the bourgeoisie gave its caricatural aspect, wherein *subjectivity* is mixed with *things*. But communism accentuates this hostile attitude toward subjective life, particularly because it is still obsessed with primitive accumulation, which is not compatible with that enjoyment of the moment, whence comes the subject's presence to itself.

My study tends rather to show what, in distinction, could not be suppressed without destroying the *subject* at the same time, that is, the *sovereign end* of objective activity. To do this I needed to reveal what is hidden behind the grimaces of human life; these differences may be transcended, but after having grasped what they denoted in the first place.

PART FOUR

The Literary World and Communism

ONE

Nietzsche and Communism

1. The Apparent Disproportion between Nietzsche and Communism

One is immediately struck by a disproportion between Nietzsche and communism.

In a rather general way, Nietzsche's work exerts an irresistible attraction, but this attraction does not entail any consequence. These dazzling books are like a liquor that excites and illuminates, but leaves a basic way of thinking intact.

Relative to an inconsequential tragedy, the problems of communism have an incomparable importance. No matter, in a certain sense, if the tragedy involves something whose value, in my view, is greater. But I cannot forget that only communism has raised the general question.

Communism claims, on behalf of each human being, the right to live, which he is deprived of in part by the juridical system in force. All around me the interest of the multitude is at issue: even if I suppose that it is less painfully so than was that of the proletariat of Marx's time or than is that of the disadvantaged nations (like India and China), I recognize the importance of the forces that communism sets in motion. What is more, communism, represented by powers that occupy a considerable place in the world, challenges the right to live of those who benefit from the advantages of bourgeois society, who benefit, for example, in order to write. Thus, communism is the basic problem that is posed to each one of us, whether we welcome it or reject it: communism asks us a life-and-death question. For their purpose, the militants have at their disposal not only a coherent body of doctrine, based on the lucid thought of Marx, but an active organization to which discipline has given its exemplary effectiveness. Unquestioning doctrinary submission, devotion unto death and the relinquishment of individual will are expected of each adherent, without the promise of a reward commensurate with his sacrifices (the reward may even be, for some, that destruction by the others which is the aftermath of great revolutions). The truth is that, the *cause* being given, nothing counts more, for the adherent first of all but finally for whoever takes part in communist society. The personal commitment of the adherent stems from an obligation that falls on all men, but it was not the commitment that created this obligation. Indifference or hostility change nothing in this: nothing is more important, for the neutral or the enemy, no matter, than the communist endeavor. The conviction of the militants gives it the sole value today, for all men: it was able to place the fate of the world at issue; nothing remains outside it.

Concerning Nietzsche's thought, I am free to believe or say that it is actually no less important, or more important, than communism. But then I should at least clearly acknowledge that, not having been understood, this thought is for the moment as if it did not exist. The thoughtlessness of those who showed an interest in it is the most common attitude. I leave aside those who devoted professional studies to it, frankly dismissing it. Nietzsche's life is viewed as a tale, a tragic one to be sure. The naive longing for a living mythology easily gives a meaning to this tale, but this mythology is scarcely less removed from the contemporary world than are the myths of the ancient world. The worst thing is the importance that, for the purposes of their own ambition, some individuals tried to give to a thought whose essence is in not being reducible to service, in being sovereign. It was easy for them not to take account of Nietzsche's previous refusal. They could be all the more cavalier as Nietzsche died *without descendants*. His mobile, concrete thought, tied to historical conditions, completely vanished with him. He found commentators, but they treated him like a dead man stretched out on a dissecting table.

2. Nietzsche's Doctrine the Same As That Set Forth *in* The Accursed Share

I am the only one who thinks of himself not as a commentator of Nietzsche but as being the same as he. Not that my thought is always faithful to his: it often diverges from it, especially if I consider the detailed developments of a theory.[1] But that thought is placed under the same conditions as was his. There was nothing sovereign that the historical world offered him that Nietzsche could recognize. He refused the reign of things, and science could not be in his eyes mankind's limit and end, since, assumed as such, it ensures the mind's subordination to the object. It was essential to him to rediscover lost sovereignty. These few principles reveal, at the same time, the situation on which Nietzsche's thought depended and the one in which *The Accursed Share* perceives a basis for starting anew.

The communists are opposed to what seems sovereign to them. But for Nietzsche, a world deprived of what I call sovereign would no longer be bearable. With respect to traditional sovereignty, he had the same attitude as the communists. But he could not accept a world in which man – *in which each man* – would be a means and not the end of some common endeavor. Hence the insulting

irony with which he addressed the forerunners of National Socialism, and the curt refusal, but free of contempt, that he offered
to the social democracy of his time, from which communism
derives. The refusal to serve (to be useful) is the principle of
Nietzsche's thought, as it is of his work. What turned Nietzsche
away from God or from morality was not a personal desire for
enjoyment but rather a protest that was directed, at the same
time, against moralizing (enslaving) sovereignty mired in Christianity, and to the order of things where reason viewed as an end
confines subjective life together with thought.

If one understands what I am saying, Nietzsche's thought, identified with the positing of sovereignty independent of its mired
forms, the kind of sovereignty that my long study was meant to
bring out, no longer looks like a miserable agitation when contrasted with communism. In fact, today there are only two admissible positions remaining in the world. Communism, reducing
each man to the *object* (thus rejecting the deceptive appearances
that the subject had assumed), and the attitude of Nietzsche –
similar to the one that emerges from this work – free the *subject*,
at the same time, of the limits imposed on it by the past and of
the objectivity of the present.

3. The Thought of Nietzsche, That of Hegel, and My Own
The isolation of two philosophies with respect to all others that
men conceive is odd, no doubt, appearing to be inappropriate,
more like a provocation than an unavoidable formulation. In principle we are, Nietzsche and myself, two "thinkers," taken from a
mass that clutters the history of thought in the bourgeois world.
It is common to ascribe to Nietzsche an importance of the first
order, but this importance is suspended, as it were; it is not connected with anything, except at times with the backward, nation-
alistic forms of violence.

Be that as it may, it seems arbitrary to assert that only two positions coincide. Other men asserted their independence, the sovereignty of their thought in a world where values are generally called back into question. It is banal to note that Hegel's "absolute knowledge" takes the place of God, and that "absolute knowledge" was not different from Hegel himself.

At the risk of appearing too narrow, when other questions might be raised, I will speak only of Marx's teacher.

The gist of my intention is given in Hegel's will to autonomy (for Hegel this means the autonomy of thought, but Hegel is incapable of separating thought from the other contents of this world). According to Hegel, the philosopher, associated with the dominant forms in the same way as the mind is associated with the body, and in the same unity, indisputably, attains the autonomy that the master did not attain (in a sense, in the language of Hegel, the sovereign): in the final state of things possible, the philosopher in fact could not will anything that was not the dominant reality, and the latter could not bring about anything that did not correspond to the philosopher's thought. The difference between my *dialectical* thought and that of Hegel is difficult to formulate, since contradiction can constantly resume the development of both.[2] There is nothing that I do not follow in the overall movement that Hegel's thought represents in my eyes. But the autonomy of Hegel's "absolute knowledge" is that of discourse unfolding in time. Hegel situates subjectivity not in the object's disintegration (always begun anew) but in the identity that the subject and the object attain in discourse. But in the end, "absolute knowledge," the discourse in which the subject and the object become identical, itself dissolves into the NOTHING of unknowing, and the vanishing thought of unknowing is in the moment. On the one hand, there is an identity of absolute knowledge and this evanescent thought; on the other, this identity is

369

THE LITERARY WORLD AND COMMUNISM

reencountered *in life*. "Absolute knowledge" closes, whereas the movement I speak of opens up. Starting from "absolute knowledge," Hegel could not prevent discourse from dissolving, but it dissolved *into sleep*.[3] The vanishing thought of which I speak is the awakening and not the sleep of thought: it is reencountered in an equality – in the *communication* – with all the *sovereign moments* of all men, insofar as the latter do not want to take them for things.[4]

It is reencountered above all in the moments that preceded the awareness or thought of unknowing.[5] I am talking about the discourse that enters into darkness and that the very light ends by plunging into darkness (darkness being the definitive silence). I am talking about the discourse in which thought taken to the limit of thought requires the sacrifice, or death, of thought. To my mind, this is the meaning of the work and life of Nietzsche. It is a question of marking, in the labyrinth of thought, the paths that lead, through movements of vehement gaiety, to that place of death where excessive beauty begets excessive suffering, where all the cries that will ever be heard are mingled, cries whose powerlessness, in this awakened state, is our *secret* magnificence.

Nietzsche's cry recalls the cry we would need to give out, with all our strength, in dreaming, and which we know in our terror emits no sound. It is nonetheless a cry of joy: it is the cry of happy subjectivity, which the world of objects will no longer deceive, and which will be reduced to NOTHING. Within an apparent despair, it gives rise to a burst of malice (this is the wisdom to which we can aspire). Nietzsche joined the intelligible to the sensible in himself and there is nothing that he gave as the purpose of his thought, unless it be the sovereign moments that give humanity its countenance. No cause, no commitment issue from an empty generosity, with which no expectation is connected. But Nietzsche is on the side of *those who give*, and his thought cannot be isolated from the movement that tried to promote a resumption of life in the moment, in opposition to the bourgeoisie, which accumulates. Hegel was drawn along by romanticism at first, but he repudiated it and his break led him finally to support the bourgeois State (he did not break in this way with the revolutionary ideal of his youth; he sided with the bourgeois State, with the bourgeois-minded functionaries, not with the feudal State). Nietzsche himself combated romanticism, but his hatred of Wagner led him to do so: he objected to the inflatedness and lack of rigor, combining as he did an intellectual severity and a depth of emotional life, but he remained completely on the side where calculation is unknown: Nietzsche's gift is the gift that nothing limits; it is the sovereign gift, that of subjectivity.[6]

Two

Nietzsche and Jesus

1. Nietzsche's Ambition To Supplant Jesus

Nietzsche's position is the only one apart from communism.[7] To my mind this is an obvious fact. I want to make clear that it is not enough for me to show that Nietzsche is the object of a misunderstanding; I also wish to bring out the extent and inevitability of it.

I will start from an observation by Gide.

"Nietzsche," Gide asserted, "was jealous of Jesus Christ, jealous to the point of madness. In writing his *Zarathustra*, Nietzsche is ever harassed by his desire to write a counterpart to the Gospels. He even adopts at times the form of the Beatitudes the better to make a mockery of them. He wrote the *Anti-Christ*, and in his work, *Ecce Homo*, he poses as the adversary triumphant of Him he sought to oust."[8]

Gide thus emphasized, not without reason, a trait that sets Nietzsche apart from all the others. This quite evident aspect could not escape notice, but usually no one stresses it. I imagine that some people avoid thinking about it, for it is difficult – or think of it as Gide does: with a feeling of discomfort – and fear. Would being jealous of Christ be unacknowledgeable in principle?

But Nietzsche avowed it.... Strangely, for the megalomania of *Ecce Homo* (where the title, chosen by the author, repeats the

373

words of Christ) is comical in its ambiguity. An insolent gaiety carries it along and retracts the acknowledgment while affirming it at the same time. This book has the sense of a *testament*, but Nietzsche disclaims this: "I am no man, I am dynamite. – Yet for all that, there is nothing in me of a founder of a religion.... I want no 'believers'; I think I am too malicious to believe in myself.... I do not want to be a holy man; sooner even a buffoon."[9]

The disavowal is so closely bound to the admission that the latter was fully expressed only in madness. The crisis in which Nietzsche's mind broke down came soon after the writing of *Ecce Homo*. It underscored that work's audacity: the notes that he signed "the Crucified" reiterated and completed the admission, but what madness admitted was, clearly so to speak, what the rational man dissimulated.

The first impulse is to take this (I mean the illness) as a basis for situating what Gide called Nietzsche's jealousy. A modern man, whose life is devoid of mystery, who was a professor, and who, up to the end of 1883, behaved as a civilized man, could not of his own accord slip into the mythological realm. He could not himself attain divinity. No one can doubt this (and Nietzsche had a presentiment of it): the ambition to be better than a man can only have a "comic solution."[10] Yet this was the rather firm resolve (which he apparently could not escape) of a man whose basic lucidity and refinement are beyond question. The madness properly so called is late and does not permit us to reduce to illness a kind of invasion by the divine domain, whose consequence was, as early as 1882, the painful failure of *Zarathustra*.[11]

Nietzsche's Problem, or the Deserted Beach

It is difficult to arrive at a sufficiently clear understanding of the problem to which Nietzsche's attitude seems to have responded. Gide's humanism is antithetical to that irrational dis-

374

tress. Nietzsche's concern is inconceivable for Gide, who writes: "Nietzsche's immediate and deep reaction was, it must be said, jealousy."[12]

Although it had nothing to do with possession of a woman, nor of a power or a prestige, Nietzsche's reaction was not in fact different from jealousy. But, leaving aside the wretched and lamentable stories, Nietzsche was not jealous of any other man, neither of Plato nor of Buddha, nor of anyone else who matters.... The problem of God and the divine status of Jesus alone motivated his attitude. This is a paradox, but the object of Nietzsche's jealousy is God.

Doubtless he is the only one who could say: "No God! no man above me." Jaspers declares that his "moderation was even more dominant after *Human, All-too-Human*.[13] But he himself cites Nietzsche's sentiment as a boy of fifteen who wrote:

None so bold be ever
To ask with rash endeavor
Where I might have my home.
Ne'er by space I'm captured
Nor by fleeting hours enraptured....[14]

Thus the sentiment that Gide calls jealousy, that I relate to sovereignty, takes on, in light of the chapter by Jaspers, the sense of a leitmotiv. It was Nietzsche's peculiarity not to accept the limits to which a human life is conventionally restricted. He thus reverted to the theme of Feuerbach, but in his case it was not a matter of idle words. His life showed that for him this idea had consequences: "All the beauty and sublimity we have bestowed upon real and imaginary things I will reclaim," he said. He did not reclaim them only for himself, but "as the property and product of man."[15] The game that was played in this way was that of the being that we are against the being that we have created, that we have imagined, and for which we have renounced the possibility of seeing the magnificence in ourselves.

For Nietzsche, God was only our limit. "God," he said, "is a gross answer, an indelicacy against us thinkers – at bottom merely a gross prohibition for us: you shall not think!"[16] The *objectivity* of God answers to those who ask for the origin of things: the shoemaker made the shoe and likewise God created the world. With this answer the lasting and the reassuring take the place of the problematic. For theology, God is subjectivity nonetheless, but creating the world of things and giving Himself in this manner, above Him, an objectivity like His own. Apparently, it was of the love given to the divine objectivity that Nietzsche was jealous.

The meaning of this paradoxical jealousy cannot be drawn from a superficial examination.

Let us imagine a deserted beach, the veiled light of the afternoon and the land restricted to the insignificance of the dunes, whose lines add nothing to the boundlessness of the sea and sky. I can include myself at will, subjectively, in this immensity (I can do so, myself being NOTHING; the subject, which I am, is NOTHING). I can at will, objectifying myself, exclude myself from it. But if I posit myself as an object, I also objectify the immensity. Consequently, the immensity transcends me (it transcends that given object, which is there). It is no longer the NOTHING in which I myself am NOTHING (it is neither it nor myself being objectified: the immensity becomes *something* of which I speak, *something* that speaks to me. Let it be said: At first a beautiful and terrible animation results from the game. But speech (my speech) completely invades the object, that object, immense perhaps, but an object, which transcends me. I can still, sheltered from transcendence, save the ineffable part of the object (although words define Him and He finds His expression in them, God is also *silence*).

An operation of this sort does not compel me. If I wish, I can say of it after the fact: this is NOTHING, this objectivity is only a *game*. The immense shadow that my thought extends over the world is NOTHING. I might choose *not to withdraw the adorable phantom from the game!* In a general way, I can at will bring into the *game* that which captivates me; that *thing* which captivates me is no longer anything but the object of my desire or my passion, which transfigure and deny it as an object, which affirm it as a *subject* (as NOTHING), which annihilate it. From that point I can still feign, like the child, the *reality* of my *game*: this is the height of luxury.[17] But where God is concerned the waste product of the operation (the *thing*) ultimately wins out over the imperceptible.

What is involved finally, if not *withdrawing* the object of theology *from the game?* and bringing man out of the world of *play* (the world of desire and of the NOTHING which desire pursues) into the world of the *thing*, of seriousness, of duty and morality. So that in the person of God (as in that of the kings, but for more logical reasons), sovereignty leads desire to the dupery of abdication. What is involved, if not *labor*, to which it was necessary to give the advantage?

This was supposed to be brought about, this thing that supposedly would have revolted the free men of the past: *the domination of labor*. The thing was to prevail over the sovereign moment and the object over the subject; whereas sovereignty is the affirmation of the preeminence of the end, which is the subject, over the object, which is the means.

Can it be said that, all in all, men could not have avoided going through this? Possibly so, but the opposition of the man of play to the God of obligation is clumsy nonetheless. It is not that of the supernatural Being to the natural being: man and God are

377

on the same plane. If Nietzsche sets himself against Jesus, he speaks of Dionysos. It is always an ensemble of human and divine forms opposing another ensemble, on one side Nietzsche and Dionysos – and the Dionysian world – and on the other, the believer and the God of reason – between whom Jesus is the mediator. The essential point is that on one side the seduction of Dionysos is a prelude to tragedy and that of Jesus to the arranged marriage. Nietzsche's jealousy is that of the passion that is forsaken for the match dictated by utility. In the end, the difference between the two sides has this sense: I don't say Jesus, but the believer *withdraws from the game,* and the disciple of Nietzsche *throws himself into it.*

On the beach I spoke of, nothing separates me from the immensity except for the certainty of being *at issue:* I have recognized my equality with the emptiness and boundlessness, for I know that at bottom I am this subjective and contentless existence, but memory ties me to objects, to contents, in the midst of which I situate myself, one object among the others. If I objectify the immensity, which then transcends me, I open the way to the regular dispositions of speech.... But I can simply stop short and tell myself: What separates me from the immensity, those differentiated contents that memory represents to me, does not signify that I am a given object in the order of objects that God rules over, but that, in the immutable immensity, equal to itself, what I am is *at issue.*[18] I am not this that I name in the same way that I name each particular thing in the order where it has its place and has a sense that accounts for it; I am an object *in question,* an object whose basic content is *subjectivity*, which is a question, and which its differentiated contents bring into play. As a subject I am NOTHING within the immensity that is NOTHING – as an object, in the feeling of being at issue that sets me against the self-sameness of the immensity, I rediscover an equivalence. If this distinct reality that I am as an object were not at issue, if it took shelter, it would definitely separate me from that equality with the immense NOTHING, but precisely that by which I differ from NOTHING is that by which I am at issue. Objectifying myself, I exclude myself from the undifferentiated immensity, but this object *at issue,* which I am, places itself at the mercy of the game, which destroys it as an object, which delivers it over, as an aleatory object, to that intangible NOTHING that the subject is. This aleatory object is at the same time the form in which we offer ourselves to the other's desire; it is the sovereign object, which does not serve, which does not let itself be grasped in genuine reality, that of effi-cacious, risk-free action. In a word, it is sovereignty, but that of man: divine sovereignty is different in that the myth can be, if we wish, withdrawn from the game, but this only happened slowly: there was the immortal God, but, having all the privileges, He also gave Himself that of dying, and the Eternal itself, in the person of Jesus, let itself be put to death. But the object that the God of reason is, which created the world and over which nothing has any hold, which, as the immense NOTHING, knows nothing of birth and death, is no less than this NOTHING *outside the game.* It is nonetheless offered to man's desire, but only to better ensure the reign of labor and morality. Nietzsche's jealousy is that of the man who means to be sovereign without illusions, toward the imagined being who captured the love of all men only to deceive them. Sovereignty died of the maneuvers that brought about the general submission to the concern for the future: Nietzsche alone restored it to the reign of the moment.

3. Sovereign Thought

It is not easy to understand Nietzsche's attitude, even when one's personal sensibility would lead one to do so. Even if our sensi-bility is intact, we still belong to the world in which we speak, in which no one can escape from the Christian system without being immediately obliged to adopt a system that is just as closed (or more so). Every day the sovereignty of the moment is more foreign to the language in which we express ourselves, which draws value back to utility: what is *sacred*, not being an object, escapes our apprehension.[19] There is not even, in this world, a way of thinking that escapes servitude, an available language such that in speaking it we do not fall back into the immutable rut as soon as we are out of it: how can we imagine, in spite of Kant, an ethics that does not *commit itself*, that does not place us in the service of some means? Our inclinations do not alter this circumstance in the least. Nietzsche himself could do little more, in this sense, than appeal to the sensibility: his language is inimitable, and no one was able to connect with him starting from the common discourse. It is easy, on the other hand, to pass by him without any recognition of what he tried to signify. Gide is not the only example of this.

It is common to retain only one aspect of Nietzsche, suiting the one who assumes the right to choose. The significance of his thought has remained inaccessible up to now. Ever since he became famous, has he been anything but an occasion for misunderstanding? I strive to show this, but the foregoing propositions, or those that follow could not make it clear if the set of analyses I have undertaken, whose cohesiveness is apparent in spite of everything, did not tend to do what no one ever did before, but that Nietzsche hoped someone would attempt after him: give the ins and outs of a position by which the order of values is overturned. Nietzsche assumes the sovereignty of man in this world of subjugated sovereignty, or of sovereign subjugation.

He did not set his mind on forgetting the efforts in which mankind of all epochs exhausted itself, while having no deeper aspiration than the sovereign moment freeing itself from subordinate activity. He was aware of this, but at the same time he weighed the powerlessness of that "moment" in the domain of thought: beyond the "sovereign moment," Nietzsche sought "sovereign thinking," whose inexpressible significance he experienced. He wrote: "To be alone with a great thought is unbearable. I am seeking and calling to men to whom I can communicate this thought without their being destroyed by it."[20] Or:

> I have presented such terrible images to knowledge that any 'Epicurean delight' is out of the question. Only Dionysian joy is sufficient: *I have been the first to discover the tragic!* The Greeks, thanks to their moralistic superficiality, misunderstood it. Even resignation is not a lesson of tragedy, but a misunderstanding of it. Yearning for nothingness is the *denial* of tragic wisdom, its opposite![21]

Apparently the moral problem took "shape" in Nietzsche in the following way: for Christianity the good is God, but the converse is true: God is limited to the category of the good that is manifested in man's utility, but for Nietzsche that which is sovereign is good, but God is dead (His servility killed Him), so man is morally bound to be sovereign. Man is thought (language), and he can be sovereign only through a sovereign thought. Now, just as the original sovereignty (that of the gods and kings) is tragic (before the reduction of tragedy to morality), but only at the end, *sovereign thought* is boundless tragedy. That triumph which it basically is, is first of all a collapse; it is the collapse of that which it is not. In its immediacy, sovereign thought is "off its hinges"; it exceeds the bounds of knowledge; it destroys the world that reassures, that is *commensurate* with man's activity.

But if sovereign thought is far removed from vulgar, practical morality it is nonetheless the hypertrophy of the basic demand that is at the origin of morality:

You see what it was that really triumphed over the Christian god: Christian morality itself, the concept of truthfulness that was understood ever more rigorously, the father confessor's refinement of the Christian conscience, translated and sublimated into a scientific conscience, into intellectual cleanliness at any price. Looking at nature as if it were proof of the goodness and governance of a god; interpreting history in honor of some divine reason, as a continual testimony of a moral world order and ultimate moral purposes; interpreting one's own experiences as pious people have long enough interpreted theirs, as if everything were providential, a hint, designed and ordained for the sake of the salvation of the soul – that is *all over* now, that has man's conscience *against* it, that is considered indecent and dishonest by every more refined conscience – mendaciousness, feminism, weakness, and cowardice.[22]

The simultaneous explosion of language and practical morality is the principle of the operation. What is sovereign has no other end than itself. Now, language (discursive and not poetical language) carries within itself the "signification" by which words constantly refer to one another: definition is the essence of language; through definition each word gets its meaning from another word, so that, taken as a whole, language is ended only by the word God, – or by words with a *sacred* meaning, ultimately devoid of intelligible meaning (hence of any meaning), or by the prohibition of their use. The sovereign operation of thought is given, at its origin, in the use of the word God, as the final meaning of all things. But insofar as the use of the word God is the guarantor of this meaning (and is bound by this meaning) of things that it creates, the operation has two values: with the first, things get their meaning from what is sovereign, but with the other, what is sovereign gets its meaning from things. The use of the word God is deceptive therefore; it results in the distortion of its object, of the sovereign Being, between the sovereignty of an ultimate end, implied in the movement of language, and the servitude of means, on which it is based (*this* is defined as serving *that*, and so on...). God, the *end* of things, is caught up in the game that makes each thing the means of another. In other words, God, named as the end, becomes a thing insofar as he is named, a thing, put on the plane with all things.

4. From Gide's Anxieties to Nietzsche's Sobs

Nietzsche's passion brought to light this reduction of exceptional sovereignty to the general servitude. Nietzsche wrote: "One is most dishonest to one's god: he is not *allowed* to sin."[23] "A god who would come to earth must not do anything except wrong: not to take the punishment upon oneself but the *guilt* would be divine."[24] Contrary to vulgar atheism, he never aimed at the divine domain, as being irreducible to profane measures, but at the reduction that morality carries out within that domain, in the form of a personalized god. He did not hesitate to say: "The refutation of God — in fact, only the moral God is refuted."[25] The concern with saving the divine domain, or the sovereign domain of thought, from the moral reduction took precedence in him over the desire to escape from the moral code. Renée Lang, speaking of Gide's Nietzcheanism, points up the difference between the *Cahiers d'André Walter* (1891) and *Les Nourritures terrestres* (1897) or *Le Prométhée mal enchaîné*. She situates "Gide's metamorphosis" between these two points, going from the disgust with sin to the pursuit of happiness, to the affirmation of life. In her view, the change occurred gradually, accelerated "however by two powerful incitements: Nietzsche and Africa."[26]

Gide denied having been specifically influenced by Nietzsche, especially in regard to *L'Immoraliste*, whose detailed conception preceded the reading of Nietzsche. He was even mistaken for a time concerning the date at which he began that reading. But he himself furnished the elements that allowed the correction to be made. The publication of some peculiar letters has established that at the end of 1895 he had "not yet tackled Nietzsche" but, as Lang had supposed at the start, through the reading of journals Gide had formed a clear enough idea of Nietzsche to write: "I was a little afraid of him: he attracts me the way it happens in vertigo...."[27] The trip to Africa where, the ascesis given up, Gide found the possibility of a happiness without remorse, no doubt preceded even the indirect acquaintance with Nietzsche. Yet Nietzsche's ideal "subsequently helped him legitimate" his new ethic and *his new life*. It was very different with Nietzsche: "his sickly constitution...made what he preached *unattainable* for him."[28] Indeed he was so far from his affirmations that one day he wrote these unsettling words: "It is easy to talk about all sorts of immoral acts; but do we have the strength to endure them? For example, I could not *bear* to break my word or to commit murder; I would languish for a longer or shorter time, then die, that would be my fate. Whether the crime and its punishment were made public or not."[29] He was so far from the power of which he spoke (where in my view he was wrong to place explicitly an emphasis that in his work is placed implicitly on sovereignty, which is not the same thing: sovereignty requires power perhaps, but the pursuit of power reduces man to action, which is a *means*; it is the contrary of sovereignty), that he had the right to assert: "As far as torments and renunciations go, my life can be measured against that of ascetics of all times." So it can be said of Nietzsche's intellectual scheme (and Nietzsche himself said this) that the immoralism in it is the consequence of morality. I quoted earlier the aphorism in which he sees in the denial of God, his denial, the demand of Christian morality. He gives here the general form of a surprising line of reasoning: "We want to

be the *heirs* of every ancient morality and not to begin afresh. All
our activity is only a morality that turns back against its ancient
form." "In order to comply with morality, one no longer eats a
certain food; likewise to comply with morality one will eventually end up no longer *doing good*." Life's demanding nature is
at play in Gide's attitude if he affirms the rights of life against
morality, of desire against duty, of the moment against the calculation of interest. Something different is at stake in Nietzsche:
in Nietzsche man demands — fully, in a general way and in the
very movement of thought — to escape from the reduction of
being to thinghood. Joy and sorrow no longer matter; it is no
longer a question of pleasure protesting against an obstacle once
given, but of rescuing being from the strictures of a thought that
is essentially concerned with ensuring *the judicious order of things.*
Whether or not there is a judicious order of things is not the ultimate question either. But will man serve that order? Will he get
value and meaning from it? Or will that order serve him, in the
way that food and roofs do? Will man have, beyond the judicious
order, a sovereign life, one that is problematic, useless and dangerous, deriving meaning only from itself and decidedly tragic?

These problems take us far from Gide, who doesn't care about
any general inquiry. It is not a matter of deciding whether he is
mistaken. We would distort Nietzsche's attitude by using it to
define Gide's mistake. I imagine, on the contrary, Nietzsche de-
claring, against himself, that Gide is right. He didn't make the
demand he felt the analogue of a universal moral law. It is a question of what is sovereignly real, which counts at the moment
when man *wills*, if only once, *to be in a sovereign manner*. What is
sovereign has an incomparable value no doubt, but value does not
signify the obligation that weighs on everyone. Moreover, *to be
in a sovereign manner* is easy: every moment lived for its own sake
is sovereign, but the thinking of the one who lives it can, in the

385

moment itself, assign him to servitude (in the form, for example, of a literary project). There is no resolve that is not a vertigo, where the conscience is never satisfied, where the game appears paltry measured against a sovereignty – manifest but inaccessible and unthinkable – that belongs only to the totality. Whence a lasting kind of self-contempt, no less than the inevitable audacity. "Why am I thus?" Nietzsche said. "What madness to think oneself free to choose to be, and to be in such and such a fashion. Behind this, the need to imagine for oneself a being who could have *prevented* a being such as I, a self-despiser, from ever being born. To feel oneself to be an argument against God."[30] This note illuminates rather painfully the distress that is connected with the feeling of jealousy Gide speaks of, but – it is the same with every sentence that Nietzsche wrote – one mustn't get stuck on it. Zarathustra spoke another language: "God's woe is deeper, you strange world! Reach for God's woe, not for me! What am I? a drunken sweet lyre – a midnight lyre, an ominous bell-frog that nobody understands but that *must* speak...."[31] I don't know if one will grasp, by following these sentences, a slender thread connecting a being to the abyss of a totality in which he dissolves. Nietzsche said of music that he couldn't see any difference between it and tears.... The conclusion of Zarathustra is that "JOY IS DEEPER THAN WOE...."

The essential point where Gide met Nietzsche is doubtless the affirmation of joy. But the joy of Gide is crude. In the often indirect expression it received, that of Nietzsche is like the uncontrollable rise of the sobs that he stifled.

5. The Extent of Gide's Mistake
Nietzsche's jealousy toward Jesus must be considered with regard to this balancing act, this wavering between audacity and contempt, between joy and distress. Doesn't jealousy itself swing

from the purest feelings to derision? When the jealousy is expressed with humor, reversing itself, what Nietzsche would prefer to be to being Jesus (he says "to being a saint," but Gide is right, we may read "Jesus"), is first a "satyr";[32] then the feeling heats up and it becomes a "buffoon." Thus, Nietzsche is led by a feeling of jealousy to the contrary feeling of derision. But this could not be explained if some sovereign demand had not corresponded to the object of his jealousy. We know that this was the case. But Gide was mistaken about this to the point of being indefensible. Either things became so distorted in his memory that they were reversed, or his knowledge of Nietzsche was so superficial that he didn't have the authority to speak.[33]

Gide writes in his *Journal*:

> I cannot set up against Christ that proud and jealous resistance of Nietzsche. When he speaks of Christ, his marvelous perspicacity seems to me to fail him; yes, truly, he seems to me to accept an already second-hand and distorted image of Christ, and, in order to oppose him better, to hold Christ responsible for all the clouds and all the shadows projected on this earth by the sorry misinterpretations of his words.
>
> I feel in Christ's teachings as much emancipatory power as in Nietzsche's; as much opposition between the value of the individual and the state, or civilization, or "Caesar," as much abnegation and joy. What am I saying: as much? I discover still more, and a more profound and more secret opposition; more assured and, hence, calmer; more complete and, hence, less tense, in the Gospel of Christ than in the Gospel of Zarathustra.... It belonged to Nietzsche to rediscover under the shrouds and resuscitate a true Christ, but, rather than rally to Him whose teaching surpassed his own, Nietzsche thought to increase his stature by opposing Him, he resolutely misunderstands Christ; but for this misunderstanding, which is to be his spring-

board, the Church is even more than he responsible; by annexing, by trying to assimilate Christ, instead of assimilating herself to Him, she cripples Him more – and it is this crippled Christ that Nietzsche is fighting.[34]

Lang, who examines Gide's whole attitude toward Nietzsche, cannot omit to point out that even if he "often identified one with the other" (but, it seems to me, this "often" is a matter of convenience), Nietzsche "clearly distinguishes the message of the deliverer from Jesus of Saint Paul's dogmas, a message that seems to him to be annuled by the death on the Cross which the Church makes its real foundation." Lang also points out that

> scattered throughout Gide's books there are recriminations against the Christianity embodied in Saint Paul, nearly identical to those of Nietzsche and only slightly less ferocious: a leveling, suffocating, hypocritical morality, they say is contrary to life, to the creative impulse, to the heroism of culture, protecting the weakness and mediocrity of the throng at the expense of the individual.[35]

Anyone who has read Nietzsche attentively will be surprised at such an error. In a little book published under the title *Nietzsche and Christianity*,[36] Karl Jaspers has called attention, on the contrary, to the interest of an image of Jesus projected by Nietzsche which stands in contrast to the Church's formulation. "Gide," writes Lang, "has always defended Jesus against Christianity; he has long promised us a treatise by that name." *Christ Against Christianity*: the title would fit the chapter that Jaspers has devoted to the image that Nietzsche constructed of Jesus, titled "Who was Jesus?"[37] Moreover, Jaspers titles the following chapters: "The Distortion of Jesus' Christianity" and "The Roots of Distorting Christianity." He even takes note of a diametrically opposite interpretation. Ernst Benz, a contributor to the *Zeitschrift für Kirchen Geschichte*, where he published, in 1937, *Nietzsche's Ideas on the History of Christianity*, says that Jaspers,

> in his treatise [e.g., *Nietzsche and Christianity*] comes to a strange conclusion. Having repeatedly pointed out the mendacity of the nineteenth century's liberal and positive theology, this theologian finally considers Nietzsche's picture of Jesus and its significance "in the sense of a positive contribution to the realization of a new form of Christian life and thought." He then speaks of Nietzsche in these terms: "The Anti-Christ turns into...the teacher of an imitation of Christ which the Church, in its weakness and indolence has suppressed. The enemy of the Church turns into the prophet of a possible new Christianity, which the Church itself, afraid of its relentless and uncomfortable consequences, has preferred to conceal: He becomes the herald of a new evangelical order which would unite a new community of His king for a new imitation of Christ, and by acting out a life in His manner would strike the paper creeds from the hands of mere Christian believers."

"Astounding sentences," concludes Jaspers, "to emanate from a theologian – astounding for those who envision the whole of the portrayal of Jesus just drawn in Nietzsche's words."[38]

I am inclined to think that Gide, before Benz, having tried to reconcile the irreconcilable, Jesus and Nietzsche, having imagined, dubiously, the inadmissible figure of a Christ with Nietzschean traits – having in any case *placed the figure of Nietzsche opposite that of Jesus*, was no less troubled by having done so than Nietzsche, who had done it first.[39] But Gide felt at a loss, and harbored toward Nietzsche, whom he reread only rarely, a feeling of malaise and suspicion. Doubtless, Nietzsche made him feel that he had little originality. *Les Nourritures terrestres* can be seen as a rather thin extension of Nietzsche's teaching. Nietzsche frightened Gide, but not as he did at the start, when he represented sin (Gide never again stopped granting himself sin). Nietzsche reduced him to insignificance: his only outstanding book derived from that all-too-heavy influence, but he didn't understand a difficult work. He saw the value of the present moment only in the light of enjoyment. This is not *contrary* to that thought, but Gide could not feel the abandon of a positively sovereign man who, no longer being subordinate to others who would answer him (and answer for him), question joyfully perhaps, but silently, and to the point of death. Gide was a timid questioner; he sagely asked limited questions, having no feeling for tragic, or serious, play. He was a man like any other: I could not offer him any higher praise.

He undoubtedly had the desire to "take hold of the evangelical doctrine, knock down its barriers and defenses, divest it of its promise of a hereafter, of all mysticism, and transfigure the life of Jesus into a reign of liberating joy."[40] Such was the best means of reconciling the irreconcilable and of living in harmony with oneself, which he could do only by forgetting Nietzsche. I don't know if he realized the extent to which his love of Jesus was a game. The name Goethe sums up the secure feeling that human life gave him.

Jaspers (and Benz) made the comparison that he might have drawn, and that he should have drawn if offhandedness — and thoughtlessness — had not prevailed over conscientiousness. But it seems to me that he was right to make this mistake. Jaspers has assembled those texts that assume, in the history of sovereignty, an altogether surprising, but decisive meaning that Gide's mistake clearly underscores.

Jaspers quotes Nietzsche:

If there is anything unevangelical...it is the hero concept. The very opposite of all struggle has here [in the Gospel] become instinctive: the incapacity for resistance here becomes morality.... But how surprised we are to see that Nietzsche can *speak of himself in very similar terms* [in *Ecce Homo*]. "I have no memory of ever making an effort – no trace of struggle can be shown in my life; I am the opposite of a heroic character. To want something, to strive for something, to have an end, a desire in mind – all this I have never experienced. I have not the slightest wish for anything to become different; I myself do not want to change." There are several such analogies between Nietzsche's language about Jesus and about himself. "Everything else...all nature is useless to him except as a sign, a parallel," we quoted him as having said of Jesus. And about himself he says, "But what has Nature been created for, if not so I shall have signs in which to talk to souls?"

As we read on, our astonishment increases. Nietzsche not only makes such analogies unconsciously, but he explicitly claims Jesus for his own position "beyond good and evil" – for his own amoralism in the fight against morality. "Jesus sided against those who judge: he wanted to be the destroyer of morality." "Jesus said: What do we sons of God care for morality?" And last, explicitly, Nietzsche says: "God is the Beyond good and evil."

The problem of the presence of eternity, of experiencing bliss, which Jesus solved by his way of life, is Nietzsche's own problem. "What seems to distinguish Christ and Buddha: it seems to be an inner happiness that makes them religious," he says with evident appreciation, indeed with approval. Nietzsche's way of achieving this inner happiness differs from theirs: it is to experience the abolition of all aims, and simultaneously the aimlessness of genesis in the realization of the eternal recurrence. Nietzsche experiences this mystically, not in the practice of a way of life, but the feeling that "bliss is here" is nevertheless familiar to Nietzsche, as it was to Jesus.

391

In Nietzsche's eyes, the great antagonist of Jesus was Dionysus. Almost all his theses are phrased against Jesus and for Dionysus. In Jesus' death he saw an expression of declining life, an indictment of life; the dismembered Dionysus impressed him as life rising in tragic exultation, constantly regenerating itself. And yet, in a curious bit of ambiguity, Nietzsche could, if only for rare moments, strike the pose of Jesus, and the scrawls of Nietzsche the madman, so meaningful in his case, were signed not only "Dionysus" but "the Crucified."[41]

Jaspers does not at all forget Nietzsche's opposition to Christianity ("against which...he had repeated Voltaire's 'Ecrasez l'infâme' "[42]). Nietzsche accused Jesus himself of decadence, of childishness, and – doubtless in the sense given to the word by Dostoyevsky in *The Idiot* – of "idiocy." But, as with all those who had the power to set things in motion, there was something in him that began anew, following in the line of his predecessors. Lucidity, passionate resolve, and detachment from the ties that the past had formed, joined to the desire to give and the certainty that the gift decides, establish a deep kinship between Nietzsche and Jesus. Above all, both were moved by the feeling of sovereignty that possessed them and by an equal certainty that nothing sovereign could come from *things*. Nietzsche sized up this resemblance. He was in a position opposite Jesus! But the self-assurance and abandon of Jesus were precisely what he lacked. Jesus claimed a legacy, and the possibility of Christianity – in which things absorbed him, when he thought he had prevailed over them, as he meant to do – spread out in front of him. Nietzsche was alone and his teaching compared to that of Jesus is an unfortunate joke, which no one took seriously.

I would venture to say that no one *could* have taken seriously, and perhaps, a bit further, that no one should have.... Gide's absurdity in this regard is perhaps less bothersome than Jaspers' rigorous description. At least Gide's superficiality and that muddled shame, so full of twisted feelings that it changes into ingenuousness, are not professorial. Perhaps it was Nietzsche's luck to be condemned to mockery by those who loved him. The mockery of Mann is no less striking to me, and seems to me no less worthy of attention than that of Gide.

THREE

Nietzsche and the

Transgression of Prohibitions

1. Nietzsche, Doctor Faustus, and the Myth of the Defeat of the Ambitious Spirit

As everyone knows, *Doctor Faustus*, one of Thomas Mann's last novels, is in a sense a life of Nietzsche fictionalized under another name. But this "life of the German composer Adrian Leverkühn, as told by one of his friends," far from illuminating the figure of the philosopher, blurs its features, so much so that one is obliged to delineate it anew.

Maurice Colleville writes:

> With *Doctor Faustus* the very persona of Nietzsche, the living man, the man in the flesh, thrusts itself on the novelist, focuses the narrative, determines the general structure of the new novel. Here it's not a matter of thematic influence, it's the very life of Nietzsche that Thomas Mann has transposed into the existence of the composer Adrian Leverkühn.[43]

Yet the elements drawn from Nietzsche's biography only roughly determine the traits of character in the novel. Mann has recently submitted an essay in which he relates the circumstances in which Nietzsche must have been infected.[44] It is assumed, and

Mann assumes, that Nietzsche owed his mental breakdown to the infection (with syphilis): Leverkühn of *Doctor Faustus* is himself stricken with general paralysis; the slow progress of the disease is for him, as it was for Nietzsche, a slow and nearly constant torture; like Nietzsche's, and at about the same age, his mind is overcome. And like Nietzsche, he dies on August 25, after twelve years of stupor.

And yet, Nietzsche died in 1900 and Leverkühn in 1940. Except for the secondary studies at "Kaiseraschern," in a school similar to Schulpforta, the theology studies begun quickly and quickly abandoned, and an ineffectual attempt at marriage, recalling Nietzsche's dealings with Lou Salomé and Paul Ree, on the whole the details of Mann's story do not follow the biography of the author of *The Gay Science*. Were it not for these few facts, probably no one would have assimilated the characters of the two personages.

On this point Colleville writes:

> Much could be said about the resemblances and spiritual affinities that one can detect between Nietzsche and his counterpart, Leverkühn. We lack the space to note many of the novel's details where, in the statements of the characters, purely Nietzschean principles are affirmed. It would be easy to show that the Devil, whom Thomas Mann introduces in the flesh, deliberately upholds the thesis of the will to power or a parody of it – that, as in Nietzsche, the life that is depicted in *Doctor Faustus* takes no account of morality, is not concerned with moral actions...; that the good is here only called "the flower of evil."[45]

Most of the events of the life and career and the basic intentions of Nietzsche and Leverkühn are different. Leverkühn's character remains remote from the sense of historical mission, from the absolute moral distress and the absolute affirmation of the philosopher of the overturning of values. In return, Nietzsche is very far from a pact with the Devil, which is, albeit involuntarily, the lot of Leverkühn.

There is definitely something disturbing about the figure put forward by Mann. In particular, the Paul Ree of the novel, Rudolf Schwerdtfeger, before meeting Marie Godeau (another Lou Salomé), was the homosexual lover of Leverkühn. I don't know if Mann is echoing a tradition deserving of credence (this is the case for the visits of the young Nietzsche to a Cologne brothel); the homosexuality of Nietzsche is doubtless a conjecture!, perhaps even a conjecture that exists solely, though unavoidably, in the minds of readers of Mann, so that the homosexuality of Leverkühn would have nothing to do with Nietzsche, and the same would be true of a thousand different traits: the birth on a Thuringian farm, the death on a farm in the Bavarian mountains, the musical theories analogous to those of Schönberg, or the death of a nephew, of a little child.... This last trait apparently related the author himself, and the homosexuality perhaps.... But the pederasty does not cease being accursed; its image brought into the life of Nietzsche has something underhanded, shabby about it: Leverkühn is a genuine damned individual, visited by the Devil, to whom he is bound by a pact.

Mann undoubtedly meant to construct a figure of the sort that mythology and legend can produce, combining the traits of different heroes, and the real personage with the legendary one. The novel's title refers to the most recent – and the most significant – of Leverkühn's musical works: the intention to place Leverkühn in the lineage of Faust is obvious.

After Colleville, Geneviève Bianquis points to a perhaps closer parallelism with the oldest account of the adventures of Faust, the *Faustbuch* of 1587. "Not only," she says, "is the musician's last work directly inspired by the last chapters of the *Faustbuch*, but Leverkühn's entire life is copied from the existence ascribed by legend to the accursed magician."[46] In fact whole sentences from the *Faustbuch* are carried over into Mann's novel, and Leverkühn, like the Faust of legend, "was the son of honest and pious Thuringian peasants." Other details tally. The composer occasionally speaks an archaic language similar to that of the *Faustbuch*; he speaks in this way with the Devil; he is steeped in the magic of numbers, and in the mathematical relations of music he seeks something other than the sensible ordering of sounds....

Apparently, it was pity – which he acknowledges in the essay and relates to veneration, but which inclines him painfully to contempt – that led Mann to combine the figure of Nietzsche with that of Faust, in order to reduce it to the theme of the will as victim of its excessiveness. "I experienced... the mixture of veneration and pity. I have never ceased to experience it."[47] Such is the origin of *Doctor Faustus*. In it the transfigured Nietzsche is no longer anything but the myth of defeat, of the catastrophe of the spirit: what he embodies is the impotent exasperation of an impious will the limits of which the exceptional man has to go beyond.

With a good deal of precision and delicacy, Mann has linked, in his study, the illness and the genius of Nietzsche (as he does in the novel about the genius and the illness of Leverkühn). "The point is *who* is afflicted with the disease: an average numskull in whose case the disease of course lacks any spiritual and cultural aspect, or a Nietzsche, a Dostoevsky."[48] This sense of proportion does not lessen the harshness of the final judgment. Nietzsche wanted to make *Zarathustra*

an achievement measured by which the entire remainder of all human activities appears poor and confined, when he claims that a Goethe, a Shakespeare, a Dante would never for a moment be able even to draw a breath in the heights of this book, and that the genius and the goodness of all great souls put together would never be capable of producing as much as one single oration of Zarathustra.[49]

Mann seems justified in contrasting these pretensions with the poverty of the results. "This faceless and formless monster, Zarathustra...often touching and mostly painful to watch – an unhuman wavering at the borders of the ridiculous...."[50] Mann even writes: "Who takes Nietzsche at face value, takes him literally, who believes him, is lost."[51] Nietzsche is a brilliant intellect, stripped bare by his illness, but the spectacle he offered to his fellows is something like, say, a farmhouse burning in the night. Nietzsche: "a figure full of delicate and venerable tragedy and enveloped by the flashing summer lightning that heralds the dawn of a new time."[52]

2. Nietzsche and the Myth of Defeated Germany

Further, Mann is disposed to mix Leverkühn's misfortune with Germany's disaster.... Insofar as it transfigures the life of Nietzsche, that of Leverkühn transposes it into the period of the wars, which was the period of Germany's collapse. The story, which the author attributes to one of the musician's friends, is supposed to have been written during the second of these wars, the current, oppressive preoccupation with which adds to the heaviness of the preoccupation with past events.

In Germany, people took from Nietzsche's teaching those elements that drew them willingly into war. But the historical effect is negligible: Mann's narrative tells us of the immense joy that exploded, literally, with the declaration of war in 1914. Nietzsche of course had nothing to do with this. But a salient aspect of his doctrine accords, if need be, with Hitlerism. Mann does not emphasize it in the least. He is even inclined to clear Nietzsche of that crude, sweeping accusation.

Incidentally, I am inclined here to reverse cause and effect and not to believe that Nietzsche created fascism, but rather that fascism created him — that is to say: basically remote from politics and innocently spiritual, he functioned as an infinitely sensitive instrument of expression and registration; with his philosopheme of power he presaged the dawning imperialism and as a quivering floatstick indicated the fascist era of the West in which we are living and shall continue to live for a long time to come, despite the military victory over fascism.[53]

But if the Nietzsche–Nazism connection is superficial (for Nazism, Nietzsche's contribution was not only useless or uncertain but awkward), it is nonetheless easy and unavoidable to draw a parallel between the fate of Germany, its efforts and vain exasperation, and the unhappy impotence and miserable destiny of Nietzsche: "a figure full of delicate and venerable tragedy," standing in the storm of history. An obvious efficacy *(who takes Nietzsche literally... is lost!)* depriving the philosopher of significance, reduces him to the visible sign, to the figure of tragedy. Mann's *invalidation* is so complete that Nietzsche emerges from it muzzled, confined to musical expression. This book is in fact an abdication, if not by the writer, then by Germany (on behalf of which some Germans have reproached the exile for speaking): *Doctor Faustus* is the funereal panorama of a nation, the account of a collapse, the dirge of a world into which the Devil brought confusion and error: this *lamento* is the execration of excess, it is the confession and the cry for mercy of a diabolic resolution.

3. Homage and Insult
I won't say more about Germany and its destiny, but however justified the judgment condemning that country's excess may be, it is not necessary in this connection to yield to the disarray that

is provoked by Nietzsche's elusiveness and mobility. It is simple to say, "Who takes Nietzsche literally... is lost." Or to resign oneself and no longer to expect from him, like Jaspers, anything but an initial shock, an incitement to the movement of thought. I imagine, on the contrary, that Nietzsche's is the only philosophy that wrenches one away from the servitude inherent in philosophical discourse, the only one that restores sovereignty to the free spirit. It's true that Mann is right: "Who takes Nietzsche literally... is lost!"[54] But: "Who tries to save his life shall lose it." No one is – for a moment – sovereign who does not lose himself.

There is a glimmer of truth in Mann's impression, perceiving the link between the impulses that led Germany to the monstrous, and disastrous, attitude of its wars and Nietzsche's thought, open to the derangement of thought. The very form of this thought participates in the beginning of a disequilibrium, a rebellion, but Nietzsche himself felt the need for a restrained form. It seems that "escaping from Germany" had a vital significance in his eyes, that he clung to the idea the way a drowning man clings to a line, and it is in this, rather than through the doctrine of toughness, that he can be seen as having a presentiment of shameful events. To his mind, it was crucial to deny Christian morality, which utterly condemns the animal play of strength. He sometimes did so inordinately, without having sorted out the concordant demands of prohibition and infraction (he fell into the impasse of power...). But his attitude is closed to us if we relate it to the concern of the man of action. Nietzsche aspired to the sovereignty of a "free spirit"; he would not have wanted, if such were possible, to abandon restraint, but he could not ignore the *horror* of that defenseless position.[55]

> You will never pray again, never adore again, never again rest in endless trust; you do not permit yourself to stop before any ultimate

wisdom, ultimate goodness, ultimate power, while unharnessing your thoughts; you have no perpetual guardian and friend for your seven solitudes; you live without a view of mountains with snow on their peaks and fire in their hearts; there is no avenger for you any more nor any final improver; there is no longer any reason in what happens, no love in what will happen to you....[56]

I don't know if Mann is sensitive to such accents. He is surprised rather by Nietzsche's inability to revere. He is a little alarmed himself by the terms in which he has spoken of Zarathrustra: "unhuman, wavering at the borders of the ridiculous." "When I say this," he adds,

> I remember the desperate cruelty with which Nietzsche spoke of many, really of all things he revered: of Wagner, of music in general, of morals, of Christianity – I nearly said: also of all things German, – and how apparently *even with his most furiously critical attacks against those values and powers which he always respected deep within his innermost self, he never had the feeling of really impairing them, but rather seemed to feel that the most awful insults he hurled at them, were essentially a form of ovation.*[57]

But Mann has misunderstood the significance of these remarks: later we find this conclusion: "One can say that Nietzsche's relation to the preferred objects of his criticism was fundamentally that of passion: a passion basically neither negative nor positive, for one continually changes over into the other."[58] These alternations are not unimportant.

If we wish to judge Nietzsche's way of thinking, we must first consider the two basic attitudes of those who want to give their life a value independent of their useful works. Within the limits of Christian religion, the concern with reserving value for grace, irrespective of useful works, always played the greatest role. However, I will pass over the oppositions represented by the names of Augustine and Jansenius, Calvin and above all Luther. Libertinage and satanism are closer to the Nietzschean negation. I must recall, to begin with, the need for prohibitions without which the *possibility* of life as we know it is not given. We know that the observance of prohibitions relating essentially to sexuality and death founds the difference between man and animals. They are the respects that we impose on ourselves, which give that human quality which we prize above all else. No one can say, without being naive, concerning these prohibitions which press upon him, that he would be what he is, that he would have that eminent dignity, if he had not observed them: who could go back to animal behavior? But on the other hand, no one would have a sovereign attitude if he sometimes did not lift those prohibitions, if he had not situated, beyond the rules he observes and even reveres in some way, the sovereign moment of being within himself. The most ancient men – and, in agreement with them, the archaic peoples – dimly perceived the need for these alternations. Only the rationalism of our age has scorned the primitive rule, which is not grounded in reason.

Rationalism's contempt for the irrational rule is complex. It is a matter of reducing value to reason, that is, to the useful (even if it is absurd that an action should have value only in relation to something else, itself being useful for something...[59]). But rationalism itself *utilizes utility* when it deems it right not to follow a bothersome rule. Sometimes it gives a utilitarian interpretation of an interdiction, such as incest (thus the alleged degeneration of children born of the incestuous unions). Other times, reason is the pretext for liberties taken with custom, but a decision made rationally because of an irrational desire takes away the savor of the object of that desire. In a sense, rational judgments are favorable to license, but by judging it reasonable they make of it what nudism makes of nudity: nudity that is not miraculous, that is not desirable.[60] Nietzsche had a new attitude.

Nietzsche did not have the archaic attitude. It is true that he was susceptible to that moral law whose violation, in its principle, responded to a deeper demand within him, and one more deeply moral than the coarseness of the law. But in this fact I only see the key to a somewhat different position. Nietzsche has an attitude that was symmetrical and opposite to that of the heroes of the Greek tragedies – whom a fatality condemned to violate the rules they held sacred. But I could not adequately situate Nietzsche's paradox, that insult which is a homage, without relating it to other transgressions of the law in the context of modern life.

4. Nietzsche and Don Juan

The violation of the most seductive law (it is not the most serious) is doubtless the one that was assumed by the mythical character Don Juan: I am thinking of the portrayal by Mozart and Da Ponte. Kierkegaard, who came under its spell, contrasted the spirit of devotion with the seduction of a music that is the soul of eroticism. But Don Juan's libertinage goes beyond the delight in which the sexual prohibition is lifted: it is from the breaking of the law that assures the dead of the horror-stricken respect of the living that the figure of the "seducer" has derived its greatest charm.

I can violate a law in two ways. I can neglect to observe it, violating it through ignorance; this is the attitude of rationalism. But I can consciously, without disregarding it, violate it with exuberance. In a first movement, Don Juan is content to ignore the fear that most people have of the dead: he is the Commander's killer, but the irony of his invitation is not a sacrilege if nothing is sacred to him. But when the statue walks into the house the evidence is clear and Don Juan no longer defies that which he had the strength to ignore, he defies that which towers over him. He passes from levity to a consciousness of the *law*, when the hand of the statue chills him and, thunderstruck, he shouts *No* to the one who, in vain, commands him to repent.

It is insofar as the Commander acts in the real order that Don Juan's attitude resembles that of Nietzsche. The feeling of Don Juan, certain that hell is swallowing him up and not yielding, is in my view comparable to the surmounted terror, which will never cease terrifying, that Nietzsche links to the certainty of the death of God. Neither one yielded, they did not surrender at the moment when there was nothing left around them that did not overwhelm them. The libertine's death was not his defeat if in the hand of death itself he was unable to admit he was beaten, to the point where one must speak of his moral triumph. The Commander would win if the killer acknowledged the crime and repented: he fails since he cannot get the lawbreaker to admit his wrong.

The story of Don Juan enriches men with a possibility they lacked in the archaic world. In the archaic world, the transgressor acknowledged the crime in advance. He committed it nonetheless. The advantage remained with the one who dictated the prohibition. However, a radical difference separates the legendary lord from Nietzsche. The former is brought, in spite of himself but through sovereign action, to the knowledge that the law prevails. He does not yield and remains conscious, in dying, of not yielding. But this force overwhelms him *from the outside*. The moral demand never ceased to impress itself on Nietzsche *from within*. Nietzsche could not rely, as Don Juan did, on the errors of reason.[61]

405

5. *Baudelaire's Satanism and Sartre's Interpretation*

Sartre has stressed the *minor* character of satanism. Satanism is perhaps more foreign to Nietzsche than Don Juan's invitation. But he
also comes near to it in a different way, which allows us to define
another possibility open to present-day man, one that only Christianity has provided: "The revolutionary," says Sartre, explaining
Baudelaire's attitude,

> wants to change the world.... The rebel is careful to preserve the
> abuses from which he suffers so that he can go on rebelling against
> them.... [He] does not want to destroy or transcend the existing
> order; he simply wants to rise up against it. The more he attacks it,
> the more he secretly respects it. In the depths of his heart he pre-
> serves the rights which he challenges in public.[62]

Or further on:

> The atheist doesn't bother about God because he has made up his
> mind once and for all that God doesn't exist. But the priest who cel-
> ebrates a Black Mass hates God because He is kind and flouts Him
> because He is respectable, He applies his will to the negation of the
> established order, but at the same time he preserves this order and
> asserts his belief in its existence more strongly than ever.[63]

Sartre has said of this position that it was that of a man who
"never progressed beyond the stage of childhood."[64] (Is Satan
himself anything more than "the symbol of disobedient sulky
children who asked that their father's look should freeze them
in their singular essence and who did wrong in the framework
of Good"?[65])

Apparently missing from these formulas in which Sartre wished
to enclose Baudelaire is the awareness of a contrary problem: that

encountered by revolutionaries who, if they overthrow the established order, have the responsibility of establishing a new order, a better one no doubt, but an order nonetheless. No serious and sustained objection can be made against the need to give everyone's activity rules that limit it and place it in the service of good.[66] So we are faced with a dilemma: we are adults [*majeurs*], we actually overthrow the established order, but we cannot intend to put freedom in the place of constraint, we have to impose some new constraint, less burdensome perhaps, but a constraint such that society as a whole does not cease to acknowledge the primacy of useful activity. Just as before, we must deprive ourselves of access to a too costly luxury, a certain freedom that is conventionally called *evil*. We would not be able, in a roundabout way, to satisfy the need for license in the name of the necessity that is condemned by the law. Only rebellion gives access to the unjustifiable disorder whose meaning is in not being compatible with the law. But, like the crowds, rebellion is childish. Lucid revolution submits to the necessity whose empire blind rebellion denies.

If I go back to the archaic forms of prohibition and violation, the dilemma is posed in different terms.

In the pre-Christian world the prohibition that an irrational nausea prescribed was empirically in accord with necessity. This nausea resulted from the disequilibrium that exuberance introduced, but, restrained for a long enough time, the exuberance would give itself free expression without any danger and what it experienced at that moment in a sovereign manner was what it had at first forbidden itself. But the prohibition lifted in this way was lifted only *childishly*: those rules transgressed *in broad daylight* during the festival were those that the transgressor preserved *in the depths of his heart*. Revolutionary action, the only adult action, cuts us off from those cunning possibilities to which, in the guise of satanism, Christianity gave a more shameful form of itself, one

407

that was more deeply untenable and at the same time more accessible to us. The sexual prohibition is mainly the occasion of this modern form of rebellion. Baudelaire, whose prosecutor Sartre took it on himself to become (which also involved some ingenuousness) expressed this possibility, unknown to archaic man, very well: "As for myself, I say: the supreme and unique pleasure [*volupté*] of love lies in the certainty that one is doing *evil*. – And man and woman know from birth that the whole of pleasure is to be found in evil."[67] If God, who placed evil in pleasure, did not exist, or at least was not the object of some mistaken certainty, the sovereign moment of pleasure would no longer be available to us.

In other words, eliminating the mysticism connected with religious representation:

– the rule of life establishes the value of irregularity;

– the sovereign attitude, which is established by respect for the rule, is linked to the conscious violation of the respect it fails to observe.

– pleasure, unjustified by any utility, is sovereign insofar as it denies to the point of ecstasy a world that is infinitely deserving of respect.

It is characteristic of Christianity to have given a coherent (rationalized) form to the respect that the world of efficacious activity deserves. The basic theme of archaic humanity attains absurdity in the "logical" opposition of God and evil, of angelic purity and criminal obscenity. Eroticism is doubtless only a particular aspect, but it is a touchstone: the question is always whether we are exceeding the limit *despite* the awareness we have of exceeding it dangerously, and *despite* our respect for the weakness of a world predicated on the limit. If we are aware of the danger and of the destruction of *things*, we acknowledge in some way (in the feeling of sin, but also in the vexation that intended to pay no heed to anything) the respect that is deserved by the prohibition we violate: the prohibition and the immense world, whose most studied form is the Christian God, which is associated with the prohibition. Would Don Juan be what he is for us if he had not encountered it, and if, encountering it, he had not refused it to the end — in the gasp of death? Would sensual pleasure be dreadful, which it is, without that curse by God that oppresses us when we are ravaged by pleasure?

Nietzsche is the atheist who bothers about God, because he once recognized that, not existing, the place that God left vacant laid all *things* open to destruction. At the same time, Nietzsche demanded *freedom* and was conscious of a breakdown that goes with it. Freedom is, first of all, a political reality: in this case, it corresponds to the oppression of one class by another. (It can also be the occasion of a philosophical chatter, as if the metaphysical question concerning it did not immediately call for the silence of unknowing.[68]) But beyond politics and the domain of efficacious action, freedom signifies a sovereign attitude in the domain of sensible values (I can act in order to be free but the action immediately deprives me of the freedom that I have to respond to passion). It is remarkable in this respect to see Nietzsche, to a certain extent, share in Baudelaire's "childishness." Nietzsche's behavior apparently has nothing to do with an opening, in evil, to the voluptuous moment. But where Mann sees a futile agitation, in the entanglement where the insult clung to the homage, the dual impulse peculiar to the sovereign attitude is revealed.

Nietzsche had perceived from the start that paradoxical impossibility of yielding in either direction. As early as 1875, after *The Birth of Tragedy*, he wrote these few words that break down the door opened by Mann's judgment: "Socrates, I must avow, is so close to me that I am constantly at war with him."[69] He never stopped taking stock of the immense effort — represented by

409

Socrates and morals, Christianity and God – that attempted to organize into a single block all the conflicting possibilities of the human being. That is why he never saw *evil*, which makes this desperate effort useless, anywhere else but in the rent where Baudelaire glimpsed it. Vis-à-vis unavoidable evil, the evil that alone is sovereign because it alone escapes from necessity, Nietzsche did not just have the attitude of the child who would like for a delightful situation to last: he knew (but wasn't Baudelaire aware of the fact?) that it can't last, he knew that the void opened up beneath the feet of anyone who assumes it, to whom the sovereign moment is given, who, in this moment, experiences as his own dissolution the dissolution of the *thing* and of everything...he knew that once the keystone of the edifice was struck, "the earth was severed from its sun" and that we were already "in the breath of empty space."[70]

FOUR

The Present Age and Sovereign Art

1. The Situation of the "Sovereign Subject" in Today's World
It seems to me at this point that the usual tie linking thoughts
among themselves and linking men to the limited propositions
of language is coming undone. At this point, admiration and adhe-
sion are passing over into oblivion, into indifference. In this ambiguous world, which is breaking up, where others sought God,
where in our turn, certain of attaining NOTHING, we seek – the
time comes, finally, to embrace all the perspectives in which the
drama's protagonist, the *subject*, or the authentic sovereign, seems
to us now to be lost – so clumsily.

Might there actually be a place in this world for that impossibility? One kind of figure is banished from communism, that of
the sovereign writer or artist. In Soviet society, the writer and
the artist are *in the service* of leaders who are not sovereign, as
I said, except in the renunciation of sovereignty. (An unprecedented situation results from this. Not only has Soviet society
banished the sovereign writer or artist, but in general it no longer
allows anything but the art or literature of the past.) The bourgeois world, which is basically even more closed than communism to positive sovereignty, does welcome the sovereign writer
or artist, but only insofar as he is not recognized as such.

2. Sovereignty in Sacred Art and Literature

But the broad perspectives I want to speak of can be embraced only if we start from an earlier situation. Archaic society itself essentially excluded the sovereign writer or artist. But sovereignty dominated it. The writer or artist could not be sovereign in that society because of their artistic production alone. Literature or art, subordinate either to the city or to the person of the sovereign, were nonetheless the expression of an autonomous subjectivity, not of an objective activity or an alienated subjectivity (involved through action on things in the negation of itself). In particular, art was an expression of the subjectivity of the sovereigns, who did not work and could not have any action that might subordinate them to anything but themselves. Moreover, Greek tragedy, which expressly considers man's sovereign subjectivity, always deals with the subjectivity of traditionally sovereign personages, which goes to show that ancient democracy, which had repudiated the person of the king, maintained the values that he embodied. The situation of artists or writers in archaic society, prior to the possibilities of profane art, was actually quite variable, but in any case they were in the service of that archaic sovereignty which we can justifiably call *real*, as it is connected with some *thing*, with an institution, a given objective reality. The principle of such a service lay in the sovereign's inability to express, by himself, that subjectivity which, being the objectified subjectivity of all the others, had to be *communicated* to them: this principle was equally valid for kings, for priests and for sacerdotal bodies. Dignitaries could speak but they could also keep silent and use the voice of others. Were they not themselves in the service of a sovereign *reality*, of an institution that transcended them personally, and that they only temporarily embodied? Within this sacred system, splits [*déchirements*] could occur; a man might say to himself – and proclaim – that, over and above those who

412

claimed to embody it, he served the true sovereignty, which was independent of all its embodiments. But the principle was not changed in the slightest. The writer or artist served in any case a *real* sovereignty, outside their personal objectivity, save in the affective tie connecting this latter to *real* sovereignty.

3. Profane Art and Literature

As the sacred world declined and profane society had more importance, profane art and literature apparently took on profane forms. But was this so-called profane ever anything but a degraded aspect of the sacred? Considering them as a whole, imposing as they are, profane art and literature still did not bring men anything more than a substitute for the emotions that were found first in the sanctuary where the most terrible truth appeared to them.

It would be difficult to state briefly what profane art is capable of expressing. The only general character it has is its extreme diversity.

Derision and confusion constantly and limitlessly distort it. But for all that, it continues to fulfill the initial function of art, which is the expression of subjectivity, of that subjectivity which, from the outset, claimed to be the purpose of all objects.

This point is essential: the sacred and the profane are defined by a formal discontinuity, by the sharpness of their contrast. But if we contrast sacred art with profane art, this discontinuity is absent.[71] Sometimes profane art borders on sacred art, and nowhere is there any clear difference, any *threshold*, in the continuous multiplicity of the various forms of profane art. Even if it is easy to be mistaken in the matter, *genius* is *altogether different* from talent, but just as prose is not separated from poetry by any *threshold*, art that expresses anguish is not truly separate from that which expresses joy; the chapters of a manual that deals successively with dramatic or lyric poetry, the novel, the journal or the essay, are

413

only arbitrarily distinct. Profane art, *regarding itself as such,* can even, whenever it likes, express as well as it can the subjectivity of those sovereign forms that long dominated society. But it still differs from sacred art in that it *adds* to the expression of this definite subjectivity that of human subjectivity isolated from those dominant forms.

4. The Connection between Profane Art and Eroticism

In particular, it expresses the subjectivity of eroticism (which is out of place and gives rise to disconcerting comments if it is assumed in the context of sacred art). In principle, eroticism is linked to the profane world in that it cannot be the object of general communication, which the expression of the sacred is in society. The communication of erotic subjectivity, even if it is literary, appeals confidentially to the one who receives it as a personal possibility, separate and apart from the multitude. It does not address itself to the admiration, to the respect of everyone, but to that secret contagion that never rises above others, that does not advertise itself and calls only for silence.

5. The Artist's Distress Linked to Sovereignty, Which Is Inaccessible to Him

We nonetheless lose, in the dispersal of the profane world, the ability to communicate sacred terror, which is the province of religion; there is a deterioration even though a compensation might appear. Sacred art got its power from repetition: the greatest shocks provoking the strongest emotions were repeated without variants; weariness came only in the long run. Profane art no doubt has the capacity to renew, but the artifice is perceptible from the moment when expression no longer has the immutable form that the centuries had allowed. It is no longer the subjectivity of mankind, independent of that of a *servile* artist, concerned

414

with finding the most effective *means*. It is that of any man bustling about in the world of things and deriving from his agitation an existence on a par with the subjugated crowd. Genius itself does not do away with the necessity for the artist to wretchedly seek his way, often passing through intrigue, rivalries and ingratiations. Nor does it do away with that megalomania based on error, which substitutes grandiloquent chatter for the simplicity and the silence of royal personages, on whom chance had bestowed effortless majesty. But, usually without knowing it, the artist accedes to sovereign subjectivity *himself*, by expressing it.

For a long time, what kept the artist from feeling himself to be sovereign – rather the opposite – was propriety. The artist made the work of art. Who was more conscious than he of the skill, the work, not to mention the trickery, without which he could not have expressed anything? Insofar as it exists, subjectivity is sovereign, and it exists insofar as it is communicated. But his honesty diverted the artist from the movement to which his situation condemned him. His integrity and the feeling he must have had that he would be committing a crime of "lèse-majesté" if he assumed a sovereignty that the institutions reserved exclusively for themselves. Sacred art at first had been for the artist an expression of the subjectivity of others, not of his own. Profane art found its integrity in maintaining this modesty. While on the whole it gave up expression of the dominant sovereignty, at all events it confined itself as best it could to expression of the subjectivity of others besides itself. This kind of art became mainly the expression of personages who were not aware of being sovereign and whose fleeting subjectivity, necessarily sovereign, would have slipped away if they had been tied to their daily action with its narrow reality – trips to the office or purchases in shops: there is a conventional suppression of objective elements in the representation of the personages of art, but this kind of sovereignty, that of anybody, acquired in the suppression of servile elements, is not offset by the clear consciousness of a sovereign situation in the world. In spite of everything, these personages are apprehended, if not in an insignificant attitude, then at least in their ability to take upon themselves the totality of being. This slide that characterizes profane art has the following consequence: if the artist manages in spite of everything to express his own subjectivity, it is always a fleeting subjectivity that is attributed to others, the subjectivity that does not recognize what it is.

In the period of art I am speaking of (from which romantic art stands apart perhaps, but with the awkwardness that wonders at its audacity and vainly calls attention to it), the artist remained within the humbled society, suffering, like anyone else, the ascendancy of a traditionally sovereign world. He was no longer in the service of the incarnations of that world, as his predecessor was in the time of sacred art (think of the anonymous image-maker of the Middle Ages), but he was nonetheless, like anybody, in search of the dignity that was given by proximity to the great ones or to the throne. In what he imagined of his own subjectivity, nothing seemed sovereign to him: the honesty to which he clung did not allow him to think differently. His place at the court, not his value, entitled him to that share of the magnificence to which he aspired with the feigned modesty that is the essence of modesty. He confined himself to the role of decorator and art to that of embellishment.

6. Sovereign Art

The sovereigns themselves recognized to a degree, but heedlessly, this mistaken self-perception that artists had. But they drew artists to their court and could not help but see a work of art in the splendor that defined their sovereignty. Without the effect of art, the sovereigns could not have communicated the splendor of their subjectivity. For the splendor of a king consisted of nothing but appearance, and appearance was the domain of the architects, painters, musicians and writers that surrounded him. It was insofar as these latter had the power to give the sovereign's splendid subjectivity the signs that expressed it that the king was radiant to all others. He drew them into closeness with him, therefore, because in his eyes art brought them near to his own essence. But the artist could not himself be any less heedless than the king was. He did not see the magnificence within himself, but only in his works or in their royal aspect. It was never a question of man's fundamental subjectivity, which, differing only in a random way from that of other men, instead of being radically separate, like that of God or the king, belonged to the artist to the degree that he was able to communicate it. Sovereign subjectivity remained linked to the universal, to the *totality*, which the king had the function of claiming, and to the *power* he believed he derived from the subjective sovereignty that the others attributed to him. In this way, the road toward a sovereign subjectivity merged with his own oneness and the magic power that belonged to him personally was blocked for the artist. The divine condition and the possibility of attaining it through an intimate participation (of which the artist was capable, but outside the work of art) sanctioned this estrangement, in which he kept himself, from that which he might have discovered in himself, directly[72] (which exists provided the subject discovers it by expressing it).

When the occasion presented itself, a few artists glimpsed a possibility that is theirs. But they could not grasp its significance so long as the feudal edifice was not strongly shaken. Until then, God, surrounded by saints, priests and great ones, made them feel there was a subjectivity that necessarily carried more weight than their own, in the sense at least that their own was bridled and reduced to worrying about the contestation of others.

417

It was a long time before solitude spread out before the man to whom the work of art – expression – opened up the riches of subjectivity, once there were no longer at his side those shadows madly in love with themselves, anchored in the sense of grandeur elevating them far above the multitude, of which Louis XIV is the last chilling example. In an immense spiritual agitation, the idea of God had itself lost that undisputed power of vertigo, whose existence alone made the inadequacy of *all* men bearable (their profound servitude and the way they had of lowering themselves to the level of things, while pretending to place themselves not quite so low as their neighbor). Nothing subsisted but that deep, and elusive, subjectivity, slipping away from anyone who tried to reduce it to that which things are, a subjectivity of which God and kings were obviously nothing more than the antiquated form, reduced in fact, alienated in the very effort to grasp it. In the depths of this solitude the problem of art finally ceased to be ridiculous, or if it seemed a bit more so, this was because absolute, aggressive ridicule was now the contrary of wretched, humiliated ridicule; unlimited ridicule opened "the man of sovereign art" to art finally free of respect for others and to sovereignty not limited by any prohibition, but only by the consciousness of an unbearable tragedy, at once dreaded and desired.

7. The Poverty of "Art for Art's Sake" and the Extreme Limit of the Possible

Yet, recently still, the miserable idea of "art for art's sake" showed how difficult it is to perceive the simplicity of the problem that art poses to existence. "Art for art's sake" meant that art cannot serve any other purpose than itself, but this formula makes little sense if art is not first extricated from the insignificant position it has in society. Art for art's sake was a response to the yearning for the feudal situation, where those whom the artists served, and on whom they completely depended, were themselves in the service of institutional sovereignty. What was at issue was still a decorative art, but this time one for the use of dilettantes detached from society. What the protagonists of art for art's sake wanted was merely to escape from the preoccupations of a society that had set itself goals that had nothing to do with pure sovereignty, goals that were not different, on the whole, from the basic goals of Soviet society. The formula would have been truly meaningful only if art had directly assumed the legacy of sovereignty, of all that was once authentically sovereign in the universal figure of God as well as in the figures of the gods and kings. It was necessary finally to claim the legacy with a force that corresponded to its boundlessness, but without ever resorting to *discourse*, in silence and in the *sovereign* moment of a definitive indifference.

If art is heir to the sovereignty of the kings and of God, this is because sovereignty never had anything in it but general subjectivity (except for that power over things that was attributed just as arbitrarily to sovereignty as to the operations of magic). But at first, men saw only in *others* (whether these others were the imaginary Being or their fellow men) that which their subjectivity generally contains that is disturbing, leaving one on the verge of tears. Could we, even today, perceive without the *beloved being* that staggering truth of the *self*, whose absence we cannot endure and whose presence we cannot bear as it is, since in our eyes it is doubtlessly the subjectivity of being, but only at the price of destroying that thing in it – the limited object – which it might be? But what love now reveals to us more dangerously than God could once reveal in a different way has the defect of being unbearable: we cannot detach the beloved being from the ties that bind it to chance and that constantly toss us back and forth between error and suffering: we live thrown back, beyond love, into the heartbreaking expression of a subjectivity that we have in common with that indeterminate fellow being to whom literature appeals, and who makes us alive to that subjectivity at the moment when we communicate it to him. This sovereignty is doubtless but a suffocation in the unbearable.[73] It brings to mind the ejaculation that makes one empty, the ecstasy that makes one cry: "I am dying from not dying." But it is no longer a matter of dilletantism: sovereign art reaches the extreme limit of the possible.

8. *The Example of* Zarathustra

The situation of the artist discovering the dignity that belongs to him is ridiculous nonetheless. The work of art cannot express without misrepresenting it that which his sensibility suggests to him and reveals to him only in impotence finally. Traditionally, the work of art invites one to give some *real* form to the subjectivity that offers itself and yet is only a refusal of the *real* order.

I now come back to *Zarathustra*, whose weakness I could not have considered apart from the preceding reflections, and whose example will help me define my thinking. Isn't *Zarathustra* the transposing onto *others* of the expression given by Nietzsche to his own subjectivity? It is the plagiarism of sacred literature, bringing onto the stage a character from the sacred world, recognized as such, or meaning to be. But in the tradition of profane literature, *Zarathustra* is the expression of a fictitious subjectivity, a piece of objective literature. We have to wonder whether it was possible to feign the existence of a sacred personage without going against the requirements of a world that knows nothing of the gratuitousness of fiction: mythology never professes to be anything other than real. But this book, being neither completely sacred nor completely profane, does not completely satisfy the requirements of a sovereign art either. It falls short to the extent that it conceals the author's deep subjectivity under antiquated forms. This book is the *fiction* of sacred *reality*, although

420

it is the immediate expression of sovereign subjectivity: this discordant multiplicity involves a considerable slide. Nietzsche, with the aid of profane liberty, disguising himself as a recognized (or recognizable) sacred entity, potentially assumed the functions of such an entity, connected with the reality of power. The sovereign subjectivity of which I speak, drawing its consciousness and very existence from literary expression, cannot give itself functions possessed only by real and recognized entities. The *real* sovereignty of Zarathustra striving to act in the world is not the useless fiction of profane art, whereas the movement of thought is very much the expression of sovereign art. But sovereign art is such only in the renunciation, indeed in the repudiation of the functions and the power assumed by real sovereignty. From the viewpoint of power, sovereign art is an abdication. It throws the responsibility for managing things back onto things themselves. In *Zarathustra* we can no longer see, at present, anything but the suffering of Nietzsche bewildered at feeling the sovereign subjectivity within him, suffocating and, out of despair, with the aid of fiction, looking on deserted paths for the way out.[74] But *Ecce Homo*, which according to Gide expressed Nietzsche's *jealousy*, the insistence on a sovereignty *equal* to that of Jesus, is nonetheless a disavowal of the dubious claims of *Zarathustra*. The suffering of sovereignty weighed upon him and, possessed by a great passion, he rose from a hopeless yearning for archaic forms, to that abandon of sovereign art, which made him finally prefer "being a buffoon to being a saint."

9. *Where Sovereignty Chooses Not To Subordinate*
"I am NOTHING": this parody of affirmation is the last word of sovereign subjectivity, freed from the dominion it wanted – or had – to give itself over things.

In this world, the man of sovereign art occupies the most common position, that of destitution. Whether or not he enjoys paltry resources, destitution is his lot, only the bottom of the ladder is the right level for him: even this is on the understanding that he does not demand a leadership privilege for the class that occupies it. Not that he opposes the leadership of the poorest, but even if they remain destitute, those who lead – or intend to lead – are opposed to him. He remains on the side of the *led*. Those who mean to lead the world – and change it – opt in this way for accumulation. Those who prefer that others lead it, even if their refusal to lead were but the consequence of the refusal to be led, aim at nonproductive consumption. The *led* of our time are the only ones who restrain, if the *leadership* troubles them, that vast movement of growth whose excessiveness is the promise of disastrous consumptions.

There is always something extravagant about the "man of sovereign art" (what Jaspers calls "exceptional"). But I would like to forestall any extravagant interpretation of what I've said about this, which I limit to experience, concerned that I will not get to the end of it. This affinity with destitution comes into play, at the bottom, only in the aversion for enterprise. It is merely paradoxical: at the bottom of the ladder the worker demands the improvement of his condition, with a view to a greater consumption throughout his life, but he does not want to extract it from an increased amount of labor, on the contrary; it's true, only technical progress and acquired accumulation make it possible to satisfy him, but he *may* be indifferent to these factors; his first impulse is directed against growing accumulation. In general, the working masses I speak of would reduce, if the decision were theirs, the share allotted to accumulation: they would increase that allotted to wages. I am not saying they are right, nor that the "man of sovereign art" is in principle qualified to judge in the matter, but the impulse of *immediate* subjectivity goes blindly in that direction.

This doesn't signify a general affinity between the "man of destitution" and "the man of sovereign art." From a different standpoint than that of accumulation and expenditure, it merely signifies the *déclassé* existence of the sovereign artist. The profane artist could also socially lower [*se déclasser*] himself, but nothing obliged him to do so, whereas the sovereignty of art requires that anyone who bears that sovereignty within him come down in the world. This loss of social standing [*déclassement*] is not opposed to the inner knowledge of the human possibilities that classing alone opened up, but it involves itself in the negation of those possibilities insofar as they attain the cohesion that bestows rank. Indeed, sovereign art signifies, in the most exact way, *access to sovereign subjectivity independently of rank.* This does not imply the meaninglessness of the behaviors that raised men above themselves as well as above animals, but rather their complete *dislocation* and their constant calling into question. In any case, sovereign subjectivity can never tie itself to such behaviors, except on condition that they do not raise any objection to existence at the bottom of the ladder. Not that they do not differ from that existence but the one who upholds them can never feel free of the abhorrence of contrary behaviors. Nothing, in fact, could make him regard himself as being above another, even if this were a criminal or someone repugnant to him, except insofar as the other would himself imagine he had some superiority of rank or race.

This is not a moral attitude or, at least, it is not a judgment good for all times. It is particularly when accumulation prevails over its contrary that class differences have a meaning they did not have before.

The world of accumulation is the world rid of the values of traditional sovereignty, in which things have "value." Subjectivity has the most limited place in it. But rank maintains, as I said, a constant importance, in hidden forms. In spite of everything, rank has kept part of the allurement it had in archaic society, but fortune alone determines it and, though everyone may be tormented by it, no one talks about it.

I call attention to the immense hypocrisy of the world of accumulation. In principle, it is completely contrary to archaic society's two main forms of activity, to the positing of *rank*, established by some form of ostentatious expenditure, and *war*, which is assuredly the most costly form of the destruction of goods. In actual fact, accumulation developed insofar as it effectively opposed both these forms. But while the world of accumulation remains their moral condemnation, it was only able to give them an increased importance, however, since it ultimately increased wealth. But this importance goes hand in hand with a disgraceful delusion. The world of accumulation cannot use up its wealth except through differences of rank and through war. These trappings, in the archaic world, had human dimensions, and the virtues of man thrived on them, not always happily, but at least in an exalting manner. Whereas, owing both to their condemnation and to their increased necessity, the generalized pursuit of rank is today, in its hypocrisy, the final humiliation of a multitude that has become comical, and war looks as if it will become the *fraudulent* bankruptcy of the human race.

Communism has opposed and still opposes the pursuit of differences of rank, but it is facing a dilemma: peaceful policy is causing it to shift from a frantic accumulation to modes of consumption [*consommation*], which in the current framework are bound to foster, in everyday life, not a rise in the standard of living, but a fight by every one for a higher standard than his neighbor. I'm not saying that the communist leaders could not in any way orient their economy toward a rise at the base, but such an

424

orientation is more difficult than it appears at first. Proletarian opposition to the wage scale is perhaps not strong, the proletarians considered in the aggregate being themselves inclined to rise on the scale. The idea of a "communist" society, in the strictly egalitarian sense the word has in its contrast with the merely "socialist" stage of development, has never taken on a concrete meaning since the anti-egalitarian turn of Stalinist policy. An opposite turn would imply, I imagine, a reversion to constraint, and constraint leads back to that tension which only war maintains. Now, it would be impossible to overlook the fact that communist accumulation, which doesn't necessarily lead to war, leads to it insofar as constraint ensures unlimited accumulation, if need be, and insofar as the leaders' sovereign renunciation of sovereignty is contrary to nonproductive consumption. The way out is undoubtedly egalitarian consumption and it would be inadmissible not to see that, in the world of renounced sovereignty, egalitarian consumption is what's wanted. Unfortunately, egalitarian consumption runs counter to the sovereign movement that demands consumption, and only renounced sovereignty ensures it, a renunciation that may be achieved by the leaders, or at most by a party elite, but not by a mass of people always open to outstripping one another. Thus, given the fact that egalitarian consumption remains the way out for the Soviet world, and the easy roads or tracks that most often guide movements do not lead to it, the easy roads leave the communist rulers facing this dilemma: either consumption in the pursuit of rank – moral bankruptcy – or catastrophic consumption in war. For, turning aside from these outlets, accumulation generates those return shocks – all the more dangerous because they confound the will – with a decisive force.

Doubtless, if the communist bloc existed by itself this dilemma would seem easily avoidable, but opposite the bourgeois world, twisting on the horns of the same dilemma (and perhaps more *dizzily?*).... Soon, developed accumulation permitting, the Soviet populace will be disjoined by an increased, easy and unequal, consumption, or, in the disorder universally maintained by a blind bourgeoisie, some unacceptable provocation by its enemies will cause its leaders, frightened by a consumption that disgraces them, to plunge it into war.

FIVE

1.

Communist thought is not equal to this situation. The solution that it envisages theoretically is logical; it is consumption at the base, but this thought does not address the problems that go beyond the construction of the USSR. It restricts itself without renewal to the basic ideas of Marxism and to the immediate experience of internal Soviet policy. The first communist to come along will be quick to reply to me: he will do so with that blind sincerity that leads straight to dishonest provocation. I will listen to him with the feeling that, after all, the vacuousness of noncommunist thought justifies him. But contempt or insult cannot alter the fact that communism, having earned the credit for raising and keeping open the problem of egalitarian consumption, has not solved it for all that. In particular, nothing in the world enables us to *glimpse* a changed humanity, renouncing, in its inner being, the pursuit of rank and war. Moreover, that is not what's at issue.

The problem that confronts us is not whether within the limits of the USSR and the communist bloc, or even in a uniformly socialized world, it will be possible to use up the accumulated resources.[75] The current problem is altogether different: it's a matter of using up, *without war,* that unprecedented accumulation, which has turned the whole world into a colossal powder keg. I'm not talking so much about nuclear explosion as I am about the general movement of production, which has not become any less terrifying since the USSR began to take part in it. Indeed, the development of the USSR has coincided with the atomic discoveries, which finish the business of making wars of accumulation an enormous return shock.

In principle, sovereign thought is not concerned with problems of this nature. Sovereign thought considers the possibility of sovereign moments that are not grasped as things, and that stand in contrast to archaic sovereignty. Archaic sovereignty offered itself to the things that slaves and subordinates became, and to the things which the products of these latter were, as their purpose. In this way, it came under the sway of the world of things in order to dominate the world: in order to become the purpose of things, it grasped itself as a thing, and took on the efficacy of a thing. Sovereign thought, which corresponds to the "man of sovereign art," who first expressed himself in the work of Nietzsche and whom I've tried to describe in a quick but systematic sketch, envisages a complete separation from the world of things (from objective activity) and from subjectivity. It has two aspects, then. The first is the world of free subjectivity; the second is that of objectivity freed from subjectivity insofar as the latter frees iteself from objectivity: these two aspects are interdependent, whence the ambiguity of this work which, wanting to reach the sovereign moment, considers practical questions so as to separate them from it, *and conversely.*

The problem I speak of – exhausting the surplus *without war* – is that of a world of production that would escape the control of subjectivity.[76] We must seek exhaustion through rational means, as against the subjective means of the pursuit of rank and of war.

Free subjectivity is not at issue. In a world of productivity that would consistently obey its own laws, expenditures *freely* devoted to art might be great, but they would not depend on a sovereign concentration of resources and *remaining haphazard,* they would never pose as a solution to the problem. The solution depends on rational behavior alone, with the capitalist states considering the gift in a *rational* manner, with a view to a less unequal distribution of resources in the world, in the framework of a narrow policy and a traditional diplomacy. Today revolution is nothing but an emotionally charged word, an incitement to war that doesn't have the clarity to give its name: nothing more is involved than a change of direction.[77]

If the view of today's world that is manifested in thought linked to the primacy of *conscious* subjectivity were to spread, the world of things would escape the irrational government of an objective thought that is constantly distorted by the action of an unconscious subjectivity.

2.

I could not define the place and the meaning of the "man of sovereign art" in this world without calling attention to the rational consequences of a less dim-sighted way of looking at things. But the masses are only interested in the consequences of his thought and his sensibility is alien to them. The strangest thing is that he measures up to that measureless catastrophe under the threat of which we are living. This is because he always lives rather as if he were the *last man.* In the same way, sentiments opposite to those of the multitude, or the lack of sensibility, measure us against death. At every turn, I necessarily distance myself from that normal condition to which ordinary thought rivets us. Arriving at the end of this work, whose progress led only to the distant point where thought loses itself, I have a troubled feeling.

Have I not led my readers astray? Or have I misled them twice? My thoughts direct me toward an undefinable region to which it is vain to try to lead. But I would like, once more, to laboriously roll my Sisyphean rock; I would like to open up another perspective if I can. Thus far, I have spoken of Nietzsche and I will now speak of Franz Kafka. I don't want to lose sight of the main thing. The main thing is always the same: sovereignty is NOTHING.

Notes

PREFACE

1. *"J'exposais le rapport de la production à la consumation (à la consomma-tion improductive)."* Bataille opposes *consumation* – a noun that doesn't exist in French – to *consommation*, or consumption proper. His neologism recalls the etymological sense of consuming, as in a fire that utterly destroys. It is his own concept of fire, sacrificial consumption, with a sense of nobility, as opposed to the bourgeois consumption of production and accumulation. Hereafter, Bataille consistently uses *consumation*, which will be translated here as nonproductive (or useless) consumption, or simply as consumption. – TR.

2. This work will doubtless have a third volume (see *Sovereignty*, begin-ning on p. 193, below). In a manner of speaking, the second presents the basis of the movement that animates humanity (the basis being the simplest form); the first describes its effects in human activities considered as an ensemble, in the economic and religious spheres; the third would set forth the solution to the problem of autonomy, of the independence of man relative to useful ends; it would be concerned directly with *sovereignty*. But I do not intend to write it for some time. For the moment, the first two books – each of which, more-over, constitutes a separate study – together have a coherence that suffices in itself.

3. In particular during a lecture [*The Relations Between the World and the Sacred, and the Growth of the Forces of Production*] that François Perroux had asked me to give at the Institute [of Applied Economic Sciences, on June 8, 1949].

PART ONE: INTRODUCTION

1. For example, the world of the police, or that of undertaking.

2. Where thought would express its object (its sole object), the concrete totality, only on one condition – that it would no longer rise above it, that it would itself be a constituent part of the totality, *lost within it.*

3. Which itself is a reflection, is a totality only insofar as it is a reflection, but a reflection moved to turmoil as well as to rigor by the diversity and the contradictions of its contents.

4. Even the thought of Jean-Paul Sartre is far from being at ease with sexuality. Or rather, its ease is conditioned: by an exceptional disgust, which relegates eroticism if not to insignificance, at least to a world of depression; and on the other hand, curiously, by the lack of a sense of sin, that is, a sense of prohibition, of the necessity of prohibition, which founds the human, and of the equal necessity of its transgression. Without such a sense, elusive eroticism is an unsuccessful construct: this is what my book will show.

PART TWO: THE PROHIBITION OF INCEST

1. It is precisely a question of two worlds that tend to be separated by a partition; but an understanding of these two worlds presupposes a total view across the partition. And it should be understood that ethereal eroticism includes mystical love, which is to say, divine love.

2. The phrase in brackets was crossed out in the author's manuscript and reinserted by the editor of the Gallimard text translated here. – TR.

3. Lévi-Strauss, *The Elementary Structures of Kinship* (Boston: Beacon Press, 1969).

4. *Ibid.*, p. 24.

5. *Ibid.*, p. 13.

6. *Ibid.*, p. 19.

7. *Ibid.*, p. 21.

8. Lévi-Strauss refers in his note 1 to A. L. Kroeber, "Totem and Taboo in Retrospect" [which appeared in *American Journal of Sociology* 45 (1939), pp. 446–51].

9. *Ibid.*, p. 491.

10. *Ibid.*, p. 99.

11. *Ibid.*, p. 438.

12. *Ibid.*, p. 438.

13. *Ibid.*

14. [Translated into English as *The Gift: Forms and Functions of Exchange in Archaic Societies* (New York: Norton, 1967).]

15. Lévi-Strauss, *Elementary Structures*, p. 52.

16. *Ibid.*, p. 52.

17. *Ibid.*, p. 63.

18. *Ibid.*, p. 62.

19. *Ibid.*, p. 63.

20. *Ibid.*, p. 481.

21. *Ibid.*, p. 38. There is an obvious exaggeration on this point: the situations differ greatly according to the case in question. And likewise, one can wonder to what degree, for primitives, the bachelor's condition is everywhere the same. It seems to me personally that Lévi-Strauss's theory is based mainly on the "generosity" aspect, although, without any doubt, the "interest" aspect generally lends consistency to the facts.

22. *Ibid.*, p. 51.

23. *Ibid.*

24. *Ibid.*, translation modified. – TR.

25. Quoted in *ibid.*, p. 137.

26. *Ibid.*, p. 138.

27. *Ibid.*

28. The expression is questionable in this sense: *obscene* refers to the prohibited aspect of sexuality, but (1) this aspect is well known, within its precise limits, (2) yet I cannot avoid using the term *prohibition*.

Part Three: The Natural Objects of Prohibition

1. It should be noted that archaic traits still appear in our societies. I will mention this example in which the very inversion of reactions (being involuntary, unconscious) has something terrifying about it: On her wedding day, a young British woman, from an upper-class milieu, became so agitated that as she was climbing the steps of the chancel, the large audience saw that the white dress was spotted down its length with blood: a grave nervous illness ensued. – A pork-butcher I knew, a very civilized one, would not allow his wife to put her hands in the salting tub if she was having her period: he was afraid the blood would spoil the pork.

2. Of course, a worker can be just as delicate as a bourgeois while behaving incorrectly according to the bourgeois code....

3. The Second Manifesto of Surrealism, in *Manifestoes of Surrealism*, trans. Richard Seaver and Helen R. Lane (Ann Arbor: University of Michigan Press, 1972), p. 186. The emphasis is Breton's.

4. This way of thinking is closer to that of René Guénon than to modern science as a whole. But René Guénon's theories appear to me to be stamped with simplification. Guénon is pretentious, rash; and if he knew as little about traditional thought as he knows about modern thought, which he criticizes wretchedly (everything he says about it – and he uses everything he says as a reason for outright condemnations – would fall down if he had so much as heard of Hegel or Nietzsche, let alone Heidegger), he would only merit a shrug. At all events, one would need a facile mind to read with any confidence an author whose haughtiness is so unwarranted.

5. "Drive out what is natural and it will come back at a gallop." [Usually translated as, "What's bred in the bone will come out in the flesh." – TR.]

6. Indeed, in the mind of a humanity living under the primacy of reason, it is as a disappointed anticipation that the death of a man is represented as being momentous and awful, in contrast with the insignificance of animal death. It is because he lives in anticipation of the future, to which his activity has committed him, that the death of a man is so important in our eyes.

7. See *The Accursed Share*, vol. I, Introduction, ch. 2: "The Three Luxu-

ries of Nature: Eating, Death and Sexual Reproduction," p. 33.

8. On the life of doctors in the United States. The qualifying subtitle of [the French translation of] Frank Slaughter's novel is, however, *Sans le secours de la médecine* [that is, *Without the Aid of Medicine*. The novel's English title is *That None Should Die* (New York: Doubleday, Doran, 1941). – TR.]

PART FOUR: TRANSGRESSION

1. *L'Homme et le sacré*, 2d ed. (Paris: Gallimard, 1950), pp. 152 and 153 [*Man and the Sacred*, trans. Meyer Barash (Glencoe, IL: Free Press of Glencoe, 1959), pp. 115 and 116].

2. If need be, one can still say that nature includes man, that the movement I speak of occurs within nature. This is true, but the human domain in nature is a new domain, which surpasses nature, which is not enclosed within its general laws. I will not address in the present book the problem that this raises.

3. That is, at any rate, laughter whose object is *comical*.

4. P. 78, part 3, ch. 2, sec. 5, *Eroticism Is Essentially, from the First Step, the Scandal of "Reversed Alliances."*

5. P. 77, part 3, ch. 2, sec. 5.

6. I don't deny that in its way profane life is itself capable of great changes. But I must first make it clear that war, love and political sovereignty cannot genuinely enter into profane life. The profane world does not change of itself except in terms of techniques and juridical modes of production, and then it is a question of *continuous* changes. One can even say that if there is *discontinuity* of change (revolution), it implies the intervention of elements heterogeneous to the profane order, such as armed mobs and so on.

7. We shall see further on that only animality viewed by scientific thought as a thing presents a real unity with profane life.

8. Think, for example, of the completely unsustainable daring of the characters of detective novels.

9. Animal sacrifice is the earliest type, but after a period in which human sacrifice developed, animals had to be substituted for human victims. See *The Accursed Share*, vol. I, pp. 55–56.

10. We know that the ancients identified, at least in poetry, the possession of a woman with sacrifice. It seemed that except for the dying, women were treated in this instance like sacrificial animals. Here I must stress the fact that woman, more than man, is the center of eroticism. She alone is able to devote herself to it, provided she doesn't have children in her care. Whereas man is nearly always a working or warring animal first of all. However, I have spoken of eroticism mainly in reference to man. I did not think it necessary to examine each of the situations I have spoken of from a woman's point of view. I was less anxious to fully describe the different aspects of eroticism than to grasp the movement whereby human existence encounters the totality in eroticism.

PART FIVE: THE HISTORY OF EROTICISM

1. See H. Hubert and M. Mauss, "*Essai sur la nature et la fonction du sacrifice*," in *Année sociologique* (1897–1898) [*Sacrifice: Its Nature and Function*, trans. W. D. Halls (Chicago: University of Chicago Press, 1964)].

2. According to the *Petit Robert* dictionary, "the right a lord had to put his leg in the bride's bed on her wedding night, and, in some places, to spend this first night with her." – TR.

3. To avoid useless complications I will speak only in this note about the place of sorcery. For Frazer, magic (sorcery) was on the side of the profane, by reason of its technical ends. (But its modalities are closely related to those of religion; the *evil spell* corresponds to *sacrifice*, and so on.) For Mauss, it was on the side of the sacred (H. Hubert and M. Mauss, "*Esquisse d'une théorie générale de la magie*," in *Année sociologique* [1902–1903]). Mauss considered magic to be religious, at least *lato sensu*, and his position, a cautious one, doesn't have the clearly questionable character of Frazer's.

4. R. Hertz, "*La Prééminence de la main droite*," in *Mélanges de sociologie religieuse et de folklore* (1928).

5. This is an incomplete sentence in the Gallimard text. – TR.

6. The editor of the *Oeuvres complètes* notes that here the manuscript breaks off in the middle of a page. – TR.

7. The author's manuscript was not clearly legible here, so the Gallimard editor guesses that the word is *assigne*. – TR.

8. Twenty years ago this prescription was commonplace: in religious institutions a girl entered the bathtub in a long nightgown. There is no misinterpretation here, for the alluring figure of eroticism is virtually the same for women and for men – it is feminine nudity.

9. *Ronces? Rosiers?* The author's manuscript is not clearly legible here. – TR.

PART SIX: THE COMPOSITE FORMS OF EROTICISM

1. Possibly of Arab origin. See my article "La Littérature française du Moyen Age, la morale chevaleresque et la passion," *Critique* (July, 1949), p. 598.

2. I leave aside homosexuality, which contributes only odd variants, of secondary importance, to the general picture; and masochism, which in my view is only an alteration of the sexual disposition, with the man displaying feminine behavior toward a woman of masculine behavior – unless it corresponds to the excess of sadism, wherein the subject's cruelty is finally turned back against the subject himself.

3. Jean Guitton, *Essai sur l'amour humain* (Paris: Aubier, 1948), pp. 158–59.

4. Nor do I wish to associate myself with the narrow views of the author I quote, who writes: "If it is true that religion originates in mysticity and mysticity in sexuality, then the highest is brought down to the lowest, and the idea of God is reduced to the level of the glands." (*ibid.*, p. 159).

5. *Lautréamont et Sade* (Paris: Minuit, 1949).

VOLUME III: SOVEREIGNTY

PART ONE: WHAT I UNDERSTAND BY SOVEREIGNTY

1. How childish it is to deny the force of the Gospel. There is no one who should not recognize Christianity for having made it the book of humanity par excellence. That resolution of stinginess into indifference, irony and sympathy does not undermine the edifice of prudence so completely as it may have ap-

appeared to; but how can one aspire to be sovereign without the vehemence that it opposes to the concern for self-interest, without the ingenuousness that it opposes to vehemence? The *evangelical* ethic is as it were, from beginning to end, an ethic of the sovereign moment. Narrow-mindedness did not originate with the Gospel, but that is what it kept, in its restraint, from the rules that it largely denied. True, its transparency allowed the rules to return, and even made their weight easier to bear. Apart from the use that fear and prudence made of it, this transparency has kept its virtue. In theory, transparency has never survived our practical *application* of the maxims on which it is based. Transparency is nonetheless the inaccessible object of a fundamental desire, which is the anticipation of a miraculous moment. Forgetting the Gospel's embeddedness in the world of its time, the concern for what was possible, linked to the acceptance of rules that have become odious in our day, and the masses' hatred – degrading in fact – of deviations that are inconsistent with the possible considered in a general way, ponderously, it has remained, for anyone capable of understanding it, the simplest, most human, "manual of sovereignty." Even the myth of the slaying of the king, which is its plot, contributes to this virtue, difficult to grasp perhaps, but raised to the level at which transparency and death are identical.

2. See Roger Caillois, *L'Homme et le sacré*, 2d ed. (Paris: Gallimard, 1950), ch. 2, L'Ambiguité du sacré, pp. 35–72 [*Man and the Sacred*, trans. Meyer Barash (Glencoe, IL: Free Press of Glencoe, 1959), "The Ambiguity of the Sacred," pp. 33–59].

[*Crossed out in the author's manuscript*: In his preface (1939), Caillois says about the interest we both have in the subject of his study: "It seems to me that with this subject there was established between us a kind of intellectual osmosis which, on my part, does not permit me to distinguish with certainty, after so many discussions, his contribution from mine, in the work that we pursued in common." There is a good deal of exaggeration in this way of representing things. If it is that Caillois owes something to our discussions, whatever this is can only be quite secondary. At the very root I can say that if Caillois attaches an importance that was not attributed before him to the problem of the ambiguity of the sacred, I could not help but encourage him to do so. Along with "The Sacred as Transgression: Theory of the Festival" (pp. 126–68), it is, I believe, one of the most personal parts of his book, to which I don't think I contributed in any way, but which the whole of my thinking constantly draws upon. I take this opportunity to express my indebtedness to the near perfect reformulation of the question of the sacred that Roger Caillois's little book constitutes. Moreover, it seems to me that it would be very hard, without having read it, to grasp the basic arguments of *The Accursed Share* in the context that justifies them. *Man and the Sacred* is not only an authoritative book but also an essential book for understanding all the problems to which the sacred is the key. – Note that, in much the same form, but with the title *Le Pur et l'impur*, Roger Caillois's study constitutes one of the chapters of the *Introduction* to vol. 1 of the *Histoire générale des religions* (Paris: Quillet, 1948), for which it was first written, in 1938.]

3. But I will go ahead and indicate the existence of a point where laughter that doesn't laugh and tears that don't cry, where the divine and the horrible, the poetic and the repugnant, the erotic and the funereal, extreme wealth and painful nudity coincide. This is not a fanciful notion. In fact, under the name of *theopathic state*, it has been the object of an implicit description. I don't mean to say that in the theopathic state this coincidence always appears in its full scope, but it *may appear*. The therapeutic state implies at the same time the coincidence of complete unknowing and unlimited knowledge. But only in this sense does absolute unknowing seem to respond, to be *the* response to the state of questioning that is brought about, beyond utility, by the search for knowledge. But this unlimited knowledge is *the knowledge* of NOTHING. Negative theology, which tries to carry the implication of the theopathic state over into the realm of knowledge, might merely take up the thought of Dionysius the Aeropagite. *God is nothingness,* but I prefer to say God is NOTHING, not without linking this negative truth to a perfect laughter: the laughter that doesn't laugh. What I said about this state, a coincidence . . . of the poetic and the repugnant, etc., does seem contradictory with the negation of any content that seems to define it. But the principles put forward in Volume II prepare us for this and, as I will show further on, the object of laughter or tears, of horror or the feel-

ing of the sacred, of repugnance, of the awareness of death...is always NOTH-ING, substituted for the anticipation of a given object. It is always NOTHING, but revealing itself suddenly as a supreme, *miraculous, sovereign* response. I define unalloyed sovereignty as *the miraculous reign of unknowing.*

4. I am aware that sobs in most cases signify unhappiness. I will return shortly to the scant difference that exists between unhappiness and happiness in the unfolding of some of our reactions. But at all events, in unhappiness sobs maintain the sacred moment of rift, and deliver us for a while from the *difficulty* in which the rift left us, so that in tears we find a strange comfort.

5. I have spoken of this experience in *L'Experience intérieure* (1943), *Le Coupable* (1944) and *Sur Nietzsche* (1945) [*Inner Experience*, trans. Leslie Anne Boldt (Albany, NY: State University of New York Press, 1988), *Guilty*, trans. Bruce Boone (Venice, CA: Lapis Press, 1988]. These works will be brought together in a second edition under the general title of *Somme athéologique* (Gallimard), and will be followed by a Volume IV, *Le Pur Bonheur*, and a Volume V, *Le Système inachevé du non-savoir*. Only the second edition of *L'Experience intérieure* has been published; that of *Le Coupable* is in preparation.

6. Needless to say, this NOTHING has little to do with *nothingness.* Nothingness is a metaphysical concept. The NOTHING I speak of is a datum of experience, and is considered here only insofar as experience implies it. No doubt the metaphysician may say that this NOTHING is what he has in mind when he speaks of *nothingness.* But the whole impetus of my thought demands that at the moment when this NOTHING becomes its object, it stops, it ceases to be, giving place to the unknowable of the moment. Of course, I admit that I valorize this NOTHING, but in valorizing it I make NOTHING of it. It's true that I confer on it – with an undeniable (but deeply comical) solemnity – the *sovereign* prerogative. But would *sovereign* be what the crowd imagines it to be? *Sovereign* is what you and I are – on one condition, that we forget, forget *everything.*... To speak of NOTHING is really only to repudiate the enslavement, reducing it to what it is (it is useful); it is finally only to deny the nonpractical value of thought, reducing it, beyond the useful, to insignificance, to the honest simplicity of imperfection, of that which dies and passes away.

7. Which I came across in Edgar Morin's book, *L'Homme et la mort dans l'histoire* (Paris: Corrêa, 1951). It had not struck me when I read the *Conversations with Eckermann*.) "Everyone," writes Morin, "has been able to note, as Goethe did, that the death of someone close is always 'incredible and paradoxical,' 'an impossibility that suddenly changes into a reality' (Eckermann)." Let it be said here that Morin's big book on death teems with truth and life.

8. It is, according to Goethe's phrase, "an impossibility that suddenly changes into a reality." See p. 209, above.

9. The term is from Morin, *L'Homme et la mort dans l'histoire*, p. 22.

10. *Ibid.*, p. 63.

11. Needless to say, I do not intend to address the political problem of royalty. In fact, I think that to anyone who has followed me the question would seem to have faded into the distance, if such a thing is possible. The same is true of the problem of God. To my mind, what faith calls God can only be an object – or rather the absence of an object – of unknowing. This does not mean that a world without God is complete, as naive atheism imagines. The place left by the absence of God (if we prefer, by the death of God) is enormous. But to see in God the object of a positive knowledge is first of all, to my mind, an utter impiety. It is also the preeminent delusion (it is to speak with assurance of something we know NOTHING about). Finally, it is the most ridiculous compromise with the world of useful works (the Creator, the God of goodness); it is the monstrous misconception whereby the religious world dissolves into that of useful works.

12. It would assume, in fact, the unity of the tragic and the laughable, of the pure and the impure, of chaste, mad passion and cunning eroticism.... But the unity of laughter and tears requires "Laughter that doesn't laugh, and tears that don't cry." The unity I speak of requires cruelty that isn't harsh and fear that isn't afraid of anything.... In this unity, the object of the contradictory effusions dissolves into NOTHING and *silence reigns*.

13. The gift in particular was the main object of the whole of Volume I of this work.

14. But as late as 1840, following the return of Napoleon's casket to Paris,

indignant that the delegates under the vaults of the Invalides were long in removing their hats, Victor Hugo could write: "Most had kept their hats on until the entry of the casket; some, taking advantage of the darkness, never bared their heads for a single moment. And yet they were in the presence of the King, of the Emperor, and of God; in the presence of majesty, living, dead, and eternal majesty. M. Taschereau, in a buttoned redingote, was stretched out over six benches, his nose pointed vaultward, the soles of his boots turned toward Napoleon's casket..." (*Suppléments inédits aux "Choses vues,"* published by Henri Guillemin [*Figaro littéraire*, June 12, 1954, p. 5]).

15. The custom of sovereigns saying "my subjects" introduces an ambiguity that I can't avoid: in my view the *subject* is the *sovereign*. The subject I speak of has nothing *subjugated* about it.

16. The most rationalist of us still grasps a part of this if he considers the emotion that their king – or their queen – communicates to foreign crowds.

17. "Among the Malays, 'not only is the king's person considered sacred, but the sanctity of his body is believed to communicate itself to his regalia, and to slay those who break the royal taboos. Thus it is firmly believed that anyone who seriously offends the royal person, who touches (even for a moment), or who imitates (even with the king's permission) the chief objects of the regalia, or who wrongfully makes use of any of the insignia or privileges of royalty, will be *kena daulat*, *i.e.* struck dead, by a quasi-electric discharge of that Divine Power which the Malays suppose to reside in the king's person, and which is called "Daulat" or "Royal Sanctity"'" (Walter William Skeat, *Malay Magic* [London: 1900; reprinted London: Frank Cass, 1965], pp. 23–24; quoted in H. Webster, *Taboo: A Sociological Study* [Palo Alto, CA: Stanford University Press, 1942], p. 267).

18. I always use the words *recognize* or *recognition*, not in the sense of gratitude, but in the Hegelian sense. For Hegel, what is in us only insofar as it appears such does not truly exist until others so *recognize* it: thus it is evident, for example, that no one is king before others have *recognized* him as such.

19. See the ethnographic particulars in A. M. Hocart, *Kings and Councillors* (Cairo: P. Barbey, 1936).

20. It was there that he wrote, in 1786, *The 120 Days of Sodom*, the manuscript of which was lost due to the looting that followed July 4, 1789, a riot in
which Sade participated in his own way, urging on the crowd from his window.
He would shout into a pipe that was used to empty his waste: "People of Paris,
they are slaughtering the prisoners!" The warden de Launay had him transferred
for this reason to Bicêtre. In this way, the manuscript of the *120 Days*, which
he couldn't take with him, was lost. Sade lamented his loss with tears of blood,
but the manuscript was found again, in a sale, a century later.

21. I will come back to the place that art occupies in the history of sovereignty. All the parts that follow tend to make clear this movement that goes
from archaic sovereignty to the sovereignty of art, but in particular chapter 4
of part four deals with the change that art underwent, from being the expression of sovereign subjectivity existing in an institutional form to being that of
the author's subjectivity.

PART TWO: SOVEREIGNTY, FEUDAL SOCIETY AND COMMUNISM

1. I speak here of communism considered in general as a political doctrine
in action, seeking to change the world, and not as the communist theoreticians
speak of it when they envisage the final, communist stage of the world's trans-
formation, in which each will receive according to his needs, contrasting it with
the immediately preceding socialist stage, where production is completely taken
over and organized by the collectivity.

2. To be exact, these thoughts occurred to me on reading Isaac Deutscher's
Stalin (Gallimard, 1953) [*Stalin: A Political Biography* (New York, London: Oxford
University Press, 1949)], which appeared in French translation after the death
of the head of the Russian government. The work by Deutscher, who has taught
me a great deal concerning a question I have always followed, commands attention for a number of exceptional reasons. It is the work of an author whose
detachment recalls that of historians speaking of Roman, or Egyptian, history:
clearly, Deutscher set out to understand, and not to meet the fixed requirements
of supporters and opponents. It is possible, in spite of this, that he did not arrive
at the truth. All things considered, the truth may be more anti-Stalinist – or

more Stalinist. Whatever the case, the search for truth seems to have had more importance in his eyes than the desire to damn or to praise. That is extraordinary when delicate subjects are involved, especially if it is added that Deutscher was at first very close to the events. He was born in Poland in 1907; in the early years he was a communist. He spoke Russian fluently and he traveled a good deal in Russia. He wasn't excluded from the Party until 1932. Today he is nonetheless very far from the communist hostility to ordinary people who are indifferent to communism. He seems to be completely rid of the concern with changing the world: he is simply a reporter like the others. But while his former opinions don't enter into his writings, he nonetheless benefits from firsthand information that few noncommunists have available. Starting from that base, he was able to take advantage of the numerous Russian publications that alone make the search for detail possible. His critical studies are both brilliant and careful: they will be questioned on many points, but in the obscurity in which the truth of events and of their causes has remained hidden, no one can honestly disregard the coherent ensemble which their statements form. On the whole, Deutscher justifies Stalin without concealing the harshness of his politics. Everyone can tell him, obviously, that such harshness was not justifiable. Whether or not the state of the world is better after Stalin's intervention is another matter. But Deutscher is content with showing that Stalin successfully carried out the projects that were apparently dictated to him by a compelling need: if he had not reacted with that energy that shrank from nothing, if he had not had a feeling for the violent solutions that were called for, it seems in fact that the ground would have finally given way beneath him. This is easy to say after the event, and the assertions of eleventh-hour sages will always appear ridiculous. But to seek the logic of what first appeared to be an inexplicable series of horrors is nonetheless the task that the historian has assumed. In the first instance, history must consider facts as elements in a determinate process. It must not, cannot, stop there, but without attempting this, how would it be possible to go on speaking of the place – the quite extraordinary place – that Stalin occupied in history?

3. *Ibid.*, p. 72.

4. *Ibid.*

5. *Ibid.*, pp. 72–73. The author refers to Stalin's *Collected Works* (in Russian), vol. 1, pp. 138–59.

6. These words quoted by Deutscher (*ibid.*, p. 73) are Stalin's.

7. Deutscher, *ibid.*, p. 140, quoting N. Sukhanov, *Notes on the Revolution* (in Russian), vol. 3, pp. 26–27.

8. Deutscher, *Stalin*, p. 154, quoting Stalin, *Collected Works* (in Russian), vol. 3, p. 187.

9. Deutscher, *ibid.*

10. *Ibid.*, p. 282, quoting Stalin, *Problems of Leninism*, English edition, published in Moscow in 1945, p. 157.

11. Deutscher, *ibid.*, pp. 281–282.

12. *Ibid.*, p. 282.

13. *Ibid.*, p. 286.

14. *Ibid.*, p. 282.

15. *Ibid.*, p. 529; James F. Byrnes, *Speaking Frankly*, p. 228.

16. Deutscher, *ibid.*, p. 341.

17. *Ibid.*, p. 342.

18. *Ibid.*

19. Stalin, *Economic Problems of Socialism in the U.S.S.R.* (New York: International Publishers, 1952), p. 22. I have exactly transcribed the title of section four of the main section of this booklet. Stalin does specify that it is not a matter of *all* the differences, but of the essential differences. In this booklet he considers, in connection with the discussions that took place concerning a draft "textbook on political economy," some of the great questions that currently face Marxists in the economic sphere and in the context of the USSR.

20. *Ibid.*, pp. 52–53.

21. I am not saying that Marx followed Hegel on this point, but there is a direct line from Hegel's "dialectic of the master and the slave" to "the theory of class struggle." Already in Hegel, class struggle is at the basis of history, in the form of the master–slave dialectic.

22. But it is not property that confers sovereignty. Sovereignty is always a

subjective quality, even though it seems – inheritance of the quality being followed by that of land – that the quality originates in land.

23. What matters most in hunting is the element of play: hunting, noble and dangerous, has an attraction independent of self-interest. Similarly, the immediate attraction of stock-breeding is not insignificant: there may be a breeding of livestock chosen for nonproductive, aesthetic qualities (see my study "L'Elevage," *Critique* 59 [April 1952], p. 364). Moreover, the aesthetic element has a large role in stock-breeding, which is often linked to its military utility: the connection is that in warfare the element of play is no less important than in hunting.

24. Yet royalty considered as the function of the king, who would be the servant of the people, is a recent idea.

25. Everything we know about Russian revolutionary activity before 1917 and in 1917 confirms this. As far as China is concerned, [Malraux's] *Les Conquérants* and *La Condition humaine* evoke a world whose agitation is diametrically opposite to our relative inerita. Only Spain, like China or Russia, having a feudal structure (which, however, owing to its poverty in raw materials, could not in any case achieve a substantial accumulation on the basis of a proletarian domination) experienced an extreme revolutionary tension.

26. *Economic Problems of Socialism in the U.S.S.R.*, pp. 22–23.

27. *Economic Problems*, p. 33. But this unarguable definition is associated unfortunately with another, which may not be unwarranted, but which does not have the merit of contrasting, in keeping with the stated intention, basic aspects corresponding to one another: "instead of maximum profits – maximum satisfaction of the material and cultural requirements of a society...."

28. *Economic Problems*, p. 32.

29. The most conspicuous form of such a reaction is snobism. This noun corresponds in the nominative registers of English college students to the designation *sine nobilitate*, which was abbreviated *s. nob.*

30. *Economic Problems*, p. 58.

31. *Ibid.*, p. 59.

32. *Economic Problems*, p. 53. This refers to the stage of social development

that, according to Marx, was to follow socialism. To socialism corresponds the formula, "from each according to his ability, to each according to his work." The communist formula is "from each according to his ability, to each according to his needs."

33. As Stalin often does for ideas he wants to emphasize, he has twice repeated nearly word for word the same phrase on the same page 53: "so that the members of society may be in a position... freely to choose their occupations and not be tied all their lives, owing to the existing division of labor, to a specific occupation."

34. Isaac Deutscher, *Stalin: A Political Biography* (New York, London: Oxford University Press, 1949), p. 1.

35. Deutscher, citing one of Stalin's childhood friends, Iresmasvili, states, "Undeserved and frightful beatings made the boy as grim and heartless as his father" (*ibid.*, p. 3). Concerning the feelings transmitted to the son by the father's desire to rise socially, Deutscher adds, "In one of his first brochures, Stalin illustrates a point of Marxist theory by the experience of his own father: 'Imagine,' he wrote, 'a shoemaker who had a tiny workshop, but could not stand the competition of big business. That shoemaker closed his workshop and hired himself, say, to Adelkhanov, at the Tiflis shoe factory not to remain a worker forever but to save some money, to lay aside a small capital and then to reopen his own workshop. As you see, the position of that shoemaker is *already* that of the proletarian, but his consciousness is *not yet* proletarian, but petty-bourgeois through and through.' There can be no doubt which shoemaker served the writer as the illustration of his thesis. The tiny workshop, the bad luck in business, even the name of the employer, were part of Vissarion's [the father's] story." The father "died... in 1890, when his son was eleven years old" (*ibid.*).

36. He was not, properly speaking, a sovereign, but rather the opposite of a sovereign, since he was tied to the most demanding work; above all, he remained to the end the radical enemy of sovereignty in the strong sense, the writing I have cited being one piece of evidence among others. But sovereignty entered him in spite of himself, from the outside as it were, owing to his absolute power and to the power he made to reign. A sentence written by Alexandre Weissberg,

who was held for three years in the Soviet prisons, gives a striking idea of the extent of his terror: "If the Ogpu [forerunner of the KGB]," he says, "had had a means of reading the thoughts of the men of the U.S.S.R., it would have had to arrest everyone, down to the lowliest citizen. But then the Ogpu people would have been the first to go to prison, because they knew better than anyone else what was happening throughout the country" (*L'Accusé*, p. 187). It would be a mistake to overlook the fact that in creating the atmosphere of the trials and of the great purge, Stalin created an utterly new world: we can only enter that world or else seek to know it *through and through*.

37. Deutscher remarks on Stalin's nerves in connection with his stay in the Baku prison in 1908: "Convicts awaiting execution were often herded together with the rest. Executions took place in the courtyard. Nerves were strained to the limit when men saw their comrades, who might just have taken part in a debate, led to the gallows. In the tension of such moments Koba [Stalin] would, if an eyewitness is to be believed, fall sound asleep, astonishing his comrades by his strong nerves" (*ibid.*, p. 93). But one could say that his whole life is made up of a succession of analogous examples.

38. *Economic problems*, p. 30.

39. *Ibid.*, p. 31 (the emphasis is Stalin's).

40. [J. V. Stalin, *Works* (Moscow: Foreign Languages Publishing House, 1954), vol. 7, p. 14.]

41. Quoted from the translation appearing in Martin Ebon, *Malenkov, Stalin's Successor* (New York: McGraw-Hill, 1953), pp. 189-90.

42. See note 1, above, p. 433. – TR.

43. In *L'Experience intérieure* [*Inner Experience*, trans. Leslie Anne Boldt (Albany, NY: State University of New York Press, 1988), p. 4. Translation amended].

44. *Divine Names*, I.5.

45. I was referring to the most severe sensible aspect of what is sovereign in the world, the aspect most devoid of external forms and the most narrowly immanent, limited to the human.

46. *Divine Names*, I.7.

47. This is an incomplete sentence in the Gallimard text. – TR.

48. Thus, his attitude at Yalta, where Churchill presented him with an honorary sword and where, it seems, tears came to his eyes, as if he had had the same vain sensibility as those aristocrats whom he once combated and on whom this honor avenged him. Yet, the truly miraculous character of such an homage was enough to justify those "happy tears."

PART THREE: THE NEGATIVE SOVEREIGNTY OF COMMUNISM
AND THE UNEQUAL HUMANITY OF MEN

1. The sincerity does not always exist, but the problem being considered is of no interest unless it does.

2. Marx wrote as early as 1846, "Society has...always developed within the framework of a contradiction – in antiquity the contradiction between free men and slaves, in the Middle Ages that between nobility and serfs, in modern times that between the bourgeoisie and the proletariat. This explains, on the one hand, the abnormal, 'inhuman' means with which the oppressed class satisfies its needs, and, on the other hand, the narrow limits within which intercourse, and with it the whole ruling class, develops. Hence this restricted character of development consists not only in the exclusion of one class from development, but also in the narrow-mindedness of the excluding class, and the 'inhuman' is to be found also within the ruling class. This so-called 'inhuman' is just as much a product of present-day conditions as the 'human' is; it is their negative aspect, the rebellion – which is not based on any new revolutionary productive force – against the prevailing conditions brought about by the existing productive forces, and against the way of satisfying needs that corresponds to these conditions. The positive expression 'human' corresponds to the definite conditions *predominant* at a certain stage of production and to the way of satisfying needs determined by them, just as the negative expression 'inhuman' corresponds to the attempt, within the existing mode of production, to negate these predominant conditions and the way of satisfying needs prevailing under them, an attempt that this stage of production engenders afresh" (*The German Ideology*, ed. C. J. Arthur [New York: International Publishers, 1973], p. 116). I needed to quote this passage providing a remarkable illustration of my analysis, but the object

449

of the latter is by no means the doctrine of Marx: I did not mean to consider anything else but the state of mind and the moral reactions of contemporaries, specifically persons I have known, communists or others. The fact that the texts of Marx help to underscore the precise terms of the problem is undeniably interesting, but for the purposes of this inquiry that is not the main consideration, for the essence of Marxism is given independently of Marx or else there is no such thing; in my view, it is the common inner experience, irrespective of the study of texts.

3. I met a communist forest ranger with whom I had the friendliest conversations. He had worked in the equatorial forest and on the subject of black people, he told me simply: "They are beasts." There was no insistence or hatred in his voice, more like a rough graciousness. Communist though he was, he could not help sharing the *interest* that the "bestiality" of the blacks has for colonizers as a whole. – But a particular fact determined his judgment: according to him, black people themselves treated each other like things, lending their wives for a fee as if they were things. There is no question that men of color have their prohibitions, which are not rudimentary, but they are different from ours and Europeans only see violations in the ones they observe. In this case, even more than in class difference, interest plays a large role, in that the victim's servitude (the fact of oppression) excludes the possibility of a counterpart of the master's interests. It sometimes happens, however, that the white oppressor gives the native, whose prohibitions he does not observe, an impression of bestiality. Actually, the value judgments, which justify the subjugation and facilitate it, would operate in the same sense in regard to unemployable lepers.

4. Nietzsche had a very strong reaction prompted by the prohibition of antisemitism. I point out later that prohibitions in general are a way of magnifying what they prohibit. But what is magnified the is the unmitigated explosion, a pure, or more exactly, a blind animality. The appeal to the idea of a so-called inferior race in order to justify the explosion has an element of cowardice, of baseness, that is completely contrary to the spirit that receives the prohibition in anguish.

5. On the "taboos" affecting chiefs, kings, magicians and priests, see the

general survey by H. Webster, *Taboo: A Sociological Study* (Palo Alto, CA: Stanford University Press, 1942), ch. 7, pp. 261–79.

6. *Ibid.*, p. 261.

7. *Ibid.*, p. 270.

8. This equilibrium no doubt is precarious only apparently. There exists a general equilibrium that the particularity (that we considered in space, individually, or in time, in the different periods of history — which, moreover, in space are not everywhere the same) does not disturb except insofar as it is absorbed beforehand in a kind of definitive stability. We are still free to imagine other formulas. In principle, it is not when there is no agitation left in this world that we can say: "Now we have turned the last pages of the book: it's all settled." It's been a long time, however, since anything has appeared that we can consider new: the storm is stronger, its waves are fuller, the last one did not break before it had reached the highest degree of intensity where, in the half-light illuminating all things, perspectives emerge that seem unprecedented. But these are the perspectives of reason, which exclude precisely that unforseeable, *impossible* element that I call miraculous. The transformations that result from new techniques (quite different from those brought about by social revolutions, acting in the juridical order) surprise us to the extent that we are still living in the anticipation of miraculous changes. But they do not reveal anything deeper than the permanence of such an anticipation. The radio voice comes from farther away and is heard by more ears, but it is the same voice; the means of transportation are faster and surgery increases the cure rate, but these differences are quantitative. The same is true of the atomic explosion whose disastrous effects could no doubt prove *much greater* than those of natural cataclysms — but we cannot hope for anything miraculous to come of it except in a negative sense. Nothing is comparable to the creative effects that determined labor, whose combined repercussions produced the man that history makes known to us, and accumulation, which put an end to the age-old equilibrium and introduced catastrophic production. Accumulation had at least this qualitative result: it altered the structure of the human being, it engendered utilitarian man, who strives rationally to get rid of anything sovereign within

him: in this way it creates the possibility of a new man, who would respond symmetrically to the excesses of these industrial times and who would strive to rid himself of anything useful, of anything that is not sovereign. But this man would be new only in one sense: he would have a clear awareness of what others experienced, whose passage had enormous repercussions. Nietzsche saw what he dreamed of prefigured in his country's romantic writers (it's true that he was discouraged by a vagueness in them; he was sorry that they lacked the rigor he had found in a few representatives of the Protestantism of his time). For my part, I don't think we should expect anything more. If the edifice of the past, in which sovereignty revealed itself in its own way, is falling to pieces, we can rediscover that sovereignty only apart from those heavy structures that are, precisely, falling to pieces.

9. The examples given by Georges Dumézil (*Mythes et dieux des Germains* [*Gods of the Ancient Northmen*, trans. Einar Haugen (Berkeley: University of California Press, 1974).]) show how gift-giving led to the most generous sovereign power.

10. Cf. p. 300.

11. I could not have developed the subject of war and military organization in this work. It is not the only gap in my account, but it is the most troublesome one. I was obliged to postpone an exposition that would have indefinitely prolonged what is only a survey of the problems that I have raised.

12. In the French Revolution, power, after the king's execution, could not have in the leaders' hands the objectivity it had only in the hands of the Russians. It is possible to see in the impossible and inevitable subjectivity of Robespierre's power a sign of his actual suicide.

13. I must forgo speaking here, other than by illusion, of that element of celebrity akin, so far as it is on the side of glory, to military fame. I must give up the idea for the same reason, as I have said, that I generally forgo speaking of the interferences of the army, of force.

14. Corresponding to this impossibility of a well-established political world there is the relative possibility of a literary world in which the claim to sovereignty is not comical, precisely insofar as it is tragic and inevitable.

15. I use the word *theological* in the sense in which Georges Dumézil uses it when he speaks of Indo-European *theology*, independently of monotheism. That is why I would prefer to say *atheological*, seeing in the sacred and in the gods, as well as in the principle of sovereignty, the negation of a perfect God, having the attributes of the thing and of reason.

Part Four: The Literary World and Communism

1. If I expressed myself at some length concerning the will to power, my thought would appear only as an indirect extension of Nietzsche's. Indeed, in my view, Nietzsche's main shortcoming is in having misinterpreted the opposition of sovereignty and power.

2. I myself can take up Hegel's thought and develop one of its points, but this still does not make it mine (that is, I don't have the right to oppose this thought, as an *other* thought, to that of Hegel). Thus, Alexandre Kojève does not develop an *other* thought from that of Hegel.

3. In a sense, into the sleep of action, which compared with the wakefulness I speak of is little different from physiological sleep, or death.

4. That is, to a certain extent, but doubtless never absolutely.

5. The passage from knowledge to unknowing is not a moment of composition; it is a decomposition of thought; starting either from the conventional idea of God, or from that of "absolute knowledge," it is atheism, in opposition to the confidence placed blindly in God, but without the compensatory resort to a confidence placed narrowly in things, or the feeling of the identity of "absolute knowledge" and NOTHING: Nietzsche *alone* has described this in the "death of God" (*The Gay Science*, trans. Walter Kaufmann [New York: Vintage, 1974], sec. 125).

6. Others besides Nietzsche have impersonally given the same sovereign gift to their fellows, doing so from a no less necessary impulse; and they were no less capable than he of ensuring the sovereignty of their gift. Indeed, others were better able to take one's breath away. The only advantage of Nietzsche, who, from the narrow perspective where I have placed myself, matters in an essential way, is that he joined knowledge to subjectivity and that, for this reason,

his thought is incompatible with those who occupy the world (the fascist vulgarity does not alter this fact in the least degree).

7. Obviously, the traditional positions are "superseded": this word is doubtless a simplification, but the reading of his work has little meaning if one has not tied his understanding of it to this way of thinking. Let us not speak of the bourgeois positions anymore. But apparently a Hegelian position is possible, which is not necessarily the communist one and is in agreement with the interpretation of communism that I offer in the second part of this volume. It consists in saying: the coexistence of the two worlds is possible and their difference will diminish, the human unity exists. But this is not a position; indeed, it means that henceforth all positions are superfluous.

8. André Gide, *Dostoevsky* (Westport, CT: Greenwood Press, 1979), p. 71.

9. *Ecce Homo*, trans. Walter Kaufmann (New York: Vintage, 1967), p. 326.

10. See *The Gay Science*, sec. 153.

11. Gide writes in a letter to Renée Lang: "*Zarathustra* has always been and is *unbearable* to me. The book has fallen from my hands each time I've tried to take it up again (whereas Nietzsche's other books constantly renew my admiration)..." (Lang, *André Gide et la pensée allemande* [Paris: Luf, 1942], p. 178). For his part, Thomas Mann (*Nietzsche's Philosophy in the Light of Contemporary Events* (Washington, DC: Library of Congress, 1947], p. 10) writes: "This faceless and formless monster, this winged giant Zarathustra with the rose crown of laughter on his unrecognizable head, with his 'Grow hard!' and his caperer's legs is no creation, he is rhetorical, impassioned wit, tortured voice and dubious prophecy, a wraith of helpless grandeur, often touching and mostly painful to watch – an unman wavering at the borders of the ridiculous." Yet Mann himself revered Nietzsche. Impossible to deny that at first these judgments do not seem unfounded. There is no doubt about the ambition of *Zarathustra*. Nietzsche meant to write a counterpart to the Gospel, but only achieved an unsuccessful, albeit profound book.

12. Gide, *Dostoevsky*, p. 185.

13. Karl Jaspers, *Nietzsche: An Introduction to the Understanding of His Philosophical Activity*, trans. Charles F. Wallraff and Frederick J. Schmitz (Tucson: University of Arizona Press, 1965), p. 47 [translation slightly altered. – TR.].

14. *Ibid.*, p. 57 [lines 1–5 of Nietzsche's poem "Ohne Heimat," 1959. – TR].

15. *The Will to Power*, trans. Walter Kaufmann and R. J. Hollingdale (New York: Vintage, 1967), p. 85.

16. *Ecce Homo*, p. 236.

17. Kierkegaard's God is the height of luxury.

18. Buddhism is radically different from this position; like Christianity, it does not accept the game, but by another means it is the negation of the object, which the subject also is in the game; it withdraws one from the game.

19. It is only through the French school of sociology, which made an *object* of it, that the sacred was once again taken into consideration (the sacred associated with Christianity, which appealed to subjectivity, within the limits I have spoken of, remained outside serious discourse). But, thanks to their error, the French sociologists said what could immediately be said about it.

20. *Volonté de puissance* (Paris: Gallimard, 1948), vol. 2, p. 115. [In this instance, as in those cited in notes 25, 29, 30, 68 and 73 below, Bataille is employing a quotation taken from the French translation of Friedrich Würzbach's German edition of *The Will to Power* published in 1940. This edition, with many notes added to the earlier Marionausgabe version, obtained little if any scholarly acceptance but was translated into French by Georges Bianqui and was the edition used by Bataille. These particular quotations were not included in Kaufmann's English translation, and so references to them have been made to the French edition cited by Bataille. – TR.]

21. *The Will to Power*, p. 85.

22. *The Gay Science*, sec. 357, p. 305.

23. *Beyond Good and Evil*, trans. Walter Kaufmann (New York: Vintage, 1966), sec. 65a, p. 79.

24. *Ecce Homo*, p. 229.

25. *Volonté de puissance*, vol. 2, p. 150.

26. Lang, *André Gide et la pensée allemande*, pp. 81–82. But it is hard not to suspect that, in a different sense from Nietzsche with respect to Jesus, Gide was jealous of Nietzsche (in the sense that the writer is anxious to ensure his "originality").

27. Lang to Marcel Drouin, *ibid.*, p. 184.

28. I take these terms from a letter by Gide, in Lang, *ibid.*, p. 182.

29. *Volonté de puissance*, vol. 2, p. 111.

30. *Ibid.*, p. 41.

31. *Thus Spoke Zarathustra*, trans. Walter Kaufmann (New York: Viking, 1966), part 4, "The Drunken Song," sec. 8, p. 322.

32. "I am a disciple of the philosopher Dionysus; I should prefer to be even a satyr to being a saint. But..." (*Ecce Homo*, p. 217).

33. This last interpretation is the more probable. "It seems to me now that I haven't gotten to know anything, except approximately," he writes to Lang (*André Gide*, p. 178). In the same letter, he says of *Zarathustra*, which is unbearable to him: "I don't think I've read, counting all the resumptions, more than ten pages of it." Gide's attitude could not have been more conscientious in principle (at least where "authors" were concerned; toward his close relations, his wife...), but his attitude toward Nietzsche is a painful example of thoughtlessness.

34. Translated by Justin O'Brien (New York: Knopf, 1949), vol. 3, p. 370.

35. Lang, *André Gide*, pp. 113–14.

36. Translated by E. B. Ashton (Chicago: Henry Regnery, 1961).

37. *Nietzsche and Christianity*, pp. 17–26.

38. Ernst Benz, "Nietzsche's Ideen zur Geschichte des Christentums," *Zeitschrift für Kirchen Geschichte* 3 (1937). The Jaspers quotations are from *Nietzsche and Christianity*, p. 26n.

39. I wish to strongly emphasize the fact that Nietzsche was, whether he meant to be or not, placed in a position opposing Jesus. There is no doubt about the ambition of *Zarathustra*. Nietzsche wanted to write a counterpart to the Gospel (but he only achieved an unsuccessful book, even it it has, as he intended and as I believe, the most profound meaning).

40. Lang, *André Gide*, pp. 112–13.

41. Jaspers, *Nietzsche and Christianity*, pp. 88–90.

42. *Ibid.*, p. 91.

43. "Nietzsche et le *Doktor Faustus* de Thomas Mann," in *Etudes germaniques*

(April–September, 1947), pp. 343–54.

44. Mann, *Nietzsche's Philosophy in the Light of Contemporary Events*, pp. 4–9.

45. "Nietzsche et le *Doktor Faustus*," p. 353.

46. "Thomas Mann et le *Faustbuch* de 1587," in *Etudes germaniques* (January–March, 1950), pp. 54–59.

47. *Nietzsche's Philosophy*, pp. 3–4.

48. *Ibid.*, p. 6.

49. *Ibid.*, p. 9.

50. *Ibid.*, p. 10.

51. *Ibid.*, p. 33.

52. *Ibid.*, p. 37.

53. *Ibid.*, p. 29.

54. Did I not myself write concerning Nietzsche's thought, that "it opens up only the void to whoever is inspired by it" (*Sur Nietzsche* [Paris: Gallimard, 1945], p. 16, in *Oeuvres complètes*, vol. 4, p. 14), wanting to emphasize the fact that it did not pertain to the world of action.

55. The difference between fascism and Nietzsche's position is sufficiently clear in my opinion, but I cannot specify it here inasmuch as this work has left aside the question of war and of the institutions that are connected with it. I would merely like to stress the bourgeois character of the military world produced by fascism: fascism remained as far as possible from the deep preoccupation that is the meaning of sovereignty. Hitler at first remained in a state of uncertainty, but at the end of 1938 he took a firm position against those who dreamed of returning, via the detour of war, to some form of religious sovereignty. "We need stadiums," he declared, "not sacred woods." I feel very far indeed from the world in which military institutions and sovereignty coincide. Doubtless, Nietzsche was scarcely any closer than I, but I imagine that a nostalgia for the feudal world delayed him somewhat and that he was not fully aware of the sharp contrast that must separate traditional sovereignty from that of the "free spirits" he spoke of. But he never became so confused that we cannot now determine, unequivocally, the direction in which his thought was implicitly heading: that of sovereignty that refuses to govern the world of things. It is the

sovereign freed from the military order, freed from any order finally, which is diametrically opposite to fascism (where the thing itself would be unreservedly sovereign, and every man overwhelmed by it, were it not for the contradictions inherent in the excessiveness and crudeness of the beginnings).

56. *The Gay Science*, trans. Walter Kaufmann (New York: Vintage, 1974), sec. 285.

57. Mann, *Nietzsche's Philosophy*, p. 10 (emphasis added).

58. *Ibid.*, p. 11.

59. I am only considering the practice of value, not the theoretical discussions, in which, moreover, faithfulness to the practice remains fundamental in fact.

60. I know that by emphasizing the connection between prohibitions and the possible, I myself am integrating them into the sphere of reason, but for me it is the result, and not the intention, that is rational. The intention is manifested, I believe, in the (irrational) disgust that man feels for the movement of nature.

61. The danger of such schemas is that they can make one forget an extreme changeableness of mood, peculiar to Nietzsche. Nietzsche also wrote: "Precisely because we are at bottom grave and serious human beings – really, more weights than human beings – nothing does us as much good as a *fool's cap*: we need it in relation to ourselves – we need all exuberant, floating dancing, mocking, childish, and blissful art lest we lose the *freedom above things* that our ideal demands of us. It would mean a *relapse* for us, with our irritable honesty, to get involved entirely in morality and, for the sake of the over-severe demands that we make on ourselves in these matters, to become virtuous monsters and scarecrows. We should be *able* also to stand *above* morality – and not only to *stand* with the anxious stiffness of a man who is afraid of slipping and falling any moment, but also to *float* above it and play. How then could we possibly dispense with art – and with the fool? – And as long as you are in any way *ashamed* before yourselves, you do not belong with us" (*The Gay Science*, sec. 107).

62. *Baudelaire*, trans. Martin Turnell (New York: New Directions, 1950), pp. 51–52.

458

63. *Ibid.*, p. 71.

64. *Ibid.*, p. 52.

65. *Ibid.*, p. 99.

66. As understood by the dominant party of society.

67. Quoted by Sartre, *Baudelaire*, p. 76.

68. Nietzsche writes: "Why am I thus? What madness to think oneself free to choose to be, and to be in such and such a fashion..." (*Volonté de puissance*, vol. 2, p. 41). Negative chatter at least has the advantage of calling immediately for silence. Positive chatter is an occasion to dodge the problem (of sovereignty) and to replace sensible values with a metaphysical value (cloaked for example in "commitment").

69. *The Birth of Tragedy*, trans. Walter Kaufmann (New York: Viking, 1967).

70. See *The Gay Science*, sec. 125, "The Madman."

71. Nor is there any discontinuity between profane art and sovereign art, which I will speak of shortly.

72. "It seems to me important that one should get rid of all, the unity, some force, something unconditioned; otherwise one will never cease regarding it as the highest court of appeal and baptizing it 'God.' One must shatter the all; unlearn respect for the all; take what we have given to the unknown and the whole and give it back to what is nearest, what is ours." This note from the posthumous papers of Nietzsche (*The Will to Power*, p. 187) sums up the whole movement of my thought.

73. Here I refer back to the note by Nietzsche already cited in note 20, above: "To be alone with a great thought is unbearable. I am seeking and calling to men to whom I can communicate this thought without their being destroyed by it."

74. *Zarathustra*, with this reservation made, is a heartrending book nonetheless: what I say about it enables one to understand it, not to reject it. That such a book is also a hopelessly entangled monstrosity, an impotent mistake, might define the pinnacle, if the pinnacle could be conceivable and it was not moving.

75. I believe it is impossible for the following reason (that I state without hoping to convince an adherent): under the current leadership, communist

humanity cannot conceive itself in terms of *play* but only in terms of labor. Play alone uses up the resources produced by labor (in its essence, war is a horrible game, from which the world of work, which meant to eliminate it, has taken away as much of its playfulness as possible). In any case, humanity is finally a game, but the "man of renounced sovereignty" places it within the perspective of labor: this is why he seems to me to be condemned, as I have already said, to that game which is no longer a game, to the most demanding form of depletion, to war. He knows this and admits it; he knows that essentially revolution commits one to war. To get out of his impasse, the "man of renounced sovereignty" would have to give up the conception of life he holds and adopt that of the "man of sovereign art." Such a thing is not impossible. It is true that the "man of sovereign art" is the first to attain, if not in the development of his life, then at least in his integrity, in the moment — and in his thought — *freed* sovereignty, but he has renounced the pursuit of rank just as completely as the communist leader. He could not have done what the communist leader did. In order to get out of feudal society, the communist leader had to set himself against play. In order to accumulate he had to completely oppose the "man of sovereign art." This does not mean that he has within him and in his thought what it takes to use up the accumulation he has created.

76. This movement is obviously outlined in Marxism. The theory of alienation is its mainspring, based on the idea that attributes the content of divinity to man alone. But in present-day communism, alienation has only taken a voluntary form (at best) and man's divine content is lost sight of. Moreover, Marx himself, who wanted the "government of things" (the separation I speak of), sought it through revolution, that is, through war that would be both the consequence of, and a prelude to, revolutions. Whatever one may think of this method as concerns the past, the question that is raised today stems from the impossibility of envisaging any result beyond war.

77. I don't intend to deal in this work with the question of the means of acting effectively. However, I will set out the principles of such action elsewhere.

Zone Books series designed by Bruce Mau

Type composed by Archetype

Printed and bound Smythe-sewn by Arcata Graphics/Halliday
using Sebago acid-free paper